Praise for *Walle* [barcode: D0561823]

"Finally! *Wallet Activism* is the book we all need to see through the marketing lies we're surrounded by and make better choices for the planet and our fellow humans. It's an ambitious deep dive into the complex factors we must consider when using our financial power, but with clear, practical guidance to help anyone at any income level make better choices."

—Vicki Robin, *New York Times* bestselling author of
Your Money or Your Life

"Tanja's gift is taking a complex and seemingly overwhelming topic and making it easier to grasp, while reminding everybody that no one is too small to spur meaningful change. This book is full of helpful information and pragmatic ideas so you can begin to thoughtfully put your money where it can do the most good—both for the planet and its people."

—Sherry and John Petersik, authors of *Young House Love*

"Tanja breathes new life into concepts like 'voting with your dollar,' without encouraging consumerism. With each chapter, she pushes us to make sure our activism isn't just symbolic. It's clear she's heard our excuses and thankfully isn't impressed by them. We all know we can do more and this book helps us take the necessary steps to think more critically, embrace nuance, and consider the true cost of our spending decisions. With each page, you'll be pushed beyond symbolic activism and into sustainable action."

—Julien and Kiersten Saunders,
authors and founders of rich & REGULAR

"In a time where people are fighting against low wages and unfair working conditions, Tanja Hester's *Wallet Activism* is more crucial than ever. This book has inspired me to not only think of changes as a consumer but as a business owner as well. It's easy to point fingers at someone like Amazon but If I expect other companies to be inclusive, I must make sure I am there, too."

—Athena Valentine Lent, *Slate* financial advice
columnist and founder of Money Smart Latina

"*Wallet Activism* is the book I was missing in my financial library. It answers so many of the questions I had about my own decisions and how I was living my life. Tanja's brilliant framework for approaching how we spend, earn, and save provided me with an invaluable tool to make better decisions for the planet and its people. She's honest about the upsetting realities we face, yet brings nuance and compassion to these complex and important decisions. I finished the book feeling educated with facts, empowered to make an impact, and inspired to take action. May we all become wallet activists so we can do our part to course correct our home before it's too late!"

—Ashley Feinstein Gerstley, author of *The 30-Day Money Cleanse*

"*Wallet Activism* dives into the most pressing issues we face as a society—inequality, climate change, corporate and political corruption—and lays out an inclusive roadmap for how we can fight back using our individual resources. Without sugarcoating the enormity of these problems, Hester empowers us to make personal changes that can, in time, enable real progress. This book will make you face harsh realities about the world we live in and your role in it, but it will also, amazingly, give you hope."

—Gemma Hartley, author of *Fed Up:
Emotional Labor, Women, and the Way Forward*

"I was blown away. From plastic straws to carbon offsets, from the mortgage interest deduction to DIY culture, you'll never think about the impact of your choices in the same way again. This book shines light on the futility of good intentions and performative efforts, and shows how to make an actual, quantifiable impact."

—Paula Pant, host of the Afford Anything podcast
and founder of AffordAnything.com

"If you're like me, you're scared and confused. You want to be a noble citizen of this globe, but you're constantly decision-making from within the thick haze created by greenwashed corporate messaging and inconsistent advice on 'being better.' I am certainly guilty of action that was merely performative, but symbolic gestures be damned! *Wallet Activism* is a necessary read that helped me blast through the pollution of internet opinions and veiled marketing tactics, and I cannot recommend it enough. Hester is brilliant. It would be my greatest wish for us all to read *Wallet Activism* and to act on it."

—Amanda Holden, founder of Invested Development
and the Dumpster Dog Blog

"There are issues bigger than the balance of our retirement accounts that impact us all, such as racial injustice, gender inequality, and climate change. In *Wallet Activism*, Tanja helps readers who want to help make a positive change but have no idea where to start. From breaking down the impact of our financial decisions, to sifting through the marketing tricks to find ways to make meaningful change with our money, *Wallet Activism* makes it clear that 'you don't have to be rich or perfect to make a difference,' 'what matters is that we do something.'"

—Chris Browning, host and founder of the
Popcorn Finance podcast

WALLET ACTIVISM

Also by Tanja Hester

Work Optional:
Retire Early the Non-Penny-Pinching Way

WALLET ACTIVISM

HOW TO USE EVERY ——— DOLLAR YOU ——— SPEND, EARN, AND SAVE AS A FORCE FOR CHANGE

Tanja Hester

BenBella Books, Inc.
Dallas, TX

BenBella Books, Inc.
10440 N. Central Expressway
Suite 800
Dallas, TX 75231
benbellabooks.com
Send feedback to feedback@benbellabooks.com

BenBella is a federally registered trademark.

Printed in the United States of America
10 9 8 7 6 5 4 3 2 1

Library of Congress Control Number: 2021026234
ISBN 9781953295590 (print)
ISBN 9781953295934 (electronic)

Editing by Claire Schulz and Alyn Wallace
Copyediting by Nichole Kraft, Paper Weight Editing
Proofreading by James Fraleigh and Cape Cod Compositors, Inc.
Indexing by Amy Murphy
Text design and composition by PerfecType, Nashville, TN
Cover design by Ty Nowicki
Printed by Lake Book Manufacturing

The wood used to produce this book is from Forest Stewardship Council (FSC) certified forests or recycled material.

Special discounts for bulk sales are available.
Please contact bulkorders@benbellabooks.com.

To Mark and Lewis,
for always inspiring me to be better.

CONTENTS

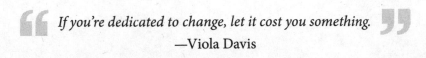

If you're dedicated to change, let it cost you something.
—Viola Davis

INTRODUCTION

You have real power. Whether you feel powerful or not, whether you feel hopeful or pessimistic about where the world is headed, whether you know exactly what change you want to see in the world or merely have a sense that things *must change*, you have power. That's a good thing, because we're staring down some of the most daunting challenges humankind has ever faced. The time to use your power is now.

First, there's the climate crisis. In 2018, the United Nations (UN) Intergovernmental Panel on Climate Change released a report outlining the impacts the world would see if we limit global warming to 1.5° Celsius (2.7° Fahrenheit) over preindustrial levels.[1] Calling the goal of limiting warming to 1.5°C "ambitious" is a massive understatement. That goal would require us to cut global greenhouse gas emissions nearly in half by 2030, achieve essentially zero emissions by 2050, and veer off the current trajectory that has us headed toward a 6°C (10.8°F) rise in the coming decades.[2] To pull all of this off would be staggeringly expensive, requiring an estimated investment of $830 billion in low-carbon energy technologies and energy efficiency *every year.*[3] Still, the report makes clear the enormous human and financial costs we can avoid if we meet this moment. Half as many people would experience water shortages in the future. Hundreds of millions of people would be less susceptible to poverty caused by climate change.

While many residents of coastal cities would still need to relocate due to rising seas, millions more could stay in their homes. Innumerable jobs and industries would be spared.[4] Spending the money now to intervene will save far more in the long term than if we continue to do next to nothing.

Second, inequality is at crisis levels nearly everywhere in the world. According to the UN, inequality is increasing for nearly three-quarters of our fellow humans living today, an effect magnified an additional 25 percent by climate change.[5] Contrary to images in media of children starving in poor countries, inequality is skyrocketing in nearly every country the UN calls "developed," another word for *rich*.[6] That translates into many more people living in poverty in countries that can afford to help. And despite an abundant supply of food around the world, billions of people are living with food insecurity and limited access to clean water.

Between the Great Depression and the late 1970s, the US and other rich nations saw an increase in social mobility, or the ability of individuals to earn more than their parents and improve their quality of life—what we often call the "American dream." But starting in the '70s, productivity gains and worker pay began to diverge, with the additional earnings from boosted productivity going to executives and stock shareholders instead of the workers generating them. Now the US is the least socially and economically mobile country in the developed world.[7] That has very real consequences: Workers desperate for income won't push back against inhumane working conditions or unfair pay. Parents working multiple jobs don't have the time to engage in their children's schooling or demand educational resources equivalent to those given to schools in wealthier areas. Children raised in poverty are extremely likely to face lifelong consequences, from worse health to worse educational outcomes, decreasing their ability to climb the economic ladder and perpetuating the vicious cycle.[8] Perhaps not surprisingly, those most likely to experience this are people of color,[9] women,[10] trans and nonbinary people, immigrants, disabled people,[11] and others who have long been marginalized by a society that privileges wealth and whiteness.

More capital exists around the world today than at any time in human history. According to Oxfam, just one year's income of the world's 100 richest people added together is enough to end global poverty *permanently* four times over.[12] The world's billionaires could give a tiny portion of their fortunes to build clean energy infrastructure and solve the bulk of the climate crisis virtually overnight. This is the scale of inequality we're talking about.

Despite how dangerously close we are to global catastrophe, our political leaders continually fail to act, citing lack of public support or simply remaining silent in the face of the greatest threats humanity has ever confronted. Political activists demanding action have succeeded in making incremental progress, but that progress alone will not get us where we need to be.

Despite all of that bad news, we have legitimate reason to be hopeful. Tackling the challenges we're facing won't be easy. But each of us has more power than we might think, because the political system isn't the only avenue open to us for creating change. Whether it's dismantling structural racism, protecting endangered species, making society more inclusive to LGBTQ+[13] and disabled people, reversing deforestation, decarbonizing our power grid, or any number of other issues close to your heart, your power lies not just at the ballot box. Your power also lies in your wallet.

———

Though we may call the American system a democracy, along with most of the other wealthy countries in the world, we are first and foremost a capitalist society. Capitalism is often described as a system that gives anyone an opportunity to improve their situation—a lofty and egalitarian-sounding goal. But what capitalism really means is putting the wants of the individual over the needs of the collective, preferencing the ability for the rich to get richer above the need of the poor not to starve. Some people win under capitalism, which means by definition that others must lose. Our vote is critically important, and who we elect to office at all levels matters a great deal. But in a flawed capitalist system like ours, one that rejects most attempts to level the playing field as antithetical to the "free" market, the driver of change is not always our vote. Very often, it's how we use our money.

Companies spend billions of dollars on advertising and marketing to attempt to persuade us in our decision-making, but ultimately, it's up to us in our role as consumers—not as voters—to determine where society and the planet are headed. For example, when I was born forty years ago, ubiquitous bottled water was simply not a thing.[14] We never voted on whether bottled water is a good thing for society or the planet, along with all its unintended consequences, but consumers vote with their dollars every day. As a result, we are producing and discarding record numbers of plastic bottles, which originate as crude oil that must be extracted and transported around the world and which most often end their lives in landfills or oceans. Also not a thing forty years ago: fast fashion, the cheap clothing found at stores like H&M, UNIQLO, and Zara that exists not in seasonal collections, but in monthly or even weekly collections that relentlessly chase the latest microtrends. These chains pump out massive volumes of new garments that, like plastic bottles, most often end up in landfills after only a short time and are made possible by exploiting already underpaid laborers, almost entirely in countries with minimal or nonexistent labor and environmental laws. Both examples (and these are only two) show the dramatic impacts on people, society, and the planet that we as consumers have made without understanding the consequences of our actions and—more importantly—without politics or elections coming into play. The question of whether we wanted all this waste and pollution was never put up for a vote. No one has ever run for office on a platform of disposable clothing.

Make no mistake: our votes matter. But changing the way things are won't happen through our votes alone. How we spend our money matters, too.

———

If you're reading this, you're someone who cares about the world around you. Maybe you've gone to marches or urged your friends on social media to change their ways or speak up. Maybe you've made the choice to buy or not buy something based on your closely held beliefs about what's right. You're not alone in this. A 2018 Cox Business survey on behalf of small business found that 71 percent of consumers would spend more at a small business if it supports an important social or environmental cause, with an equal number saying that diverse and inclusive hiring among small businesses is important and impacts where they shop.[15] According to a 2018 Nielsen study, 85 percent of millennials and 79 percent of Gen Xers believe companies should focus on improving the environment.[16] A 2015 global Nielsen study[17] found that

> sixty-six percent of global respondents say they are willing to pay more for sustainable goods, up from 55% in 2014 (and 50% in 2013). And it's no longer just wealthy suburbanites in major markets willing to open their wallets for sustainable offerings. Consumers *across regions, income levels, and categories are*

willing to pay more, if doing so ensures they remain loyal to their values. Sustainability sentiment is particularly consistent across income levels. *Those earning $20,000 or less are actually 5% more willing than those with incomes greater than $50,000 to pay more* for products and services that come from companies who are committed to positive social and environmental impact (68% vs. 63%). (Emphasis mine)

Despite being the economically worst-off generation still living,[18] millennials—even those with low incomes—are extremely willing to spend their money in ways that support their values and contribute to good causes. Similar trends hold for Gen Z and younger members of Gen X.[19]

The challenge is what to do with that willingness. As author Naomi Klein wrote in her essay "On Fire," "Even among those of us who are actively terrified of climate collapse, one minute we're sharing articles about the insect apocalypse and viral videos of walruses falling off cliffs because sea ice loss has destroyed their habit, and the next, we're online, shopping, and willfully turning our minds into Swiss cheese, by scrolling through Twitter or Instagram."[20] We're deeply concerned, but when it's not clear where to channel that concern, it's all too easy to collapse into old habits.

What's worse, companies have read that consumer research, too. They are well aware that consumers are willing to spend more for brands associated with causes. It's now ubiquitous for companies to make token efforts to *appear* to support a good cause while continuing to operate in ways that harm people and the planet. In this opaque system, it can feel impossible to know what the right choice is, and it's easy to throw up our hands and accept defeat. For too many of us, the easiest answer is to institute small changes that are ultimately only symbolic to make ourselves feel better, changes that do not lead to any actual shift in the status quo.

It's also easy to assume that "voting with our dollars" only refers to shopping, because that is where we are most aware of our financial power. (In fact, shopping is only a tiny part of the financial power you possess, and it's only one piece of this book. But let's stick with shopping for the moment.) In response to consumers' willingness to spend more on things that align with their values, we've seen the rise of "ethical consumerism" and "conscious consumerism," interchangeable terms that mean an attempt to avoid especially harmful products and instead buy things that do no harm or even do some good. It's an appealing idea, but let's be clear: we cannot shop our way out of the problems facing us. The notion of "conscious consumerism" is still consumerism. It's simply substituting one thing you might buy for another, not addressing how *much* we consume, which is an enormous part of the equation.

So how do we act as *real* financial agents of change, concerned with both the planet and its people, not just as shoppers choosing one thing over another? Is it even possible under capitalism, or is every choice too fraught with unintended consequences? These are the questions I've struggled with for years, and I suspect you can relate. I've devoted most of my life to social-change activism, working first as a journalist reporting on politics and then, for the bulk of my career, as a consultant to progressive candidates and issue campaigns in collaboration with everyone from small nonprofits to large foundations. I wrote language that became law, ran ad campaigns that convinced people to change their ways, and helped convince the public to care about things they didn't even know were problems. But even after seeing every side of the social-change sector, and working with every kind of activist, it still wasn't clear to me which individual financial choices would create real change. So I decided to take on this question, and the result of my years of research is this book. And my answer is: Yes, it is possible to use our financial power to make a difference on critical environmental and human issues, without choosing one or the other. Yes, you can make change even if you're not among the 1 percent who are able to ignore the cost of things. Yes, we can do all of this under our current capitalist system, flawed and unfair as it is. I hope you'll finish this book convinced of it. Not only can you make choices that benefit both the earth and other humans but you can make those choices while also looking out for your own financial well-being and not going broke.

During my career, I saw over and over again that large-scale change is possible—and it can happen incredibly quickly. I've seen opinions shift and behaviors change around everything from smoking in public to same-sex marriage, and I've watched us go from barely knowing that there are people without health insurance to granting universal access to everyone (even if that access is still too expensive). Some of the challenges facing us right now are enormous, and they can feel insurmountable. We can already see the impacts of climate change in our own lives. Systemic racism kills people every day. Entire species are rapidly dying. Workers are being exploited in every corner of the world. It's easy to get cynical or pessimistic and decide there's no use in trying. But the good news is that a lot of people care, and getting people to care is always the hardest part of driving change. What we must do now is focus our efforts to address challenges *meaningfully*, not just in ways that make us feel better or, even worse, that are ultimately a mere performance.

While we may wish for a world in which our votes did the heavy lifting for the change we want to see, in the world we've got, how we use our financial power is just as critical.

HOW TO USE THIS BOOK

Wallet Activism is designed to help you understand the true impacts of your financial choices, especially the many ways that companies and organizations are trying to mislead you, so that you can use your financial power to benefit our collective good. Part I focuses on cultivating an understanding of those impacts—so that you feel confident in the choices you make moving forward—and helping you ask the right questions before you make a choice. Part II is a deeper dive into specific areas of your financial life, from the things you buy and the foods you eat, to how you operate in the workplace, to where you choose to live and do your banking.

I don't like when people talk down to me or assume I can't handle the truth if it's complex, and I suspect you prefer the same thing. That's why nothing is watered down here, even when it makes the answer murkier. I believe that you can handle it. A lot of what I share here might feel bad at first. But everything in the book is focused on making us as clear-eyed as possible about the mistakes we (the collective *we*) have made in the past, so that we can be deliberate in making better choices moving forward, in ways that truly help.

Some of the research and conclusions in the book are informed by my own experiences as a woman and a disabled person, but when talking about things like racism and poverty, which I have witnessed but not experienced directly, I focus on elevating the solutions offered by those with that experience rather than speaking for them. I've done my best to use language that is inclusive and most preferred by the group the term refers to as of this writing, and I include endnotes where relevant that explain my word choice. But I've lived enough to see language evolve numerous times around these issues, and I apologize for instances where I got it wrong.

Most of all, everything I suggest in the book is offered with love, in hopes of meeting you exactly where you are now. Despite how strongly I feel about the urgency of the problems we're facing, this book takes a pragmatic approach, not an ideological one, because I live in the real world just like you do. I'm not perfect, and I don't expect you to be perfect, either. We're all learning as we go and doing our best. This book acknowledges that Amazon and Walmart exist, and they are the most affordable options for most people in their day-to-day purchases. My focus is on equipping you with an in-depth understanding of the economic forces and practices that impact people and the planet within our economy, giving you a simpler way to evaluate your choices moving forward and showing you the power you have as a wallet activist to create meaningful change, no matter your budget.

My first book, *Work Optional*, is about how to save and invest money to make work as small a part of your life as possible. Giving more power to individual workers and less to large corporate employers is something I fervently believe in, especially in our capitalist society in which the wealthiest few who run things get richer and richer at the expense of everyone else. But because of that deep inequality, the sad fact is that not everyone can afford to save and invest. If you can afford to buy all your food at the local farmers market from organic growers, to clothe your family in apparel you have time to pick out lovingly from the thrift store, to bike everywhere and avoid all fossil fuel vehicles, and to employ people for well above the median wage, I'm not here to stop you. The more we can all do, the faster we'll address the problems facing us, and those who can afford to do more have a responsibility to do so. But *Wallet Activism* has no such prerequisites, no assumptions about how much money you have. My life's work is not to help rich people get richer—it's to help us all be better caretakers of one another and the planet we call home. Sometimes that means reminding those with the most financial resources that it's not enough just to take care of yourself. And sometimes it means reminding everyone else that you don't have to be rich or perfect to make a difference.

I hope you'll take that latter sentiment to heart as you read *Wallet Activism*. None of us are too small to make change, especially when we're working together toward a shared vision of what's possible. There's no earnings minimum to be a part of steering this great spaceship of ours on a different path.

What matters is that we do *something*.

PART ONE

Becoming a Wallet Activist

*Every moment is an organizing opportunity,
every person a potential activist,
every minute a chance to change the world.*
—Dolores Huerta

CHAPTER 1

What Is Wallet Activism?

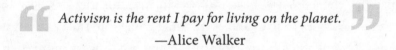

Activism is the rent I pay for living on the planet.
—Alice Walker

We all want to think that our actions are contributing more good than harm to the world. And at this time in our history, with the parallel climate and inequality crises worsening every day, many of us want more than anything to get clear, simple direction on what to do, ideally so that we'll get results we can see with our own eyes.

Several years ago, when I got serious about reducing the environmental impact of our buying habits and pledged that my husband, Mark, and I would change our ways, I was inspired by the so-called zero-waste movement. The idea behind the zero-waste movement is to avoid buying anything, especially packaging, that you'll throw away. It's a clear directive with a tangible outcome: less trash in the garbage can.

But someone attempting to live this way has to entirely change how they shop. For example, rather than going to regular grocery stores, I started shopping almost exclusively from the bulk bins at the local hippie food co-op. I'd lug heavy cloth bags full of jars that I could barely manage into the co-op, take the empty jars to be weighed before filling them so the cashier would know how much to subtract from the final weight, and then go through the painstaking process of carefully scooping things out of the bulk bins and into my jars, writing the codes for items like polenta or pinto beans on the jars' lids in chalk. I never failed to make a mess of something, my clumsy hands fumbling almond butter one day and olive oil the next. On one trip, I dropped the dozen eggs I had carefully transferred one at a time from the large stack into my reusable egg carrier, and I not only had to clean up the mess but I also had to pay for every single one. On a good day, with no major spills, it would take me almost an hour to finish the whole process, because checking out this way was slow, too, with no bar codes to scan and everything going into the cash register manually. When it was time to pay, the total was always more than it would have cost to buy the identical items conveniently packaged at another store. And every time I got hungry at home—even just for a little snack—I was faced with the daunting challenge of having to cook something entirely from scratch, the house now devoid of any prepared foods, replaced instead by Pinterest-worthy rows of jars containing only raw materials.

It didn't take long to conclude that this wasn't something I could sustain, despite all the advantages I had, like the means to afford the higher costs, no kids to entertain while shopping, and a car to help me haul all those heavy bags home. And was I even making a difference? There was less trash going out to the curb at our house, sure. But I knew I was still generating waste at the stores—I just wasn't bringing it home. It was a lot of work for an unclear impact. But the experience helped me understand that pushing everyone craving clear direction on how to do good into solutions that are incredibly hard to implement and maintain and out of reach financially is really no solution at all. We must instead channel our willingness into solutions that are both widely accessible and truly impactful.

I began looking for better solutions, ones that didn't come with negative side effects, most of which are invisible to us: from environmental degradation and worker exploitation to perpetuation of racial and gender wage gaps. But as I dug deeper, determined to find the best choices, I saw just how many deliberate efforts are happening to stymie us, wrapping brands in the veneer of "good corporate citizenship," often through approaches like "greenwashing" (making a product or company seem more environmentally friendly than it is) and "pinkwashing" (the same idea, but focusing on LGBTQ+ rights and women's empowerment). We want to be "ethical consumers" or "conscious consumers," but "conscious consumerism" is still firmly rooted in our deeply flawed capitalist ideology that puts profits above people and the planet. It still frames us fundamentally as consumers, whose main purpose and aspiration is to buy, buy, buy.

NAVIGATING THE SEA OF LIES

From the moment you were born, you've been lied to. Marketers vying for your attention have tried to instill within you a deep need for products you didn't need yesterday and probably still don't need today. Society has deemed you a consumer, rather than calling you by any of the other identities you also possess: a voter or civic participant, a resident of a place, a person with important family and friend relationships, a person who contributes to society in ways large and small. It's not just corporations who define you this way, either. Our political leaders often do, too. After 9/11, President George W. Bush famously told grieving and anxious Americans that the best thing they could do is go shopping, both to bolster the economy and to maintain the American way of life, into which shopping is inextricably intertwined.[1] Historian Sheldon Garon notes in his book *Beyond Our Means: Why America Spends While the World Saves* that the second President Bush was not alone in spreading this sentiment and that Americans have come to equate consumerism with patriotism.[2] (After all, the rhetoric around the Cold War made clear that it was between communism and capitalism, not communism and democracy.[3]) While this attitude is not so pervasive in other countries, it seems every capitalist society has forces at play working to reduce your identity to what you buy, not who you are.

Another lie you've been told over and over: It's your job to save the planet, to save the children, to save the polar bears. *But congratulations! It's easy to do! For as little as $5 a month, about the cost of a cup of coffee, you can make a difference in a child's life. And with these ten easy steps, you can save the earth!* If that were true, we'd live in a vastly different world. The realities are not quite so tidy.

The truth is that we shouldn't need a book like this. Our political leaders *should* have taken aggressive action to address climate change decades ago. All countries *should* make and enforce laws that outlaw worker exploitation and guarantee a living wage. We as a global community *should* work together through organizations like the United Nations to ensure that the excess food in wealthy countries gets to the people who need it around the world. But none of those things happen, and the primary culprit is capitalism.

Capitalism is the economic and political system in which industry is owned not by the government, but by private owners whose driving motivation is to generate profits. So-called free market capitalism is a version of the system in which government works hard to stay out of the economy altogether. Instead, government puts into place only minimal regulations meant to protect someone or something, allowing economic concepts like competition, supply and demand, and voluntary labor to set rates. Free market economists argue that we don't need things like a minimum wage, because the market will naturally balance itself out: workers will go to work for the employers who pay the most, putting pressure on those who pay less to raise their wages.[4] The problem with this theory is that it relies on everyone having perfect information—for example, workers knowing how much every potential employer pays and knowing exactly what educational pathways are available to them to qualify for higher-paying jobs—as well as everyone being able to operate from a place of comfort, not desperation. Of course, neither of those conditions exist. Most of us don't know how much the coworker next to us is getting paid, which helps perpetuate racial and gender-based wage gaps, let alone the earnings of workers in every similar position in your area.[5] Nearly 70 percent of Americans have less than $1,000 in savings[6] (and people in most other wealthy nations don't fare much better[7]). So taking time out from work to retrain for a better career, often at a high cost, is simply not an option for most people.

Capitalism is an extremely efficient system for concentrating power and wealth among a small minority of the population who has the most capital, the most information, and the best ability to take risks without facing dire consequences. Policies are made by leaders who are more interested in holding on to their power and looking out for the wealthiest among us who help keep them in power than in pushing for the change we desperately need as a collective whole. We expect poor people to pull themselves up by their bootstraps (a physically impossible task, if you've ever tried) rather than get government help to do so. And we put both the burden of trying to fix things and the blame for the problems we have in the first place on individuals.

Capitalism's job is to sustain capitalism, not to ensure the well-being of people or the planet, or even to try to scale our production down to a level that the earth's resources and labor force can sustain. It's fair to criticize capitalism, or to argue, as economist Thomas Piketty does in his book *Capital in the Twenty-First Century*, that capitalism will always inevitably lead to massive inequality. Many smart and thoughtful people have argued for getting rid of capitalism altogether. But this book is about taking action, and that means understanding how to navigate the capitalist system we have, flawed as it is: our true role in it, where the levers of power lie, and what power we as individuals possess. Some action can be spurred only by policy change at the highest levels, and pushing for that requires political engagement and organization that we absolutely must be a part of. But we can also work to understand the power of our everyday financial decisions, from what we buy to how we approach the work we do. With that understanding, we can begin to take a more critical look at the messages we receive every day—whether they're from marketers or from those who truly want to change things for the better—to determine if what they're telling us is true and if we want to act on it.

Wallet activism is that action. Wallet activism means:

1. **harnessing the power in our wallets,** our financial power as individuals to create change for the planet and our fellow humans;

2. **creating demand** for the world we want to live in, choosing what to support financially based on its true impacts (not only those we can see) and, just as importantly, choosing what *not* to support; and

3. **learning to ask the right questions,** developing the critical thinking skills to understand when you're being lied to, and to recognize when you have far more power than capitalist forces would have you believe.

Consuming at a sustainable level must always be a part of the conversation as well, so think of that as the calibration on each of the three elements of wallet activism.

THE POWER IN YOUR WALLET

When we talk about environmental and social issues, it's easy to grow pessimistic looking at all the actions we haven't taken and all the progress we haven't made. Experts say we're too late to completely dodge the effects of global warming, no matter what we do, and we're already witnessing climate change in action.[8] And the scope of the inequality that exists can feel overwhelming, beyond our own personal control. But where our leaders have failed us, we can step in to fill at least some of that void.

Corporations want us to believe that they have all the power. After all, they are multinational entities worth billions of dollars. They have powerful marketing arms and even more powerful lobbying operations. We are mere cogs in the machine compared to them. But corporations are entirely reliant on a steady stream of our dollars, and without those dollars, they cease to function. Isolated consumers have little power individually. But as a collective force, we hold all the cards. Collectively, Americans spend more than $50 trillion a year. In the eurozone, consumer spending alone totals nearly €7 trillion ($8.38 trillion US dollars) a year. Shifting even a tiny fraction of those amounts toward spending that benefits the collective good can make a massive difference. We are not just consumers. We are powerful actors on the global stage who can pressure bad companies to reform or perish. And we can be a collective force for good if we decide to change our most harmful individual behaviors, even if not all of us change our ways.

Does all of this sound hopelessly idealistic? It's absolutely not, and here's one example. If you were alive and aware of the news in the

1990s, you heard a lot about the earth's ozone layer and the techni-cally incorrect but evocative term *the ozone hole*. The ozone layer is a thin zone in the upper atmosphere that blocks the most harmful ultraviolet rays from the sun, and scientists discovered that chloro-fluorocarbons (CFCs) found in aerosol spray products like hairspray were a major cause of its depletion. World governments worked to eliminate CFCs from industrial applications,[9] but even in the absence of laws, individuals changed their behavior, too. Sales of hairspray, spray deodorant, and other sprays dropped significantly,[10] showing the potential of collective purchasing power to create real impact. If this collective action had not happened, climate change would be even worse today.[11] Because of this combination of policy change and indi-vidual financial behavior change, the ozone layer is now on track to become fully healed within the next few decades, even earlier than scientists had hoped was possible.

Transforming yourself into a wallet activist is to actively reject attempts by marketers and leaders to define you by your purchases and instead to define yourself by your values, as well as learning how to make choices in the interest of the collective good. Those choices are not always simple ones—in fact, the simpler a solution seems, the more likely it is that it's not especially impactful—but it's entirely pos-sible to learn how to make them. And often the answer for how to change something will be to pressure lawmakers to act.

There's a bit of a paradox around individual action and policy change: we simply cannot achieve all the change we want to see, at the scale we need to see, by making small individual choices, and there-fore we need to place constant pressure on policymakers. But if we believe that the only way to make large-scale change is through policy or collective action, we tend to think that our own choices are mean-ingless. They are not. As environmental journalist Lloyd Alter has written, "It is too easy and simplistic to blame the building industry, the power companies, and the oil industry, when we are buying what they are selling."[12] The truth is that achieving positive change isn't about collective *or* individual action, it's about collective *and* individual action. We will always need both. That means the collective good needs *you*.

BE THE DEMAND YOU WANT TO SEE IN THE WORLD

If capitalist society defines us as consumers, then we can talk about our potential for impact in economic terms. For those of us who care about climate change and the lives of people forced to the margins of society, that means we must shift our thinking away from simply, *What should I stop doing or spending money on?* Instead, we need to ask ourselves, *What incentives can I be a part of creating?* Let's look at an example that's gotten a lot of press in recent years: cattle ranchers in the Brazilian Amazon have been burning areas of the rainforest to turn them into pastures to raise beef. If they (and people who burn grassland and forest everywhere) don't have a viable and profitable alternative, it's unrealistic to expect the burning to stop. Many economists believe the best solution is simply to pay people not to burn down the forest, an action that only policymakers can take. But we as consumers can also choose not to consume the things that ranchers burn down the rainforest to raise, so we don't provide incentives for more ranchers to burn down more forest. If we don't eat the beef grazed in the Amazon, ranchers will have little incentive to raise the cattle that make them burn down the rainforest in the first place (and the big business firms who buy from them won't look to the Amazon for beef). Of course, this leads to another thorny problem: what those ranchers will do for work instead. That's an important problem that must be solved, ideally by policymakers paying these ranchers so they have a livelihood while finding other work. Nonetheless, removing the incentives for more people and companies to undertake obviously harmful practices is still a powerful act.

When we think in terms of incentives, we recognize that our greatest power comes from the demand we create or eliminate. According to the law of supply and demand, greater consumer demand—the fact that more people want to buy something—will spur industry to try to meet it by producing more of that thing. Unmet demand—which happens when people want something but can't buy it because there's not enough—is a missed opportunity for profit, and firms work hard not to miss out when there's money to be made. On the flip side, if consumer demand drops—if fewer people want something—and there's more supply than demand, companies lose the money they've sunk into production and distribution costs. They work hard to avoid having too much supply of something that's not in demand.

Companies spend their massive marketing budgets to manufacture demand that they are then happy to match with supply. Consider that many of us alive today can remember a time before Starbucks, when no one would dream of spending more than a dollar or two on a cup of coffee. And yet now the white and green cup is ubiquitous in nearly every big city in the world. We as consumers decided to demand expensive coffee in disposable and nearly impossible to recycle cups. But if we felt like it, we could eliminate that demand, too. It's within our power.

Standard environmental dogma tells us that the solution is to consume as little as possible. It's true that those of us in wealthy countries absolutely must buy less stuff and consume less energy if we don't wish to deplete the earth's resources at an unsustainable pace. Though the word *sustainable* has become an overused buzzword, it's still a critically important concept: we should be striving to consume no more than the planet can sustain over the long term through regenerative practices, and we should be promoting human systems and principles that we can sustain permanently without endorsing or exacerbating inequality. The earth can sustain quite a lot of us with a good quality of life if we approach things right. But in our current model, a country becoming wealthier and more developed means its residents also begin to consume at vastly higher levels on the backs of those with no economic or social mobility. That's a problem. At the same time, it's an imperialist attitude to think that wealthy countries should dictate how other countries are allowed to develop or how much they're allowed to consume as they gain upward mobility. Rather than say to them, in essence, "Sorry, you missed your chance to improve your people's standard of living back when we were doing that," we can right-size our own consumption, bringing it down to a fair and sustainable level, focus our own demand to levels others can sustainably replicate, and reorient ourselves to focus on shrinking inequality rather than growing it.

However, while overconsumption is undeniably a huge problem, working to consume less is only one half of our work. The other and equally important half is consciously creating demand for the goods and services that *do* serve the collective good. To put it in the simplest terms possible, part of the work of wallet activism is to reduce demand for everything that doesn't serve the collective good by consuming less of those things, while creating more demand for everything that does by putting our money where our values are. It's up to us to create demand for the world we want to live in.

LEARNING TO ASK THE RIGHT QUESTIONS

Throughout this book, we'll discuss the complex considerations that go into the financial choices we make. And just as the scale of our problems can quickly feel overwhelming, the complexity of choosing the best solutions can also feel paralyzing, especially as you begin to recognize more of the lies you are told every single day by those looking to get ahead under capitalism. To simplify that decision-making process, each remaining chapter in Part I will discuss one guiding question you can use to help you make choices that promote real change. Those questions are:

For whom? Does the action proposed serve those who truly need the change, because they have the most disadvantages, or does it largely serve those who already have lots of advantages?

Can everyone do this? Is this choice that I'm considering something everyone can do? And, if everyone did it, would that be sustainable? If everyone can't do it, what does that tell me?

Is it too cheap? Is something priced so low that it could not possibly have been produced or couldn't be offered without exploitation of people, the planet, or both?

What am I funding? What type of world am I helping create if I contribute profits to the entity offering something?

With practice, asking yourself these questions will become second nature as you contemplate different choices. And you may find one day that you don't even need them anymore, as your wallet activism becomes fully ingrained. But whenever you feel perplexed by new information or marketing, you'll always have these guiding questions to come back to.

A NEW FRAMEWORK FOR TRANSFORMING THE PLANET AND ITS PEOPLE

The new framework this book lays out represents a fundamental shift in mindset about the ways we interact with the world as financial beings, as well as the ways we think about the biggest challenges we're facing collectively. This framework is built on a set of core principles that permeate everything we explore throughout *Wallet Activism*:

1. Our environmental challenges and our social challenges are both urgent and inextricably linked. We cannot solve them separately or without aiming for justice.
2. The solutions most often touted are rarely the best choices for our collective good, often because it's those who stand to profit from those solutions doing the touting. But it's well within your power to learn to see through marketing and propaganda to make justice-oriented choices that weigh environmental and social factors equally to serve the collective good.
3. Consumer activism is powerful, but it cannot solve everything and must always be paired with political action and policy.
4. Only financial practices that are accessible to people of a wide range of income levels, with the full range of physical ability and disability, are worth promoting widely. Wallet activism is not just for people who can afford to buy exclusively from status brands, or who have the excess time and able bodies to bike everywhere.
5. Creating healthier incentives and right-sizing demand is at the forefront of our decision-making.
6. Perfection is never the goal, improvement is.

In some alternate universe in which utopia is possible, we might imagine a way to engage in perfect consumerism, buying only sustainably produced and high-quality goods that:

- will last a long time,
- are made from materials gathered locally without extractive practices like mining or labor exploitation,
- are crafted by local artisans who can afford to live comfortably on their income from those goods,
- are sold by retailers who pay all employees a living wage and treat them with dignity,

- have proceeds going back into the community to benefit everyone in our equitable society, and
- end their lives being repurposed meaningfully, rather than going to the landfill.

While we're unlikely to experience anything like that on a large scale, it provides a useful guide for thinking about the ideal we can strive for. A perfect financial decision would be environmentally neutral or even environmentally beneficial, neutral or beneficial to humans, practical, scalable, and accessible so that it's a viable decision for anyone, with a cost that's accessible to most people.

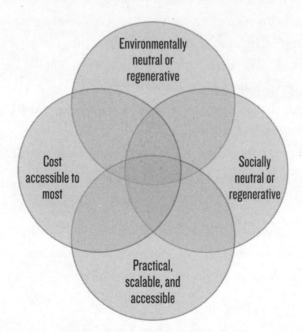

With these principles in mind, we can begin to transform ourselves into wallet activists who recognize the financial power we possess in different settings, and we can fully commit to wielding it for the collective good.

CHAPTER 2

People or the Planet?
You Don't Have to Choose

For whom?

> *There is no such thing as a single-issue struggle because we do not live single-issue lives.*
> —Audre Lorde

High in the Andes Mountains of central Ecuador, food sometimes falls from the sky. Each autumn, hundreds or thousands of brown and white plover birds migrating from the US drop into the icy waters of the Lagunas de Ozogoche to meet their death, their last sight the jagged, cloud-shrouded pinnacles that surround the lakes. Biologists have yet to explain the phenomenon, but the local Quichua-speaking

Indigenous people have witnessed this ritual for countless genera-tions. They hold a festival to celebrate the gift from above, wearing brightly dyed traditional ponchos, and feast briefly on the birds before returning to their everyday lives of subsistence farming and grazing sheep at 13,000 feet.

The landscape in Ozogoche is called páramo, a high-altitude tun-dra made up of dense but low-lying plants that give the impression from a distance of mowed grass, but which are in fact an incredibly rich store of carbon. The traditional agricultural method for the local people, as in much of South America and around the world, is to burn swaths of vegetation to create bare plots of land to farm. Even with the soil enriched by the burning, crop yields are meager and survival can be a struggle. The long history throughout Latin America of margin-alizing Indigenous people makes Ecuador's Indigenous populations 4.5 times more likely to live in poverty than non-Indigenous Ecua-doreans.[1] And without speaking Spanish, and with few ways to learn, most Chimborazo Quichua people have no opportunities elsewhere, regardless of how much they may wish to do something else.

But as word has spread of the natural mystery that happens here, adventurous tourists from wealthy countries have begun to trickle in. Those tourists have in turn told others of the spectacular beauty of the place and the warmth of the people. Now there are visitors nearly every day, braving the harrowing bus ride over rough, narrow roads, and paying for horse rides and a hot meal. While the tourism business is still small, its growth provides an opportunity for the Chimborazo Quichua that they want but have never had before: to buy some of their food and essentials rather than having to be completely self-sufficient and to improve their overall quality of life. They are beginning to be able to survive and even thrive without burning their beloved páramo.

Burning to clear land for agriculture releases large amounts of carbon into the atmosphere. This traditional farming technique, used around the world for centuries, contributes to climate change, especially in areas like the páramo that are a form of peat bog, among the most carbon-intensive places on the planet. Though it's unjust to tell Indigenous people anywhere in the world that they must change their traditional practices while billionaires in rich countries zip around in private jets, if people *want* another option, one that's better for them *and* better for the planet, we can and must support them. Deforestation is one of the biggest drivers of climate change (as much as 15 percent of net global carbon emissions each year[2]), and humanity's greatest imperative is to stop putting greenhouse gases into the sky. So supporting the Chimborazo Quichua in creating alternatives to burning the páramo must be part of our approach.

Most advice written by climate activists urges us to stop traveling, or at least to travel much less by air, primarily because of the enormous volume of carbon released by burning jet fuel.[3] And the carbon emissions of a flight to South America from anywhere else in the world are not negligible. However, if tourists stop showing up, the Chimborazo Quichua will likely need to continue increasing their burning to farm. In this case, the best thing for our climate and for our fellow humans is to support their efforts to grow ecotourism in the region.

For poor people in innumerable places in the world, ecotourism provides a near-term chance at making a living without harming the natural landscapes they love, most often with slash-and-burn agricultural methods, like those practiced widely in the Amazon rainforest to make room for grazing cattle. No one wants to chop down all their forest land—to paraphrase Joni Mitchell, their version of paving paradise and putting up a parking lot—but if that's the only option you can see to survive, you'll do just about anything. Education about how important the Amazon is for carbon storage and oxygen production doesn't go very far when people are hungry and need to feed their families.

The situation in Ozogoche, Ecuador, helps us understand that our solutions to the environmental issues facing us—most especially the urgent threat of human-caused global warming—are often short-sighted, putting the health of the planet over the well-being of its people and at times even working against the actual health of the planet by failing to recognize the constellation of holistic impacts caused by our choices.

Perhaps you've read books about what you can do to save the planet, because you care and want to do *something*. It's no accident that those books have tended to focus *only* on the planet, because that's a more manageable problem to wrap our minds around, and because the environmental movement has a long history of disregarding the impact of certain choices and decisions on our fellow humans, especially if those humans have black or brown skin or live across an ocean.[4]

Just across the border from Ecuador, small-scale farmers in Bolivia have for millennia grown quinoa, known in South America as the "queen of the Andes." Quinoa has become a darling of foodies and health nuts alike, a grain-like crop that is the food world's elusive unicorn: a complete, plant-based protein. If our goal is to eat less meat, as climate activists insist we must, logic would tell us that foods like quinoa should be what we substitute in our diets instead. Only it's not so simple.

Quinoa has been a staple of the diet in Bolivia, Peru, and Ecuador for as long as anyone knows, showing up in art at archeological sites dating back centuries before Columbus. As the global demand for quinoa has increased, pushing the price higher, some researchers believe that the price became so high that many in Bolivia—including the very people who grow it—could no longer afford to buy it.[5] It's certainly true that consumption of quinoa in Bolivia has decreased significantly. Other researchers disagree about the cause,[6] but one thing is clear: the global quinoa boom has brought harm to Bolivia. While campesinos used to grow thousands of varieties of quinoa they'd refined over generations to best suit their local climates and elevation zones, the push to commercialize the crop has resulted in their producing just a few of the highest-yielding cultivars. The land where quinoa grows best in Bolivia is scarce, and the crop's popularity has driven numerous land grabs and even armed conflict over available farmland.[7] And as global demand for quinoa has increased, more countries have started growing it in large volume, including China and the United States, pushing the price back down.[8] Bolivian farmers are now left with far less biodiversity of their quinoa, a precarious position to be in as global warming worsens. Farmers around the world are needing to turn to rare cultivars to keep crops producing when they find that their typical cultivars, those that produced best in the past, are ill-suited to the new, warmer climate. Bolivia's quinoa farmers have lost many of these rare strains. They're also left with fewer forests after clearing them to make more space for growing. And they see lower yields from their land after putting all of their fields into production rather than allowing some to lie fallow each season to avoid depleting the soil, as was formerly the practice before the quinoa boom.[9]

In our search for a perfect plant food, and in an effort to make a better environmental choice, consumers in wealthy countries have inadvertently inflicted serious pain on a huge population of people with few resources to begin with. Some undoubtedly will be worse off economically because of the quinoa boom, unable to buy a staple food or forced to continue farming a crop that fetches a lower price and is no longer profitable. But many more will find themselves far less resilient to climate change than they were before diners in rich countries developed a taste for quinoa.

Activist Chico Mendes, who was assassinated for defending the Amazon, said, "Environmentalism without class struggle is just gardening." We cannot care about the planet without also caring about the people with whom we share it. That means we need to understand the human costs of our choices made on behalf of the earth. The reverse is true, too: we need to understand the planetary and climate costs of choices made out of concern for people. And we need to let our understanding of those costs guide our choices, even if that means eating less of our beloved quinoa. Though answering these questions can often feel challenging, the guiding questions are meant to help. Let's start with the first one.

FOR WHOM?

A useful question to employ when deciding whether to do something you're being urged to do is *For whom?* Who benefits from this action? Who is harmed? Is this in the best interest of the most people, or only in the best interest of those who have the most power already?

To better understand what Mendes meant, and why *For whom?* is so important, let's consider an important episode in the history of the environmental movement. John Muir is a near-mythical figure among environmentalists. His wanderings in the Sierra Nevada mountains are legendary, the lanky Scotsman ambling up forbidding, snowcapped peaks, sleeping out in the open with only a sack of flour to sustain him. In 1892, he and other supporters founded the Sierra Club, one of the world's preeminent conservation organizations to this day, credited with inspiring the concept of the national park. John Muir saw Yosemite Valley—the centerpiece of what would become Yosemite National Park, in large part because of his advocacy—as an empty shell, a place surrounded by awe-inspiring granite cliffs in all directions, but not one inhabited for generations by Indigenous people who were forcibly driven out of the valley by army battalions in post–gold rush California.

Muir succeeded in earning federal protection for Yosemite, but *For whom?* Yosemite was protected for the enjoyment of white tourists, not for the Indigenous people who were repeatedly and forcibly driven off their homeland as late as 1969. The place names of Yosemite today serve as a silent reminder of the brutality and genocide: Tenaya Lake, named to celebrate the conquest of Ahwahnechee Miwok chief Tenaya by imperial forces; the Three Brothers, rock formations named for Chief Tenaya's sons who were captured, and one of them murdered, by imperial soldiers; and even Yosemite itself, named after a misunderstanding, when early white battalions mistook the local Miwok word *yosemeatea* for a place name. It really meant "killers," or those armed forces themselves who'd come to displace and slaughter them.

John Muir did not himself drive Indigenous people out of Yosemite, but his writings reflect his clear belief that places should be preserved for the enjoyment of "civilized" people, among whom he did not include the people who had lived there for generations, calling them "dirty" and "savages."[10] His calls to conserve Yosemite, the High Sierra around it, and much of the American West were entirely for the benefit of those with leisure time and disposable income, not for the good of everyone.

PROBLEMATIC HISTORIES

John Muir is not an outlier within the environmental movement. Early environmentalists focused on conservation of natural lands, and few of the preserved spaces included protections for the Indigenous tribes who called those lands home, which suited those conservationists just fine. We may charitably conclude that they were simply a product of their time, but unfortunately, the legacy of disregarding the needs of people of color, sometimes violently, is not merely a relic of days gone by.

As we came to a shared understanding that humankind was depleting the earth's resources too quickly, along with the realization that the planet is heating up, environmentalists shifted their focus to population. People looked at the increasing rate of resource depletion and the increasing population of humans on the planet and concluded that more people must be to blame, making *overpopulation* a buzzword throughout the 1980s and 1990s, and leading many to assume understandably that the earth must, in fact, be overpopulated.[11]

Of course, by this point in history, birth rates among predominantly white countries had dropped significantly. This meant that most of the growth in population was coming from the global south and China, predominantly poor countries at the time, inhabited almost entirely by people of color. Activists wrote books and went on television and even hosted global conferences to shout about the urgent need to address "overpopulation,"[12] apparently without ever questioning whether the problem was really more people total, or, as is actually the case, the ever-increasing consumption patterns of a relatively small number of those in the wealthiest countries. While wealthy nations could have been beginning a thoughtful conversation about how to lower their rate of burning through the earth's resources, environmentalists wasted a tremendous amount of time scolding poor countries for making so many Black and brown babies (and inspiring forced sterilization and eugenics programs around the world[13]).

For whom was this better world they envisioned? It would have left more resources to go around among the environmentalists and their friends in rich countries. Meanwhile, poor countries would be denied the ability to develop their economies and increase their quality of life to comparable levels. *I got mine, now you can't get yours.*

Sometimes this narrow-minded view of the environment also takes the form of inaction. We've seen time and again that activists are most likely to be heard—and policymakers are most likely to pay attention—when the people affected are white and middle- or upper-class. For instance, Rachel Carson successfully garnered attention in the early 1960s with her book *Silent Spring* about the pesticides like DDT poisoning people and ecosystems, and the ensuing public outcry led to a ban on agricultural use of DDT in the US. However, as of this writing, the majority-Black town of Flint, Michigan, has been without safe and clean drinking water for more than seven years despite widespread publicity, along with nine million to forty-five million Americans in predominantly nonwhite communities in any given year.[14] To this day, millions of Americans and countless people around the world are victims of environmental racism, allowing disproportionate harm to come to communities of color from poor environmental practices. Those who live around oil refineries, chemical and power plants, and herbicide-testing areas are disproportionately Black and Latino,[15] and as a result, their kids suffer higher rates of asthma and people of all ages suffer far higher rates of a wide range of cancers and chronic illnesses.[16] Yet we rarely hear any outcry about this ongoing problem from prominent environmentalists, hearing instead about dwindling populations of nonhuman endangered species.

Some environmental organizations have begun to come to terms with and apologize for their racist roots, especially in response to the Black Lives Matter movement, like the Sierra Club apologizing for John Muir's views and words. However, if you scroll through the staff pages of far too many legacy environmental organizations, you'll fly past a sea of white faces.[17] To this day, the environmental movement does very little to include and listen to Indigenous people, shutting out what could be a crucial source of knowledge.[18] It also tends to promote solutions proposed by wealthy, predominantly white donors rather than those demanded by people most affected by environmental issues, who tend to be poorer and less white. Until the environmental movement is more inclusive and diverse—including people of different races, genders, geographical locations, and class backgrounds—we must always question whom the proposed change is for.

Unfortunately, the beginnings of the humanitarian movement are no better. Early missionary work in the "New World" of Central and South America (later and more extensively in countries across Africa, and eventually around the globe) stemmed from the belief that all nonwhite people were inferior to whites. Thus, they could not become civilized to the standards of the dominant culture in white-run countries on their own, requiring fatherly help from outside. In other words, the paternalistic belief was that these "primitive" people needed "saving" and that only white people could do the saving.

This belief is often called "white saviorism" or a "white savior complex," and it's visible nearly everywhere we look, including to the present day. Numerous countries in Africa have gone so far as to ask nongovernmental organizations (NGOs) and their staffs to leave their countries,[19] because the NGOs' views of how to "fix" things completely ignore what local leaders say is needed—instead, these organizations base their approaches on what armchair philanthropists thousands of miles away think is best. But it takes more seemingly mundane forms, too: The hero in the movie that "bravely" tackles race is not the person of color to whom justice is owed but the white person who swooped in to help. Phrases like "voice for the voiceless" become popular among would-be allies. But the problem isn't someone's lack of a voice. It's the lack of listening by those who hold the most power. Well-meaning white progressives announce their allyship with people of color, only to make clear in short order that their allyship is a performance meant to make themselves feel good or, worse, to build a personal brand, not a real commitment to antiracism work. When the dominant culture considers whiteness the default, and therefore privileges whiteness—the definition of white supremacy—every person who identifies with that culture (and this includes me) needs to examine their own biases and motivation when speaking up on behalf of humanitarian causes, working to amplify rather than supplant.

Even the movement we've come to call social justice has not always focused on true justice. The women's suffrage movement culminated in 1920 when the US ostensibly granted women the right to vote, but it guaranteed that right only to white women. Suffragette leaders purposely forced women of color to the back of their protest marches, not wanting to taint their image of "purity" or give the false impression that they were fighting for the rights of *all* women. Black women would have to wait until the passage of the Voting Rights Act in 1965 to get the vote.[20] In the 1970s, this pattern would repeat itself, as second-wave feminists vehemently debated whether to allow lesbians to join them, many convinced it would hurt the cause.[21] Even today, the feminist movement is still not universally inclusive to LGBTQ+[22] people, with prominent public figures like author J. K. Rowling and many British academics insisting that trans women are not women.[23] While many feminists are beginning to examine how the movement has long upheld cisgendered, heteronormative, and white supremacist ideas, the movement still has much work to do internally.

It's natural to want to think that those who care about some of the things you care about won't lie to you. But unfortunately, given the problematic histories of both the environmental movement and the humanitarian movement, discerning the truth and understanding who benefits is complicated. Understanding those movements' histories will help us filter information we receive to make choices that do as little harm as possible.

THE VOCABULARY OF JUSTICE

Meaning well is not enough. We need to shift from focusing on our intentions to focusing on our impact. A first step to doing that is to examine our vocabulary. For too long, the word *save* has come to lead most of our statements on the change that's necessary. We aim to save the earth, to save the sea turtles, to save the polar ice caps, to save people from the Rwandan genocide, to save factory workers from abusive conditions, to save children from failing schools, and on and on. But by framing the action required as "saving," we view *ourselves* as the saviors, the heroes, the white knights to the rescue. In truth, however, those of us who benefit from a capitalist system built on colonialism and imperialism are far from the saviors—we're the attackers. Not the heroes, but the villains.

If we see ourselves as saviors, we're less likely to question our own roles in creating and upholding harmful conditions, whether it's the warming of the planet exacerbated by our own tailpipe emissions or the plight of workers forced to labor in inhumane conditions to feed our shopping habits. It's then easy to seize on small and largely symbolic tasks that make us feel good, like we're doing something meaningful, when we aren't even looking clearly at our impact. So let's strike all language of saving anything from the conversation, and instead learn to recognize how our choices harm others and the planet and focus on reducing those impacts. Instead of coming to the rescue, we're calling off the siege.

Thinking about the goals of wallet activism in terms of justice is helpful, just as the shifts toward environmental justice and social justice among the environmental and humanitarian movements have made those movements more inclusive and holistic. When we aim for justice, we acknowledge the harm done and look to reverse it by understanding its true causes and the needs of those impacted. Environmental justice looks not just at the planet, but at the people harmed by our bad environmental policies and practices, a shift pushed largely by Gen Z and millennials. And environmental justice recognizes that to transition to a future with universal clean energy, we must address the damage that will be done to workers in the fossil fuel industries when their jobs disappear. It's a recognition that we must push for change, but we must not forget about those who will be harmed by that change. Similarly, social justice recognizes that, to achieve equality[24] among everyone, we must address climate change and environmental racism, not just social forces like institutionalized racism, systematized classism, and lack of accessibility. Instead of asking what we can save, we ask who is currently being wronged. We can't ask that question without also asking who is responsible for that wrongdoing, and most often the answer is those who are wealthiest relative to most of the humans in the world. Thinking about problems in terms of justice helps us focus on those facing the greatest injustices rather than solely on our own desires, without letting us off the hook for the role we have to play in both the problem and the solution.

Social justice advocates have come to understand that injustice is rarely tidy, and it tends to cut across different demographic traits while overlapping with other forms of injustice. Legal scholar Kimberlé Crenshaw coined the term "intersectionality" in 1989 to recognize this. Crenshaw stated that traditional feminism and the antiracism movement have both failed to address the needs of Black women, because they face unique discrimination resulting from the intersecting forces of both sexism and racism. Their experience looks different from those of Black men or white women. Neither siloed movement could hope to address their needs without becoming intersectional—that is, acknowledging that many people are affected by intersecting forms of oppression and inequality and that those intersections are more complex than simply adding different forms of oppression together.

We can apply this same intersectional thinking to the challenge of bringing environmental issues and human issues together, rather than thinking about them separately, which goes against so much of the information we hear every day. The United Nations, for example, has long been involved in both environmental and humanitarian issues, but its siloed approach creates a barrier to understanding that climate change is a social justice issue and human issues are environmental, too. Separate agencies and working groups within the UN have created development goals aimed at reducing poverty and improving the quality of life in less wealthy nations and climate goals aimed at curbing global emissions enough to stop a catastrophic rise in temperatures, when these goals should be unified into one framework that addresses social and climate injustice together. And the legacy nonprofit organizations doing the most work cover only one side: planet or people. But just because that's the way it's always been done doesn't mean that's how you have to think. You can focus instead on the collective good—people and planet together—in all its intersectional messiness.

Not only can you, but you should. If you've thought of yourself as an environmentalist, or a social justice warrior, it's important to shift your mindset to think of all the problems facing us as interconnected in both their causes and their solutions. We cannot address one set of problems without addressing the others. After all, the root of virtually all of our problems is a mindset of extraction: extracting as much profit from the earth as possible, with no concern for how much is left for future generations, and extracting as much as possible from workers and customers, whether or not it's fair or just to do so. The capitalism-driven attitude that it's okay to exploit the planet also says it's okay to exploit people. There's no separation between the two. So our main task, and one that will always tend to push us toward greater justice for both people and the planet, is to root out extraction. *For whom?* helps us do that: if a solution is good for one group but not another, extraction is likely at play.

KEEPING THINGS IN PERSPECTIVE

Even people who mean well frequently push for change that isn't truly aiming for justice. Often this is due to their own unexamined biases but, every so often, it comes from a place of selfishness or unwillingness to look beyond their own self-interests.

This is not to say that only issues affecting those with the least power are important. The lack of women in C-level jobs—chief executive officer (CEO), chief financial officer (CFO), chief operating officer (COO), and similar positions—at major corporations is an important problem that needs addressing. That lack certainly contributes to workplaces that aren't women- and family-friendly. But it's important to keep a sense of perspective and make sure we aren't just fighting for those who already face the fewest barriers. Women who are in line for CEO are already among the most privileged women in society, and while they may not have as much privilege as the men who are more likely to get those jobs, they have vastly better circumstances than the factory and frontline workers who make whatever it is that the company sells. All activism that gets us closer to justice at every level is good, but the fights that achieve more power for those with the *least* power now are most important.

Asking *For whom?* also helps us understand if the action being pushed is one that's worth pushing, but with modifications. Preserving natural spaces is important, so John Muir's efforts to protect Yosemite weren't wrong, they were just aimed toward the wrong people. Efforts to conserve lands in partnership with Indigenous Americans,[25] First

Nations or Aboriginal[26] peoples in Canada, and other Indigenous groups around the world are far more likely to be about justice than those undertaken to exclude them. Fighting against "overpopulation" in predominantly poor countries without questioning overconsumption in rich countries puts the burden of fixing things onto those who didn't cause the problem in the first place and have the least power to fix it. Put your energy into supporting the solutions that advance true, intersectional justice.

CHAPTER 3

Develop an Activist's Mindset

Can everyone do this?

> *You have to act as if it were possible to*
> *radically transform the world.*
> *And you have to do it all the time.*
> —Angela Davis

Made in China has come to mean something beyond a simple label of a product's country of origin. In the 1980s, the label consumers saw most often on toys and electronics was *Made in Taiwan*, which many interpreted to mean that something was low-quality and cheaply produced. Since 2010, China has been the largest manufacturing power in the world, when it took the title away from the US. *Made in China* now suggests for many what *Made in Taiwan* once did, even though lots of top-quality items we rely on, like iPhones, are made there. But it also evokes more: the decline of American manufacturing, the downward price pressure making it hard for companies outside China to compete, the at-any-cost version of capitalism that treats humans as pawns. That's why one of the first things people often do when deciding to be more deliberate in their consumption is to question anything made in China.

If you track the rise of manufacturing in China, you also track the journey of China's huge population out of poverty. The World Bank estimates that 850 million people in China have moved out of extreme poverty in the last forty years, from 88 percent of its population in 1981 to 0.7 percent in 2015.[1] The poverty reduction in China is so dramatic that it represents a full 75 percent of all poverty reduction in the world in the 1990s and 2000s. China alone is responsible for the UN reaching its millennium development goals of reducing global poverty by half. Manufacturing brought wealth into China that has paved the way for a vastly improved standard of living among virtually all its inhabitants. It now has more social safety-net programs, like rural pensions (retirement benefits for self-employed farmers), than it did just a few decades ago, and the country is considered solidly middle-income. While only 17 percent of China's population works in manufacturing today, without the industry, the country's transformation would not have been possible.[2] We may have a knee-jerk negative reaction to the *Made in China* label. But if you care about reducing poverty, an unexpected truth is that buying things made in China *does* reduce poverty.

That's not to say that buying something made in China has no downsides. Goods made in China generally travel many thousands of miles to reach their eventual buyers, burning through fossil fuels along the way, and they are made by a workforce that usually works twelve-hour shifts, six days a week. Many factory workers leave family behind to come to the industrialized cities from rural areas and get so little time off that the most often they can hope to travel back home is once a year. Those who work in factories don't receive workers' compensation if they get injured, and they can't hope to be represented by a labor union that resembles those in the West that will fight on workers' behalf for better treatment.[3] The factories aren't held to the same environmental standards of those in wealthier countries, contributing to China's status as one of the countries with the dirtiest air, and workers are often forced to work without proper protection from on-the-job hazards. Factory owners are getting much wealthier much faster than those working for them: while the average income in China is nine times what it was forty years ago after factoring in inflation, for the top 1 percent, it's twenty-one times. And of course there's the fact that money going into China also supports an authoritarian regime that jails those who protest against it and has an abysmal human rights record for those it deems undesirable, like the estimated 1 million Muslim Uighurs being held in detention camps, many of whom are believed to be forced to work in factories and cotton fields.[4]

We can decry the exploitation of Chinese workers, an indisputable aspect of many industries in China. We can detest their blend of authoritarianism and capitalism. We can get angry that the country isn't doing more to regulate its pollution. But we must also accept that manufacturing has, without a doubt, made life better for nearly everyone in China. If we care about the well-being of our fellow humans, that means wanting people to have more financial stability and better safety-net protections everywhere—not just in our own backyard, and not just when they do things the way we wish they would.

The financial choices we make are rarely simple, as the case of China reminds us. Attempting to make positive financial choices for the collective good can quickly feel overwhelming and bewildering. This is no doubt why so much advice on how to make a difference attempts to boil things down to the simplest possible message, often at the expense of the part of the message that actually makes the difference: "Recycle!" rather than "Maybe try not to buy packaged drinks to begin with." However, while we can't take the complexity out of every decision, we can each cultivate an informed mindset for financial decision-making that best expresses our values in the world and set reasonable expectations for ourselves. Moreover, understanding the complexity of our choices and their sometimes conflicting impacts is important for assessing information we receive in the future and deciding how to act on it, because the landscape is always changing. I can't write a book that will anticipate every future choice you could be faced with—no one can. So rather than try to create a list of "good choices" and "bad choices" that will quickly become outdated, my goal is to leave you with an approach to thinking about your choices that will help you see through the lies you will continue to be told and to help you understand when you're not getting the whole story. This chapter will help you sort all of this out.

THERE IS NO PERFECTION

Globalization has plenty of drawbacks, but one of its greatest benefits is moving capital around the world so that those who haven't had access to it in the past can improve their standard of living. With 23 percent of the world's workforce employed in manufacturing and its related industries,[5] the main driver we have to improve people's standard of living is through supporting global supply chains. Opting never to buy something made overseas in favor of only locally made and locally sold goods is a valid choice, but it's not one we should make flippantly. As much as it reminds us that there are a wide range of impacts from our choices, *Made in China* also reminds us, perhaps more importantly, that there are virtually no perfect choices. Buying something made in China means supporting the deplorable and exploitative things happening there along with supporting the movement of huge numbers of people out of poverty. But buying something locally made, while it keeps more money in your community, denies people overseas the opportunity to improve their standard of living, something they surely deserve to do.

In every choice we make, there are pros and cons. Our task is to do the best we can knowing that every choice we make is imperfect. That's actually a good thing, because it frees us from putting too much pressure on ourselves to get every little thing right, and it enables us to put most of our energy into the biggest, most impactful choices.

Chasing perfection is always a losing proposition anyway, one that often holds us back from doing simple, practical things that help the collective good. The idea that you must be vegan—and never "cheat"—if you care about animals and the planet scares off a lot of people who would otherwise be completely game to eat fewer animal products and reduce the carbon impacts of their diet. The strictness and starkness of minimalism keeps a lot of people from considering the benefits of consuming less. And the ubiquitous high-end stainless steel of the zero-waste movement signals that only those who can afford such things are welcome, along with the *zero* in its actual name implying that it's perfection or nothing. So many of the social and environmental movements seeking to do good come with what is in essence an ideological purity test, and only those who score perfectly are welcome. Something to consider: If your activism has an aesthetic, it's probably more performative than impactful. At the very least, it's almost certainly scaring off people who would otherwise be likely to join in.

Another good reason not to aim for perfection is that efforts to do so often inappropriately co-opt the language or culture of one group of people to elevate a cause. For example, some white vegan activists appropriate the culture of people of color around the world without acknowledgment. Black vegans and people of color advocating for plant-based diets have pointed out that these diets have deep roots in Africa,[6] India, and west Asia[7] and that Black Americans are about twice as likely to be vegan as white Americans.[8] Dr. Lisa Betty writes about the origins of the term *vegan*, coined in 1944:

> From its beginnings, veganism . . . was unequivocally colo-
> nial, white centered-supremacist, and elitist. Culturally Euro-
> centric, veganism required moral astuteness, restriction,
> vigilance, and shame. It was not liberatory, intersectional, rad-
> ical, or decolonial . . . veganism did not emphasize or give ref-
> erence to Black, brown, [or] Indigenous cultures throughout
> the world that practiced forms of veganism and conscientious
> consumption within the narratives of veganism's history.[9]

In fact, the largest percentages of plant-based eaters in the world live in the global south: 375 million people in India, 29 million people in Brazil, and large percentages of the population in Taiwan, Jamaica, Mexico, and Vietnam.[10] And yet, the major faces of veganism tend to be white, with few efforts made to amplify voices of people of color. Worse, it's not uncommon to see white vegans or prominent organizations like PETA, People for the Ethical Treatment of Animals, using inappropriate analogies, comparing the treatment of farm animals to that of enslaved people, or likening animal slaughter to the Holocaust, comparisons that advocates of color say trivialize white supremacy and dehumanize groups that have experienced atrocities.[11] Juliana Yazbeck, an Arab writer, points out that white veganism "disregards the fact that the meat and dairy industries are inherently colonial leg-acies," and that the vegan drive to eat more cashews, coconuts, and avocados, all of which come largely from the global south, doesn't pay enough attention to the devastating impacts this consumer demand has for farmers and Indigenous peoples in those regions.[12] Erin White writes in an article for Afropunk that what's "so frustrating about too many animal-free platforms is the bizarre prioritization of animal welfare over that of the humans who produce the food . . . So often these conversations center the rights of animals to the point where they ignore the inhumane working conditions [of] poor, often undocumented laborers who provide all of our produce as well."[13] This should go without saying, but don't compare human experiences to those of nonhumans, and don't use atrocities for analogies. If we let go of trying to achieve perfection and simply focus on making progress, it's much less tempting to venture into these types of extreme rhetoric that do harm, because there is no need to depict problems in extreme terms if we're not rigidly promoting extreme solutions.

The urge to label an idea in the first place can be a big part of the problem, especially because so many of the labels we know best are absolute: *always* doing this, *never* doing that. Labels can act as gatekeepers, signaling who is allowed in and who doesn't measure up. When you label something you're doing, diverging from that label for even a brief moment—a vegan who eats a strip of bacon, say—feels like a failure instead of an occasional and deliberate splurge that's worth it if it keeps you making good choices most of the time. And we're wired to give up on things when we feel like failures. That's a big part of why diets don't work. We feel deprived by the rigid rules, and when we slip up, we conclude that we're destined to fail anyway, rather than understanding that imperfection is par for the course. If we bring a diet mindset to our financial habits and purchasing decisions, we're unlikely to make enduring changes over the long term.

This is a big part of why wallet activism is not a rigidly defined set of choices but rather a decision-making *process* that you shape for yourself with your values. Wallet activism is a practice, not a destination. The landscape is constantly changing, and a choice that was bad last year might be good now; for example, not buying a product while its employees are striking, but resuming again after new conditions are in place. A past example is the Delano Grape Strike in the 1960s, which gained prominence thanks to Cesar Chavez's involvement, urging consumers not to buy table grapes from California's Central Valley until farmworkers' demands were met. Buying during the strike was working against those fighting for better working conditions, but buying California grapes afterward sent a signal to companies that it's good business to accede to workers' demands. (Chavez was quoted as saying, "The fight is never about grapes or lettuce. It is always about people.") Give yourself the latitude to change your choices as circumstances change and you take in new information. Continual learning and adaptation are crucial.

Go into the process knowing that you're allowed to make mistakes. You're even allowed to make choices that you know are bad for people or the planet if they are the exception, not the rule. *Allowed* really has no place in the discussion, because there's no one looking over your shoulder, no test at the end. There's no one to criticize you for making a choice that breaks some arbitrary set of rules. It's far better to make choices in the interest of the collective good 80 percent of the time than to conclude that diverging from them 20 percent of the time makes you a failure and then give up entirely. Move forward with the mindset that you're aiming to make good choices *most* of the time. If we all started doing that, we'd quickly live in a different and far better world.

Beware, however, of the phenomenon social psychologists call moral self-licensing, an unconscious tendency to forgive our own unethical or problematic behaviors because of past good deeds. One study found that, after viewing different types of foods, the participants who were exposed to organic foods volunteered significantly less time to help a needy stranger, and they judged others' choices significantly more harshly than did those who viewed nonorganic foods.[14] Researchers hypothesized that just thinking about a choice deemed "good" by society (buying organic food) gave people the moral licensing to behave selfishly in other interactions. It's an easy trap to fall into if you don't watch out for it. Try to learn to spot it in your own thoughts and behaviors so you can reframe your thinking.

AIM FOR ACTUAL PROGRESS, NOT EASY WINS

In 2015, a video went viral that showed a sea turtle with a plastic drinking straw up its nose, as well as the upsetting footage of researchers extracting it. The video set off a wave of people railing against plastic straws, and within a few years, cities and towns large and small began banning them. Environmentalists hailed these policy wins, and all appearances were that this was a positive step toward reducing the plastic in our oceans, a problem of massive proportion.

However, as with so many of these stories, it's not as simple as that. Immediately after people started to float the idea of straw bans, disability rights activists spoke up: banning plastic straws would harm the disability community,[15] and none of the alternative material straws would work for their needs. Many disabled people[16] who don't have full use of their hands, or who have other mobility challenges, require straws to drink both cold and warm beverages and to take medications. The other options out there—paper, corn resins, stainless steel—all fall short in some way, whether they disintegrate in a hot drink, can't be positioned to meet mobility needs, are hard to clean, or are prohibitively expensive. Some cities responded by specifying that plastic straws would still be available upon request to disabled people. But with no enforcement mechanism for that, disability rights activists speculated that businesses would stop buying plastic straws altogether if they weren't allowed to give them out to most customers, meaning disabled customers would not get their needs met. Some environmentalists proposed that disabled people carry their own straws, demonstrating great ignorance about the finances of being disabled: disabled people are far more likely than others to live in poverty thanks to government program rules that limit how much they can save and cap the benefits they receive well below a realistic cost of living. But by and large, the activists pushing for plastic straw bans were silent in response to the pleas from disabled people.

It's also worth taking a step back to ask if straw bans were really the right solution to the problem. In anticipation of widespread plastic straw bans, large chain restaurants began introducing alternatives. Starbucks introduced a new lid for its cold beverages that's reminiscent of a sippy cup, eliminating the need for a straw for most customers. But researchers quickly determined that the new lid actually contains more plastic than the old lid and straw combined.[17] What's more, looking at the data, it's clear that if we want to prevent plastic from getting into our oceans, straws are a lousy place to start. They make up a minuscule percentage of the plastic in the oceans, while fishing nets, which we don't regulate meaningfully on a global scale, make up a huge percentage: one study found that nearly half (46 percent) of all the plastic in the Great Pacific Garbage Patch is from fishing nets.[18] In 2018, three hundred sea turtles were found dead, tangled in discarded plastic fishing nets off the coast of the Mexican state of Oaxaca.[19] But that news failed to spur the same action that the straw video did, despite the incident being far more costly to wild sea turtle populations.

In an effort to do the right thing for the environment—and for our endangered sea turtles—we instead ended up with a situation in which we're not meaningfully reducing the plastic in the oceans, and we're making dining establishments less accessible for disabled people. Worse still, we're pitting people and the environment against one another, reinforcing the false notion that we can't address the needs of the planet and people jointly.

Efforts like the campaign to institute plastic straw bans are all too common in our culture: visible efforts focusing on things that have gotten attention, but which aren't actually the problem and which might make things worse, all to feel like we've "done something." It feels good to get a law passed or make businesses change what they're doing. But when we're not looking at how the thing we're focused on fits into the big picture, disregarding its unintended consequences, we're not undertaking activism, we're performing. While there are no perfect decisions, we can defeat our own goals by focusing on *visible* actions over *impactful* ones.

That's the mindset to use when thinking about where to focus your wallet activism. It's not about receiving accolades or gaining the most likes on social media. It's about taking our responsibility seriously as part of a collective force that's destroying the planet and perpetuating an unjust and unequal society. Rather than pushing for outright bans on plastic straws, activists could have engaged the public to pressure companies to offer alternatives, so customers could choose which they prefer. Or they could have taken from the video not that straws are evil, but that there's too much plastic in the oceans, and we should first go after the biggest contributors to the problem. The lack of regulation of fishing nets around the world is a large-scale problem that will take international cooperation and years or decades to address, and more stores offering paper and plastic straws side by side would not sound quite as sexy as saying you've gotten a bunch of laws passed. That's surely why we still have so many of the issues that we've known about for as long as we can remember: people have gone for the easy or brag-worthy wins over the less visible wins that change things for the better. Aim for impact, not applause.

UNDERSTAND WHERE TO PUT PRESSURE

With the problem of plastic straws, activists could have used consumer power to push for action or aim for policy change. They chose policy change. While it had unintended ramifications in that case, often, that *is* the best course of action. (For instance, it's unlikely that we as customers could get a power company to curtail its emissions without laws or regulations forcing it to. No matter how hard we try, our consumer-driven efforts will never result in all carbon emissions being taxed.) But on the other side, when our leaders fail to act, or in instances when we as consumers hold the power to change things, it's essential to practice wallet activism. So it's important to understand where to put pressure in order to have the greatest impact.

Economists often use a metaphor to talk about how to make change happen: the carrot and the stick. Both are incentives we aim to create for entities to do the thing we want; one is encouraging, while the other is more punitive. In the metaphor, we're trying to get an obstinate donkey to move in the direction we want it to go. The carrot is what you dangle in front of the donkey to incentivize and reward it for doing the thing you want it to do, while the stick delivers a hard thwap if it does the wrong thing. While there are plenty of exceptions to this, a general rule is that consumer choices are the carrot and policies are the stick. Laws and regulations tell companies what they aren't allowed to do, and consumers signal to them what will net the greatest profits. Knowing that world governments are unlikely to ban conventionally grown produce anytime soon—we'll talk about whether they should even consider doing so in chapter seven—if we want to see a more reliable and affordable supply of organic produce on store shelves, we go with the metaphorical carrot: buying more organic fruits and vegetables to drive up demand and push producers to shift more of their operations to organics. But if we want to achieve an outright ban on an especially harmful weed killer in agriculture, we almost certainly need the stick of government rules banning or limiting the sale or use of the chemical. The most successful efforts often use both approaches in concert: making it in a company's best interest to change its ways because consumers will support it, while pushing government to pass policies that will punish business if it doesn't change.

In approaching your wallet activism, it's helpful to understand both the massive potential for change that exists if consumers demand it, as well as the limits on consumer action. Sometimes the best course of action will be to rally consumers around a cause, and other times you'll have greater success if you put on your citizen or civic participant hat and rally political action.

In financial terms, *capital* is anything you own that makes you money. Owning stock shares makes you money as stocks increase in value. Owning a home makes you money because home prices tend to go up over time. Owning a factory makes you money from selling the products manufactured there. But we can redefine capital to think of it in terms of our power in society. Capital is not only anything you own that makes you money but also anything you possess that can be a force for positive change. When we think about capital that way, we recognize that we as individuals possess a great deal of it: financial capital that we can deploy to create positive demand or withhold to shrink harmful demand, social capital we can deploy to build support among our networks of friends and family, workplace capital we can use to promote more just employment practices, political capital we can deploy to push policy change, and the list goes on.

Going back to the carrots and sticks, in general, if you want to see more of something in the world, deploying your financial capital as a carrot is incredibly powerful. If we want to see more electric cars on the road, nothing will make that happen faster than boosting demand so automakers see how well electric cars are selling and shift more of their production away from fossil fuel–powered cars. Political capital can help, too, as government can provide money to research the most efficient electric engines and longest lasting batteries. It can also put into place tax credits and other measures that will convince more people to buy electric cars, but government moves slowly while consumers can move quickly. Any entity that exists to make a profit will follow the money. When consumers can show a company there's money to be made on something that also serves the collective good, that's as powerful as anything government can put into place. Accordingly, if we want to see less of something, there is no bigger stick than policy and regulation. If you wish to see a whole industry change its ways, for example, it's still worth using your financial capital as a carrot, but focusing on policy change will ultimately be necessary. We'll talk much more about energy consumption in chapter six, but if you want to see every electricity generator in the country stop using all fossil fuels, that will certainly require action from policymakers.

An exception to the carrot and stick rule for consumer behavior is the boycott. A boycott aims to force a company to make a change, either by withholding profits from it or harming its reputation. While not every boycott is successful—often they are not sustained long enough, are not clear enough in their demands, or do not focus enough on gaining public attention—there are plentiful examples of consumer boycotts that have led companies to make meaningful, long-term changes. In the 1790s, people in England who wished to abolish slavery boycotted sugar produced in the Americas by enslaved people and instead began to buy sugar from India, giving rise to the concept of the guaranteed harm-free product, in this case sugar guaranteed to be produced without slavery.[20] That same pattern has been repeated in boycotts that have given us conflict-free diamonds, dolphin-safe tuna, and a wide range of cruelty-free health and beauty products. Boycotts have successfully forced companies to be less discriminatory in their hiring practices, like the 1941 boycott of Safeway stores led by the NAACP.[21] Boycotts have forced corporations to stop supporting harmful causes, like the campaign in the 2010s to get airlines and hotel chains to stop supporting the NRA—the National Rifle Association—through discounted rates offered to its members.[22] They've forced companies to stop inhumane practices, like the late 1990s boycott of oil company Shell over its support of a Nigerian dictatorship and exploitation of the workers there.[23] And they've forced companies to make their pay fairer, like the table grapes boycott discussed a few pages ago that led to the creation of United Farm Workers and resulted in better pay and conditions for migrant farmworkers.[24]

Of course, a boycott is not something you can do alone. The most effective boycotts are those focused primarily on hurting a company's brand reputation.[25] If you can pair a boycott with visibility for a company's bad practices—especially if it makes it into news coverage or gets a lot of attention on social media—a small number of people can successfully achieve change. Brayden King, a professor in Northwestern's Kellogg School of Management, says, "The no. 1 predictor of what makes a boycott effective is how much media attention it creates, not how many people sign onto a petition or how many consumers it mobilizes."[26] Another effective strategy is to target a company's shareholders, or to threaten the price of its stock, again with increased likelihood of success the more you can visibly spread the word. This could be as simple as getting together a group of friends and having everyone tweet at key financial reporters with credible information of a company's misdeeds and your boycott plans. Or, if you have the means, you might encourage a range of like-minded activists to purchase the minimum number of shares of a company's stock to be invited to the shareholders meeting, and then show up there and protest vocally (all the better if you can invite members of the media to attend).

A long-term benefit of boycotts is that companies that have been publicly boycotted often become more concerned about public perceptions, and they're more likely to be responsive to criticisms in the future. The athletic gear brand Nike was the subject of boycotts and intense scrutiny in the 1990s over revelations that it used child labor to produce its sneakers. Not only did it overhaul its labor practices and improve the transparency of its supply chain, Nike also became a leader in many areas of corporate social responsibility, from promoting social justice and racial equality to making major improvements to its manufacturing process to lessen its environmental impact.[27] More recently, Nike has gotten attention for its ties to forced labor in China,[28] which underscores that, while boycotts can achieve great things, they rarely achieve permanent change, and it's important to keep holding past wrongdoers accountable.

If you wish to start a boycott, do some digging first to find out if one already exists that you can join and amplify. Then get vocal: share who or what you're boycotting and why with your online networks and local reporters if it's a local issue or national reporters if it's larger. But before instigating a boycott, know whether your goal is just to get that company to change its ways, or whether it's to use the company as an example to draw more attention to a larger issue. Companies generally want boycotts to end as quickly as possible, to minimize the damage done both to the balance sheet and to the brand, and if you're just trying to get them to change a specific practice, that can be a good thing. It allows you to resolve the boycott quickly and move on to the next cause. But if your goal is to make a company an example, a longer-term boycott will be necessary. If you're successful in getting a company to change its ways, the final step of the boycott should be to praise the company publicly. This provides a carrot for that company and others to give in to boycotters' demands in the future.

It is in our nature as social beings to share what we know, especially the things that really get us fired up. And wallet activism is most effective if lots of us practice it, meaning that it's essential we spread the word rather than make different choices in silence. When deciding what to share—whether contemplating a boycott or championing a cause—we can better understand what choices are worth promoting with the second guiding question.

CAN EVERYONE DO THIS?

The question *Can everyone do this?* serves two main purposes: it helps you get a handle on how accessible and scalable a particular choice is, and it offers a lens for critical thinking about that choice.

The outdoor clothing company Patagonia has from its founding stated its commitment to sustainable manufacturing practices: it will take back any clothes you've bought from it in the past that are now worn out to be recycled, and it pays all of its employees a living wage. Patagonia is far from perfect—for example, it has been accused of using forced Uighur labor in its supply chain.[29] While not excusing that deplorable practice, many of its other practices are what we should want every manufacturing company to strive for. However, Patagonia's products are also expensive, well out of the reach of most people, and the brand is often nicknamed "Pata-Gucci." *Can everyone do this?* Can everyone buy Patagonia? The answer is clearly no. So while some may opt to buy from Patagonia if they need a new jacket and can afford it, asking *everyone* to buy their clothes only from Patagonia and companies like it is an idea doomed to fail, because most people simply don't have the luxury of making that choice. But more importantly, suggesting that the right thing to do is to buy from Patagonia will invariably shame and alienate a sizable number of people who might otherwise be receptive to your message, because the price is out of reach.

The question applies not just to monetary cost but also to scalability—in essence whether something would still work if everyone did it. The freegan philosophy, for example, emphasizes living for free off of waste streams, eating the food that others have discarded, supplemented by whatever you can forage in the wild. For those who enjoy the challenge and adventure of it, that's great. But never mind those who wouldn't dream of dumpster diving (or those who physically can't get into a dumpster), or the vast majority of us who don't have time to spend seeking out each meal. The freegan approach simply isn't scalable. If everyone started refusing to pay for food, we'd very quickly have none. It costs money to grow food, to harvest it, to transport it, and to sell it, and we have to pay for that somehow. Freeganism, and other approaches that either aren't accessible to most people or can't scale up to everyone, are great at the margins and can be rewarding for those with the time and inclination to pursue them, but they won't get us to the widespread changes that we need. And they may even be counterproductive, spreading the false notion that you have to put an enormous effort into doing things that create change. It's far more productive to promote approaches that are doable universally or nearly universally so we're growing demand in the right places.

Just because something is not doable by everyone doesn't mean you shouldn't do it if you are able. But if you decide to talk about that action, it's important to provide additional context. Often a simple solution is to caveat the ideas you share. If you wish to spread the word about the harms of single-use plastics and are inclined to mention drinking straws, you might say, "If you're able, it's great to avoid using single-use plastic drinking straws," instead of proclaiming flat out that plastic straws should be eliminated. When the reason everyone can't do something is about cost specifically, the best approach is to promote a principle instead of a specific company—for example, recommending that people make more sustainable choices when acquiring clothing—and then list resources at a range of budget levels, not just at the high end.

A final use of *Can everyone do this?* is to help you think through *why* everyone can't, and what that tells you about the potential choice. As we'll discuss in the next chapter, a low price is often an indication that something was produced through exploitation, but the reverse is not automatically true: a high price doesn't guarantee that something was produced ethically. Compare the price of the product you're considering to comparable products, and then see if the company provides a satisfactory explanation of why their product costs more. You can buy a stainless steel water bottle for a few dollars, though it may not be as aesthetically pleasing as the trendy one sold by the more popular brand that touts its eco cred. Does their bottle include much more recycled content? Do they pay their workers significantly better? Do they include in the purchase price a shipping label to send it back to them when you no longer need it so they can recycle it? Or is there no explanation for the higher price point? If there's no explanation, that's a good indicator that they're putting on an eco-friendly facade to push profits, not out of a sincere desire to change the status quo.

DEFINE YOUR FINANCIAL VALUES

The concepts we've covered so far in this chapter apply to everyone who wants to use financial power toward the collective good. In this last section, however, we'll talk about the principles that you may wish to add to your own personal approach to wallet activism, based on your own values and the causes you care most about.

Chances are good that you won't be able to do everything I suggest in this book. Each of us has only so much time, attention, and money. While you're certainly free to pick and choose what to take on based on what feels most doable in your life, I propose a different approach: letting your values be your guide. Defining what's most important to you will help you make and prioritize decisions confidently, even when they appear to be complicated. Let's say you're passionate about racial justice, and you're frustrated that we're not doing more as a society to reduce the income and wealth gaps between white families and families of color. You may then decide to make that the focus of your wallet activism, going out of your way to shop at Black-, Latino-, Asian-, and Indigenous-owned businesses and support farmers of color, even if that means being less intentional about the sources of your consumer goods and the practices that go into producing your food. Your choices will look different in some cases than they will for someone else who puts addressing climate change above everything. So long as you understand the importance of balancing the needs of people and the planet in your choices, you'll rarely be led astray letting your values guide you, because they will always help you rule out the worst choices.

The goal of this section is to help you automate some of your decision-making so that you don't exhaust yourself trying to learn every possible impact of every choice you make, large and small. In my first book, *Work Optional*, I used the analogy of being a vegetarian who is offered a burger. If you already know you don't eat meat, you don't have to waste any mental or emotional energy on that choice. You simply decline and move on. We're doing much the same thing here in identifying the choices that you can make without much thought, with a focus on the collective good.

First, begin by spending some time thinking about what issues are most important to you, the topics that really get you fired up. The range of possible answers is virtually limitless, but to get you started, some answers could include the following:

- air pollution
- animal welfare
- deforestation
- disability rights
- education quality
- food sovereignty
- gender equity
- gentrification
- global warming
- homelessness

- human trafficking
- hunger
- income equality
- Indigenous rights
- land rights
- LGBTQ+ rights
- local community development
- plastic pollution

- racial equity
- veteran welfare
- walkability of cities
- wilderness preservation
- worker exploitation

After you have a list, do your best to rank the topics in priority order, with the goal of arriving at three to five that feel closest to your heart.

To help get you in the right mindset for the next piece, consider what you already know about how your financial choices impact the issues you care most about, using your prioritized list. For example, if you care a lot about racial equity, but you haven't sought out goods and services made or sold by companies owned by people of color, you've found an area where your values and your financial choices don't currently align, and you've identified an action step for yourself. If you care about global warming and air pollution, but you travel by car and plane frequently when you have less environmentally harmful options available to you, there's another misalignment and something you can focus on changing. Think also about things you'd like to see more of in the world and things you'd like to see less of, drawing from your top-priority issues. Maybe you'd like to see more mass transit in midsize cities and fewer cars. Or more wealth for families of color and fewer wage and wealth gaps.

As you're pondering this question, it's useful to ask yourself whether you think it's more important to *know* you're a part of driving large-scale change, even if you never see evidence of it with your own eyes, or if you care more about *seeing* progress in your local community. For example, working to change the social safety nets so fewer people experience homelessness versus helping one person get into permanent housing. Both approaches are valid, but knowing which you value more can serve as a tiebreaker when you're on the fence about a decision.

As Vicki Robin wrote in *Your Money or Your Life*, your money is an expression of your life force in the world. My slight tweak on Robin's idea is that your financial choices are how you express your values to the world. So this final exercise is about figuring out your core values, or the principles you live by or aspire to live by. This is the most important piece of all, but it's often easier to figure out your values after you've thought about the causes you most care about and your vision for a better future, as they can often reveal where your heart is. Again, the list is potentially infinite, but some possible values you could write down include the following:

- compassion
- fairness (in how we treat others)
- generosity (in helping those with fewer financial resources)
- growth
- justice (social or environmental)
- optimism
- responsibility (to care for our fellow humans or look after the planet)
- self-reliance
- service
- trust (in others to make choices that are best in their circumstances)

Just like in the first exercise, choose your top three to five values, those you hold most dear. Then fill in the following financial values statement, the distillation of all of this thinking, led by your values:

I use my financial capital to promote the values of _____,

_____,

_____, and

_____ in the world, especially when my choices can make a difference on issues of _____,

_____,

_____, and

_____. I care about other values and issues, too, but these are my top priorities.

I do my best to make financial choices that support my values and the issues most important to me, creating demand for things I want to see more of in the world, like

_____,

_____,

_____, and

_____. I always strive to minimize my choices that run counter to them, denying demand for things I want to see less of, specifically _____,

_____,

_____,

and _____.

When in doubt, I lean toward choices that benefit _____ [pick one] (my community/large-scale systemic change).

There is power in doing this exercise and writing all of it down to help you commit to using your financial capital toward the collective good. If you're inspired, write or type and print this out and post it on a wall so you get a frequent reminder. If something feels like it's missing, add language to it. This is yours to adapt however best suits you. When facing a financial decision, you can come back to this statement to help you make the choice that best aligns to what you care about most, especially if you're feeling stuck between several possible options. And it's a living document, so update it if you change your mind about something or come to care passionately about a new issue. If you aren't quite ready to fill it out now, that's okay. The rest of this book may bring you more clarity on the issues that you're most fired up about. Make a note to return to this exercise when you're done.

An activist's work is to keep chipping away at a big problem over time, not giving up when things are hard and not getting discouraged when change comes incrementally rather than in big bursts. It's the same for your wallet activism: if you can use your financial power to express your values in the world, over time they will add up to something truly meaningful.

CHAPTER 4

What Is the True Cost?

Is it too cheap?

> *The real cost is always more*
> *than just the money you shell out.*
> —Jeff Nichols

It's a familiar scene: a door opens, a family walks through, shouts of "Oh my God!" erupt as hands reach up to cover mouths agape, and we cut to commercial. Then we're back, the shouts resume, and the camera pans across a newly renovated home, interspersing the ugly and poorly lit "before" pictures with the gleaming bright "after." There are tears, and hugs, and cries of "I can't believe it's the same space!" Inevitably, the renovation features a new kitchen with perfectly polished new appliances, a massive sink, and—to everyone's delight—a big new kitchen island with lots of prep space and stools where kids can eat. A home-owner will ask, no doubt prodded by a producer off camera, "What is this countertop material? It's so nice."

"Quartz!" the host replies. "And it's recycled! It's a green product."

"Wow, that's great! We care about the planet," the homeowner replies (apparently forgetting about the multiple dumpsters' worth of building materials that were hauled out of the home and to the landfill a few weeks earlier to make way for all the new stuff).

Fans of home improvement television must be forgiven for believing all of this. Because it's a lie: quartz is not a green product.

Before quartz became the material darling of home renovations, the most popular countertop material for decades was granite. Granite is a hard igneous rock that forms over millions of years deep underground as magma from the earth's core cools. It comes out of the ground at quarries, giant holes dug out of the earth's surface to extract materials that can be brought out in large chunks. It's then cut into thin slabs, polished, and shipped thousands of miles around the world to become people's kitchen prep surfaces—at least until the next renovation happens, after which the granite is most likely to spend eternity in a landfill. Because it takes so long to form, we're not getting more granite anytime soon. Though it's a common rock, all the granite that's in the ground is essentially all we'll ever have.

The countertop material we call quartz is more accurately called engineered stone, a mix of silica-rich quartz dust and a range of mining by-products, perhaps some small amount of recycled glass or stone, and a composite of plastics that binds it all together. Because it doesn't have to be quarried in slabs and doesn't require regular sealing with chemicals to avoid staining like granite does, engineered stone is certainly an improvement in environmental terms. Its actual contents can vary, so we can theoretically make an infinite supply of it in an endless array of colors and visual textures. It's also cheaper than granite, which makes it an attractive option to price-sensitive home renovators. But the price shown for engineered stone at the store does not reflect its true cost.

The process of going from raw quartz to an installed countertop looks like this: Large slabs of engineered stone are made in factories around the world (the greatest volume comes from Israel, Spain, and the US state of Minnesota) after baking together quartz dust, other mineral aggregate, and natural and synthetic binders.[1] Those slabs are then shipped to stone yards and big-box stores close to where people live so they can peruse their options before making a choice. After homeowners select their preferred finish, workers visit the home to measure the space available for the counters, then cut and polish the slabs to make sure everything fits perfectly.

Though it seems like a minor step in the process, that cutting is a big problem. When a slab of engineered stone is cut, it releases silica dust. That silica dust, if a worker inhales it, causes the deadly lung disease silicosis, in addition to other problems like kidney failure, lung cancer, and autoimmune disease.[2] In one study in Israel alone, at least twenty-two workers had silicosis severe enough to require lung transplants.[3] In response to the threat to workers' health, the Occupational Safety and Health Administration (OSHA) in the US created rules to reduce workers' exposure to silica dust. But studies have found that most of the protections offered to workers are inadequate to protect them fully, and with most countertop fabrication done by small companies and independent contractors, it's virtually impossible to monitor compliance with the rules.[4]

The price a homeowner pays for a slab of quartz countertop does not reflect the cost of the health care those workers will require. It does not reflect the cost to society or their families for their lost labor. Nor does it reflect the long-term climate impacts of the fossil fuels burned to transform it from dust in a quarry into someone's finished kitchen counter. When we think about the cost to us, we're only looking at part of the picture.

Economists call the cost of the countertop workers' health care an externality: an impact created by the production or consumption of something that's not included in the price consumers or end users pay for it. In other words, an externality is a cost you're imposing on someone else so that you can get something at an artificially low price. An externality you've certainly encountered is secondhand smoke. The price a smoker pays for a pack of cigarettes does not reflect the potential harm that may come to you from inhaling their secondhand smoke—nor does it include the cost of their own health care, for that matter. The most common and problematic externality is the pollution created by manufacturing and transporting the goods we buy. If every factory existed within a closed bubble, it would have no choice but to institute (and pay for) systems to clean up the air and water emissions it produces, so that the bubble didn't quickly fill with pollution and become impossible to operate in. And if factory owners were responsible for the cost of their workers' health care, they'd have a strong incentive to keep that bubble clean to avoid paying higher costs as workers get sick. But the only bubble is the great big one of the planet we all share. So instead, producers don't pay the price for their pollution, we as consumers don't pay directly for the pollution, and the costs to the climate and to people's health for that pollution get shifted to . . . *well, we'd just prefer not to think about that.*

To practice wallet activism, we must think about externalities. And we must go a step further, because economists generally put things in clinical- and academic-sounding terms. We must clarify that when we say *externalities*, what we really mean is unjust harm to certain people and parts of the planet especially. While it's true that electricity generated from coal or natural gas puts pollution into the atmosphere—an externality not reflected by the price on your utility bill—what's more precise is that this electricity generation tends to happen next to poorer neighborhoods, lowering property values and creating the worst health impacts for those who are least able to move to healthier but more expensive areas.[5] We do not all bear the weight of externalities equally.

To make the best choices possible, it's important to understand the full cost of something, externalities and all, not just what's written on the price tag.

THE HIDDEN COSTS OF OUR FINANCIAL CHOICES

Though a huge number of our financial choices aren't related to buying objects, let's focus for now on the physical items we purchase. The simplest way to understand the hidden costs involved in our choices is to consider each stage of existence for a physical item and what goes into that stage: extraction, manufacture, packaging, transport, retail, consumption, and disposal. For any given item we might consider purchasing, each of those steps has already taken place, or will inevitably take place, and it's up to us whether we want to support that entire chain of events and externalities or whether we wish to withhold our support. Thinking about a simple object that most of us have used, a spiral notebook, let's walk through its entire life cycle:

Extraction: A notebook is composed largely of two substances: paper (both the cardboard covers and the paper inside) and metal (the spiral coil). Paper begins as a tree that's cut down and transported to a pulp mill, as well as waste sawdust from sawmills and sometimes a small amount of recycled paper. The metal most commonly used in notebook coils is steel with a small amount of carbon added. It begins its life as iron ore that's mined all over the world, with the largest quantities coming from Australia and Brazil. Most iron ore is mined from open pit mines that harm local ecosystems and pollute both groundwater and surface water nearby, and which are often located on stolen Indigenous lands. Mining practices subject mine workers to toxic dust high in silica, causing significantly higher rates of silicosis and lung cancer, just like with quartz countertops, except that mine workers typically spend much more time exposed to the dust. To make steel, that raw iron ore goes through several energy-intensive heating and purifying processes, most often powered by coal. In that process, it is mixed with alloying metals such as manganese, chromium, and nickel, all of which also need to be mined and purified, coming with their own environmental and worker-health impacts. The mix of metals that gives our steel the desired qualities (in this case being able to be made into a thin, flexible wire without breaking—very different qualities than if we wanted the steel to become beams that would hold up tall buildings) are heated together at a steel refining facility, and the resulting product is cast into slabs ready to be shaped. The wood pulp and steel are each transported to the factories where the next steps happen, perhaps traveling thousands of miles before they become a usable product.

Manufacture: Going from tree to paper often requires two different factories—a pulp mill that turns trees into a kind of wood slurry and a paper mill that turns that slurry into finished cardboard or paper. Anyone who grew up in a paper mill town, as I did, can tell you how bad every part of the papermaking and paper recycling processes smell, an indication of how polluting the processes can be. Our wood pulp now becomes notebook paper in another energy-intensive, water-intensive process at a paper mill. In fact, papermaking requires more water to make a pound of final product than any other industrial process in the world, and the industry is the fifth largest consumer of energy globally, a data point somewhat offset by the fact that much of that energy comes from burning its own waste products. Before it can become finished paper, our pulp must also be bleached, a process that is fortunately far less harmful to the environment and workers today than it once was. If the paper includes any recycled content, old paper must be de-inked before it can go into a new paper product, a process that consumes significant energy and produces pollution from the inks that are washed off and the various chemicals used to loosen the ink from the paper. The finished paper for the inside of the notebook comes out of the paper mill on giant rolls, and the cardstock for the covers comes out in thick sheets, often from different mills, and both now move on to the factory where the notebooks come together.

Meanwhile, our steel slabs go through a reheat furnace—most often powered by coal—to make the steel malleable, and it is then milled into coils of wire. At long last, the giant rolls of paper, the stacks of cardstock, and the coils of wire are all transported to the factory that makes the notebooks, along with the inks that will create the lines typical of notebook paper and various adhesives used in the final assembly. From there, our material inputs travel through a series of machines, guided in between by humans, that print lines on the paper, stack them into notebook thickness, add covers to either side, punch holes along the edge, feed the spiral of wire through the holes, and trim the edges to get uniform-sized notebooks.

Packaging: Notebooks tend to be sold without unnecessary packaging, so most notebooks will be packed into the cardboard boxes that retailers will receive them in, though some of the notebooks will be grouped into sets of three or five and wrapped together in plastic.

Transport: Boxes of notebooks are stacked together on pallets, which are then wrapped in plastic and loaded by forklift into semitrucks bound for ports and railyards. Though the US is the second largest producer of paper in the world, it's also by far the largest consumer of paper goods, and thus it's the world's largest importer of paper, too. Notebooks bound for American stores are most likely traveling from a factory in China to one of its many large ports, where the container on the back of the truck will be lifted off by a crane and swung onto a stack of other similar containers on a massive ship, on which it will travel thousands of miles across the Pacific Ocean and arrive at a deepwater port in California or Washington State. At the destination port, a similar crane will lift the container off the ship and place it onto another semitruck or onto a railcar, on which the container will travel any number of miles inland to a distribution center, where it will be unloaded and prepared to make its way to individual retail outlets. Before any notebooks can be sold, they will travel on at least one more truck, either to a store where they can be purchased in person by customers or to the distribution center of an online retailer, but the journey could include several more distribution centers and several more trucks.

Retail: Depending on how many notebooks they need, stores will receive either pallets of notebooks in boxes or simply the boxes, and our notebooks will finally make their way to consumers' hands after spending some amount of time on a store shelf. During back-to-school periods when they're highly discounted and in demand, the notebooks may not even make it onto a shelf, with stores putting the boxes out directly to speed things along. In slower periods, notebooks could sit on the shelf for days or weeks. But finally, the notebook finds a buyer, and it's on its way to a new home. Notebooks sold online will need to be packaged for shipping, often in a combination of plastic and paper to minimize the likelihood that they are damaged in transit, though sometimes they'll be sent out in boxes much too large for the contents inside. At last, our notebook reaches the mailbox, porch, or lobby of its new home.

Consumption: You finally have the notebook in your hands. Maybe you use it right away, filling it with lecture notes and homework, or maybe you write your name in it, put it in a drawer, and forget about it. Perhaps the notebook will be in your life for many years, or perhaps its entire period of usefulness to you spans only a school term. Perhaps you spill your drink on it one day, ending its useful life prematurely.

Disposal: The day has come when you've decided to part ways with the notebook. Perhaps you simply no longer need it. Or you have too many notebooks and decide to dispose of this one in an effort to declutter. Whatever the reason, it's now time to discard the notebook. Most notebooks end up in the trash, where they are transported to a landfill and covered with dirt, entombed for all time. In some areas they are incinerated to generate electricity, their components releasing a range of pollutants into the air and water as they burn. But you care too much to simply trash the notebook, and you're determined to recycle it. You know the paper and metal can't be recycled together, so you carefully rip out all the pages and tear off the covers, placing the paper in the recycle bin. And you aren't sure what to do with the wire, so you look it up online and find that such metal can only be recycled if it's dropped off by hand at your municipal waste facility, not via curbside recycling. That seems like an awful lot of work for one little wire, so you toss it in the trash. The next recycling day, the paper is collected, and off it goes to the recycling facility, perhaps to become new paper, but just as likely to become yet more landfill waste.

———

For such a simple item, made of only two materials, it's almost shocking how many steps have to be completed and how many hands it must go through before you ever possess it. But most importantly, to get something as simple as a notebook to you, a long list of harmful chemicals are used, a massive amount of fossil fuels are burned, and many waste products—eventually including the very thing itself—are generated. Those chemicals, fossil fuels, and waste products all impact both the planet and the people involved in each step of the product's life cycle, as well as the many more people who live near the mines, near the factories, near the ports, near the electricity plants, near the landfills. And as the complexity of an item we buy increases, the steps and impacts increase, too. The vast majority of those impacts are not priced into the few dollars you spend on the notebook, even if it's a high-end notebook you pay a great deal more for.

The true cost of a physical object we buy is all of those things: It's the energy that goes into extracting the raw materials for it, manufacturing it, transporting it several times, packaging it, maintaining it at home, and eventually disposing of it. It's the pollution that goes into the air and water and onto the land from that extraction, manufacture, transportation, and disposal. It's the impact on workers' health at the mines, in the factories, at the ports, in the distribution centers and warehouses, in the increasingly overcrowded and polluted cities where people move to be close to the factory jobs. It's the exploitation of workers at every step of the process, whether it's underpaying them, refusing to properly protect them from hazardous conditions on the job, or denying them basic rights like bathroom breaks and paid sick leave. Maybe it's the impact on your health, too, if the product is outright bad for you, or if it contains substances that will harm you in the long run, even if you don't know it. And finally, it's the added demand you've helped create, ensuring that more products just like it will continue to be cranked out, all priced vastly below their true cost.

As a person choosing whether to buy something in the future, you can't expect to know what this process looks like for each and every item you might purchase. But by understanding the general process we've just discussed, you can at least take your choice more seriously than our consumer culture would have you do. And you can feel certain that choosing to consume less overall is a powerful act that reduces the total number of times this resource-intensive process is repeated.

THE RECYCLING MYTH

When talking about disposing our example notebook, you took the time to separate the pages from the wire binding and to put them in the recycle bin. Despite that, they ended up in the landfill. How can that be?

Here's a fact that none of us want to be true: a large portion of what we attempt to recycle never gets recycled at all, because the entire notion of recycling is based on a lie. In truth, very few things can be recycled. Most products that go from being one product to being another can only be *down*cycled: turned into a much lower quality product than the one they started out as. That's why it's hard to find 100 percent recycled paper: the fibers that make paper hold together get degraded each time they are processed, and thus most new paper requires virgin wood pulp. High-quality paper has virtually no recycled content in it, and newsprint, our lowest-quality paper, is typically at most 50 percent recycled content. Plastic is even worse, requiring a huge amount of energy to turn one plastic product into a far inferior one, and only with the addition of new petroleum. The only plastic product you encounter regularly made from a high percent of recycled content is the flimsy plastic grocery bag (not the thicker, so-called reusable bags that some stores charge a few cents for, and which are still likely single-use bags for many shoppers). These bags are designed to be used for a single trip home and are the bane of recycling plant workers everywhere, as they are constantly having to pull the bags out of jammed belts and sorters, forcing the process to stop and start over and over again.[6] According to the United States Environmental

Protection Agency (EPA), we're currently generating about 35 million tons of plastic a year but can recycle only 3 million tons—less than 10 percent of the total.[7] Some of that is because products made from recycled plastic are not in high demand, but it's also because a lot of items that could be recycled, especially plastic water bottles, never make it into a recycling bin in the first place.

Glass and metals degrade far less in the recycling process, and are thus closer to being what we would call truly recyclable. But we're still generating far more new product than we're recycling, and a huge volume of potentially recyclable material goes to the landfill, though with high variation between countries: countries in Europe currently recycle 90 percent of disposed glass, while the rate is under one-third of disposed glass in the US.[8] Glass is the one product for which adding more recycled content actually improves the manufacturing process and creates a higher-quality end product: previously used and remelted glass doesn't release carbon dioxide, and thus it creates fewer bubbles that can get trapped in the glass and weaken it. But even despite that, new sand—composed largely of our old friend silica— still goes into every batch of glass that's made.[9] This is hard news to hear, especially for those of us who've made a big effort to recycle in the past. But it's important that we know all of this so that we remain resolute in our commitment to make better choices moving forward.

One of the major reasons why we don't recycle more of what we discard is because of what's termed "wishcycling," when well-meaning people put nonrecyclable items in the recycling bin in hopes that they actually can be. The more garbage is mixed in with recyclable materials, the more time and expense is required to get to the material of value and the less cost-effective recycling becomes.[10] The other reason why we don't recycle more of what we dispose is that our recyclables are physically dirty. Putting an unrinsed yogurt container into your recycling bin means that container isn't recyclable. It also means that some yogurt will likely get on a bunch of other things in the bin, making *those* items impossible to recycle. Then those items go on to touch other items when your recyclables get collected, and the contamination spreads, so even your properly handled glass is now nonrecyclable. Because of that, only 40 percent of what should be endlessly recyclable glass from single-stream recycling systems—where you put all recyclable materials into a single bin rather than sorting them into different bins, known as multistream recycling—ends up getting recycled.[11]

A final reason why we're not living up to the recycling promise is another one of those hidden costs. Recycling costs money, and someone has to pay for that. Recycling rates are higher in Europe partly because countries are much smaller, and the distance from a recycling sorting plant to a remanufacturing plant is likely to be short. In large countries like the US and Canada, those distances are likely to be much greater, thus the cost of including recycled content in a new product is that much higher because everything must travel farther. With consumers insisting on the lowest possible prices and treating products as interchangeable commodities, and no incentives offered to manufacturers to include recycled content,[12] manufacturers have to choose between paying more to do the right thing or paying less to use all new material, knowing their customers are unlikely to notice either way. We would undoubtedly achieve higher recycling rates if every local system converted from single-stream recycling to multistream, but that would require local governments to raise taxes to cover higher collection costs (something no one has the political will to do), and it would also require residents to make space for several recycling bins instead of one (not something everyone physically can do).

It's still important to recycle and to do our best to ensure that only clean, truly recyclable products end up in the bin. And researchers are working on new plastics that are infinitely recyclable, which could change things in the future.[13] But we need to be honest with ourselves about this aspect of any product's true cost: in the system we have, recycling is more a myth than a reality. If you knew that everything you buy would likely spend eternity in a landfill, surely you'd make some different choices.

THE OFFSET SCAM

When trying to determine the true cost of something, in virtually all cases, we're talking about identifying factors that are keeping the retail price of something artificially low. We're shifting the cost of the pollution emitted when producing something to other people at another time, giving ourselves a type of short-term loan with an unknown amount of interest due at a later mystery date. But there's one factor that can go into the price we pay that actually raises that cost, often for no benefit whatsoever: the carbon offset.

The idea of a carbon offset is that you're paying money to fund some action that will do enough good for the climate to counteract the bad you're doing through some activity. If you travel by air, you might have seen this option offered when you bought your ticket. The calculator says that to fly from New York to Los Angeles creates 2 metric tons of carbon dioxide (CO_2), and therefore you need to buy 2 metric tons of offsets, often priced nominally at a few dollars. You pay the small price, feel good that you're not trashing the planet, and move on.

Offsets are available to consumers who want to feel better about their choices, they're available to companies large and small who want to make certain claims about their environmental impact, and they serve a fundamental role in the cap-and-trade approach to limiting greenhouse gas emissions. With cap-and-trade, a national or state government sets a limit of how much a company is allowed to emit, representing the "cap" part of the name. But that company wants to emit more so that it can make more stuff and sell it to make a bigger profit. So it can "trade" for the right to emit more, either buying unused emissions capacity from another company, or, more commonly, by buying offsets. It makes sense logically: the cap-and-trade approach theoretically limits greenhouse gas emissions to the levels we want to maintain while also creating business opportunities to those who wish to create and sell those offsets in the first place.[14]

Here's the problem: offsets are poorly regulated, and there's no guarantee that they're permanent. Most of the offsets sold to everyone from individual consumers to multinational corporations go toward planting trees.[15] That's theoretically a very good thing. Deforestation is a major issue. More trees sequester more carbon so it doesn't stay in the atmosphere, they create habitat for vanishing species, they're beautiful in the landscape, and they prevent desertification and other negative effects of having bare soil exposed to the elements. However, almost no one is checking to see if those trees actually get planted. Furthermore, the trees don't actually start sequestering carbon for many years until after they reach maturity (and we need to reduce carbon in the atmosphere now), and absolutely no one is checking to see if those trees survive long-term to fulfill their purpose of absorbing carbon over the course of many years.[16] Every year, we're seeing more numerous and more destructive wildfires as a result of global warming, and millions or even billions of trees are lost each fire season. If some of those were trees planted as offsets, there's no climate refund we receive, no emissions that can be "unemitted" by polluters whose offsets just went up in smoke. Even not accounting for wildfires, the start-up Sylvera, which assesses offsets via satellite images and machine learning for corporate clients, estimated that almost half of offsets don't deliver on their promises.[17] What's more, economists say that a big percentage of offsets just have the effect of shifting demand.[18] If you pay one landowner not to cut down their trees, calling that an offset, you've done nothing to address the demand for the wood those trees contain, and that landowner's would-be customers simply buy their wood from someone else who's willing to clear-cut their land, perhaps the landowner right next door.

There are some legitimately good offsets out there. Entrepreneurs who buy refrigerant chemicals like freon—which do disproportionate damage as greenhouse gases—from people who have them sitting around and then destroy them are permanently eliminating those drivers of global warming from our climate system.[19] But these types of offsets are rare, and not something you'll commonly be offered. If companies would sell more offsets that fund permanent, non–fossil fuel energy infrastructure, it would be a positive step. Such offsets would provide additional sources of funding beyond just tax dollars for solar and wind farms.

Because companies know that many of their customers are environmentally minded, a great many of them buy offsets so that they can make claims about their impact on the planet and climate that they would be unable to make without those offsets. *Net zero* is a commonly used phrase that tells you a company might be claiming to be climate-neutral without actually cleaning up their act. While we should encourage companies to continue providing funding for projects that improve the health of the planet and our fellow humans, it's also fair to be highly skeptical of any claims a company can make only because of offsets. You may need to do some digging to find out if a company funds legitimate and permanent offsets. And know that they may very well be offsets in name only. Natural Resources Defense Council (NRDC) recommends considering only offsets that are permanent, verified and enforceable by a third party, and additional, meaning they don't just shift demand.[20] Climate Action Reserve and

Green-e Climate are credible third-party certifiers of offset projects, and they can help you find options that meet NRDC's standard.

SUBSIDIES: ANOTHER WAY WE PAY

An additional aspect of understanding the true cost of something we buy is to know whether there are other inputs into the system that shift the cost from one place to another, often invisibly. The most common form that takes is with government subsidies, when the government uses tax dollars to support a product, industry, or behavior often resulting in an artificially skewed price for the consumer.

We'll dig into this much more in chapter seven, when we talk about our food choices, but certain types of agriculture are heavily subsidized in the US, which distorts a whole range of prices and our perceptions of them. Corn is a good example. For many decades, the US Department of Agriculture (USDA) has paid farmers to produce corn, which gives lots of farmers an incentive to grow that crop instead of whatever they were growing before. This leads to a corn surplus and apparently lower prices that not only don't reflect externalities but also don't reflect the farmers' actual costs to grow it because the government is paying for a lot of those expenses.[21] The glut of taxpayer-subsidized corn is why we're so reliant on high-fructose corn syrup in our processed foods: it became cheaper for food producers to switch to corn-based sweetening than continue to use sugar. It's why we put ethanol made from corn into our gasoline. It's why meat is a whole lot cheaper than it used to be, because most livestock in America is now fed corn instead of grass. The price you pay for a burger or steak is artificially low because your tax dollars are paying farmers to grow corn.[22] You're still paying the price—you just don't know it.

We also pay for the luxuries enjoyed by only a few of us because of the way our tax code is structured. In the US, homeowners receive tax deductions (another word for subsidies) for the interest they pay on their mortgage, which lowers their overall tax bill. About two-thirds of all households own their homes, but these also tend to be the most well-off households, and they are disproportionately white.[23] Because someone has to pay for all of the functions that government provides, tax rates and available deductions are set to bring in a certain level of tax revenue. When a homeowner writes off their mortgage interest, lowering their tax bill, that tax liability effectively gets shifted to someone else—almost certainly a person who cannot claim that deduction. We know that people who do not own their homes tend to have lower income, have less wealth, and are more likely to be people of color.[24] Tax rules like the mortgage interest deduction are why wealthy Americans pay a lower share of their income, regardless of what the tax brackets say, than lower-income Americans.[25] And these tax "benefits" extend to a range of other purchases: second homes, yachts, even electric cars, which are often eligible for tax credits and which get to travel over our roads without paying for that privilege, because we fund our road construction and maintenance with taxes on gasoline.

While these are all policy choices we make, and which we could change, they impact our financial decisions because they artificially skew the prices we must pay. Most economists agree that the mortgage interest deduction's ultimate effect is to raise home prices, because everyone who buys a home is effectively getting a retroactive discount on that home at tax time.[26] Studies have concluded that getting rid of the mortgage interest deduction would bring home prices down by 13 percent on average nationwide and by more than 25 percent in the larger cities.[27] And those higher prices also translate to higher rental costs for those who can't buy or choose not to buy, and they make it much harder for first-time buyers to purchase a home at all.[28] (This effect is further magnified by exclusionary zoning, as we'll discuss in chapter eight.) The mortgage interest deduction is meant to incentivize homeownership, but economists agree that its actual impact is to reduce homeownership rates because it drives up prices and makes home purchase less attainable.[29] The prices that lower-income people pay are often artificially inflated, while those paid by the wealthiest among us are artificially discounted by tax breaks. Almost none of us are paying the true cost, but we've built the system backward to benefit those who least need the help.

On the corporate scale, the most subsidized industries in the US are energy, agriculture, and transportation, skewing costs on most of our largest expenditures. Some of these subsidies make good sense. With energy, for example, funding research and development into renewable energy generation and storage, helping local governments build infrastructure for renewables, investing in charging stations for electric cars—these are all good uses of tax dollars to achieve the joint goals of cleaner energy and an easier transition out of fossil fuels. But a huge share of our energy subsidies actually go to the fossil fuel industry, both directly and indirectly. Commonly, oil and coal companies are allowed to explore government land for drilling and mining at rates well below market value, often without enough regard for the harm that these extractive practices will likely cause—costs that taxpayers and local residents will bear.[30] Without government supports, the prices we see at the gas pump would almost certainly be higher, and conversations about ending our reliance on fossil fuels might go very differently. But instead, with cheap gas fueling our lifestyles, few people are motivated to change their ways.

Outside of US policy choices, we see this pattern repeat itself all over the world: the people and the countries with the most money pay the least for things, while we shift both direct costs and intangible impacts onto those who can least afford them. The world's poorest people live in the most polluted places and the areas most at risk from rising sea levels and other impacts of severe global warming. Our most vulnerable workers get sick from making the cheap products that we demand, and then they're on the hook to pay for their higher health-care costs, often while earning less because they are forced to quit working. Knowing this, we can push for the policy change needed for greater equity, but we can also change our ways as consumers.

IS IT TOO CHEAP?

One of the most destructive forces in our society today is the desire to get a deal. It's understandable that we all want to stretch our money as far as we can, and getting a deal feels like beating the game. The problem isn't one person getting one deal, it's all of us demanding deals all the time. Lower prices entice companies to pay workers less and to provide fewer benefits. And worse, our obsession with cheapness stifles innovation and gives most manufacturers no incentive to make a better product, because consumers reward cheapness over quality.

In her book *Cheap: The High Cost of Discount Culture*, science journalist Ellen Ruppel Shell writes:

> Innovation is by definition risky, and it is made all the more so when stockholders overlook the long view and demand a jump in profits every quarter. When competition is mostly about price, innovation too often takes a backseat to cost cutting. Laying off workers and hiring cheaper ones is one sure way to enhance the bottom line. Another is to scour the world for low-wage workers, especially those in countries with lack-luster enforcement of environmental and workers' rights regulations. Neither of these tactics is innovative, and neither in

the long run contributes to growth. And both contribute to an erosion of income that leads to debt and a decrease in spending [among consumers].[31]

When we value cheapness over other factors, we create worse conditions for workers, and we almost certainly raise the ultimate cost of all those hidden externalities.

We also make things worse for ourselves. Good luck buying a refrigerator made today that will last you more than ten years with no significant problems. Manufacturers will blame the less polluting coolants they must use now, and the stricter energy efficiency standards. But the truth is that virtually everything mass-produced today is made with far lower quality standards than in the past,[32] and that refrigerator will end up in the landfill much sooner than its counterpart from a few decades ago. The model has shifted from charging a higher relative price so that a consumer might need to buy something only a few times in their life to charging a relative lower price but forcing people to buy the same things much more often. Manufacturers accomplish this either by producing those things poorly or through planned obsolescence, a common practice with tech products especially, making them incompatible with newer software so consumers get frustrated and "upgrade" (a dressed-up way of saying "buy the latest version of the cheaply produced thing that will also fail in a few short years"). We also make things worse for ourselves when we value cheapness because economists believe that there's not really an "over there" when it comes to wages. These economists believe that low wages in China, India, Bangladesh, and other countries where so many of our products are mass-produced have the effect of pushing down wages everywhere. By buying something cheap, we create demand only for the lowest wage and most exploitative jobs.

All of this brings us to the next question you should include in your decision-making framework: *Is it too cheap?* Given everything we've talked about in a product's life cycle—what it takes to get even a simple object into your hands, the factors that aren't included in that price, and the low likelihood that it will be recycled—this simple question will help you answer quickly whether something was likely produced in exploitative, destructive ways.

Consider a $10 pair of headphones. There's plastic on the outside and metal on the inside. That metal was mined from the earth by workers, and the plastic was created from petroleum that was pumped out. There are intricate circuits inside that almost certainly include rare earth minerals, substances like neodymium, yttrium, and cerium that exist only in tiny quantities around the world and must be mined through destructive practices, and without which most of our electronics could not function. For that low price, the headphones were certainly manufactured in a country with poor protections for workers and the environment, and the workers were definitely not well compensated for making the headphones. When they are discarded, the heavy metals and rare earth minerals within them must go to an e-waste facility, or they risk polluting the groundwater beneath the landfill. In other words: the headphones are too cheap. To be made without worker exploitation and without serious environmental degradation, they would have to cost more. (They also likely won't last long, and you'll need to spend more money to replace them in the not too distant future.)

Unfortunately, paying a lot for something isn't alone a guarantee that the product is top quality and will last forever. But buying something that's too cheap *is* a guarantee that you're buying junk and you're not using your money to express your values in the world. Given our late-stage capitalist obsession with squeezing workers as tightly as we can, a lot of us making these choices are also underpaid. That may leave you with no choice but to buy cheap stuff sometimes.

The point of asking *Is it too cheap?* is not to shame yourself for not having the means to purchase a better option. It's simply to point ourselves in the direction of making better choices when we can afford to do so, and perhaps more of the time simply choosing not to buy that thing at all. If producers know you can't live without something, they'll almost certainly price it higher to reflect its necessity. That's why food prices almost always go up, not down, while completely optional products tend to get cheaper over time. So something being too cheap is also a good indication that you don't need it.

FACTORING IN YOUR OWN FINANCIAL WELL-BEING

The final aspect of understanding the true cost of something is to put it into the context of your own life and to consider your own well-being. To put it in stark terms, for a billionaire, the cost of a Ferrari is hardly noticeable. But for most people, buying a Ferrari would lead to financial ruin. We can't assign an absolute value to anything, because it's all relative to your financial situation, how much free time you have, and what you value most. A purchase someone else deems frivolous might add tremendous value to your life, whether it's freeing up more of your time or simply giving you enjoyment, and only you get to choose what's worth it or not.

Pundits love to declare that millennials can't afford to buy homes because they're spending all of their money on lattes and avocado toast (a ridiculous claim showing they've never actually done the math on what homes cost today), but the advice not to buy those things ignores a critical piece of the puzzle: drinking a latte might be the absolute best part of someone's day, the thing that helps them keep going in a stressful work environment. If you savor every sip of that latte, it might be money well spent. If you gulp it down and barely taste it, maybe not.

As I wrote in *Work Optional*, the true cost of a thing is both the amount of time it takes you to earn enough money to buy it and the amount of future flexibility you're willing to give up to buy it by not saving or investing that money instead. *Willing to give up* is a metric only you can determine. I would add now that the true cost is also the amount of time you're taking away from other things you could be doing that have value, whether to society or to you personally. This is especially relevant when we talk about two particular hallmarks of the advice given to would-be conscious consumers: do-it-yourself (DIY) and buying secondhand.

If industrial agriculture and manufacturing are bad, the thinking goes, then making those things yourself must be better. This is one of the thoughts behind the growing homestead movement, people seeking to become as self-sufficient as possible, whether out on a large rural plot of land or on a much smaller urban homestead. And in certain circumstances, it can be true that DIY is better. For instance, if you have a yard and love to garden, growing some of your own food takes pressure off your local food system and reduces your reliance on out-of-season food flown in from far away. And any effort to reduce the size of lawns we're irrigating (turf grass is the most irrigated crop in America[33]), directing that water instead to edible crops, is a big positive. But expecting all or most of us to grow our own food ignores some basic rules of efficiency at scale. People who farm for a living are experts at maximizing their yields, and they can produce far more food per square foot of space than you as a hobby gardener can, especially if you're also holding down a job, taking care of a family, and serving in any number of other roles in your life. If we were all growing our own food, the pollution would be worse, not better. Consider:

Is it better if a few farmers have some big tractors and irrigation lines, or if every single one of us has a hose, a watering can, a shovel, a wheelbarrow, gloves, hand tools, and so on? Is it better if a few farmers get bulk deliveries of seeds, fertilizer, compost, and other materials, or if we all make several individual trips to the garden center to get what we need? Is it better if most of us live in cities, where it's more possible to live close to transit and concentrate our impact but where it's tough to grow a lot of food, or if we all spread out across the land so that we have enough space to grow our own food but also require vastly more fossil fuels to get things to us because we're so far apart?

We can collectively use fewer resources if we outsource essential tasks to those who can specialize in them and achieve economies of scale that we cannot achieve on our own. This is not an argument for industrialized agriculture, which we'll discuss in chapter seven, but rather an illustration of the point that DIY is not always better or more environmentally friendly.

When contemplating whether to DIY something, consider what you'll need to purchase to make the DIY possible and what it took to manufacture those tools. A project that requires few tools and a low start-up cost is far preferable to one that requires you to buy a lot of things that could end up being wasted resources if you ultimately decide you don't like doing that thing. Fermenting your own kombucha at home, for example, takes no special tools whatsoever— making your own is much cheaper than buying it and produces far less waste because you're not buying bottle after bottle. But if you wish to make your own beer or cider at home, you'll need to invest in significantly more equipment, much of it resource-intensive to produce. And unless you have access to a large supply of free barley or apples, the ongoing cost of materials means you'll be lucky if you break even with what you would have spent for ready-made beer or cider. If you truly love beer or cider and are confident you'll make home brewing

93

a years-long hobby, then choosing to take that on might be a good choice for you and lead to far less consumption of glass and aluminum over the long term. But if you're not so sure, a better option would be to buy a glass growler and find a local bottle shop or pub that will fill it and let you take it home and to make that the way you buy beer. It's less waste with far less work and a lot less stuff purchased.

When considering both DIY and buying secondhand, another thing to consider is simply your own limited supply of time. Buying secondhand is an excellent way to extract more useful value out of things that would otherwise be discarded, reducing the demand for newly manufactured products and costing you less money at the same time. If we're serious about reducing overconsumption, we need to normalize buying things secondhand, including for gift-giving. But secondhand shopping can also be incredibly time-consuming, just as many DIY projects can be. If DIY projects and secondhand shopping cost you less money but consume your free time, leaving you no time to relax, have fun, or take care of other important chores, then you're probably putting too much pressure on yourself. Just as you spent time thinking about the values you wish to express through your financial choices, consider what you want your time spent on this Earth to add up to. If making things yourself brings you enormous joy and you love the thrill of the hunt with secondhand shopping, then DIY and buying secondhand are just the hobbies for you. But if you try to get as many things as you possibly can through DIY and secondhand shopping and in the process leave no time to fulfill your purpose in life, then it's worth a reminder that there are plenty of ways to make good financial choices in service of the collective good without exhausting yourself.

Likewise, there are plenty of ways to make good financial choices without going broke. If it's not already, make it one of your core financial principles to remember that your own well-being is valuable and worth preserving. So often, the best choice for the environment and other people is also the best choice for your personal finances. Using less heat or air-conditioning conserves fossil fuels and saves you money. Buying fewer clothes produced by underpaid garment workers puts less pressure on them and keeps that money in your bank account. If you're spending too much and stressing yourself out over money to make choices that benefit the collective good, there's certainly another way to go about it. And given that the biggest consumers of both energy and stuff are the wealthiest among us, having more limited financial means is a good indication that you're already putting less of a burden on the planet and your fellow humans than folks who are richer than you. Just don't fall into the trap of buying only the cheapest junk, and you're good.

Regardless of which issues you're most passionate about and what you believe change needs to look like, the goal of wallet activism is to bring things into balance: more equality for people treated unequally and fewer demands on our overtaxed planet. But it should also be about balance for you: aligning your financial choices to your values, and—just as important—scaling your activism to your means. While it's true, to paraphrase the Viola Davis quote that begins this book, that fighting for the change you want should cost you something, it shouldn't cost you your well-being.

CHAPTER 5

Good Guys, Bad Guys, and How to Tell the Difference

What am I funding?

> *Il est de la prudence de ne se fier jamais entièrement
> à ceux qui nous ont une fois trompés.
> (It is prudent never to trust entirely those
> who have deceived us even once.)*
> —René Descartes

It's an exercise you might have run through: scrolling through an online form, punching in how big a home you live in, whether you drive or take public transit to work, how many kids you have, what your diet consists of, how often you travel by plane. You hit submit, and a number appears: your carbon footprint. In other words, the approximate carbon dioxide equivalent of all your habits and consumer choices, expressed in terrifying-sounding tons or metric tons. Maybe you see your number alongside the average footprint of a person living in a poor country, and you feel an immediate sense of guilt and shame that yours is so much higher. You resolve to recycle more, buy a more fuel-efficient car, or adjust the thermostat. That reaction is exactly what the inventors of the carbon footprint want. They want you to feel guilty.

Who are these inventors? Environmental scientists studying the earth's upper atmosphere? Geologists who head out on long Antarctic expeditions to drill ice core samples to compare our CO_2 levels to those from hundreds of years ago? No. The inventors of the carbon footprint were the public relations team for British Petroleum (BP), one of the largest extractors and distributors of fossil fuels in the world. In 2004, they launched their first "carbon footprint calculator," along with a massive campaign to popularize the term, and in almost no time at all, we were all talking about reducing our carbon footprints without having a clue that we'd been skillfully manipulated.

While the goal of getting each of us to understand the impact of our choices is a noble one, there was nothing noble about the campaign to get *carbon footprint* into the vernacular. It was a diversion technique to get us to blame ourselves for climate change rather than the massive corporate actors who bear far more responsibility. While they were telling us how to make choices to lower our individual footprints, BP and its fellow petroleum companies were pumping more oil out of the ground than ever, pouring billions of dollars into even more destructive practices like fracking, and lobbying world governments to lower their taxes and increase their subsidies.[1] In fact, BP is one of the biggest emitters of greenhouse gases in the world, one of one hundred companies responsible for nearly three-quarters of all global greenhouse gas emissions.[2] (Together, Chevron, ExxonMobil, BP, and Shell are responsible for more than 10 percent of all the global carbon emissions produced since 1965.[3]) A few years later in 2010, BP's Deepwater Horizon spill, caused by an explosion at an offshore drilling platform in the Gulf of Mexico, became the largest marine oil spill in history, and we all kept talking about our carbon footprints. The term had already become ubiquitous. And it's not the first time we've fallen for this ploy.

———

Andrew Carnegie is now largely remembered as a philanthropist for building hundreds and hundreds of libraries around the country. Take a look at any library built in the first half of the twentieth century, and you'll almost certainly find a plaque recognizing Carnegie's generosity in providing the funding for its construction. Those donations' impact is immeasurable, providing generations of Americans with access to information and enrichment they may not have had otherwise. Andrew Carnegie also endowed dozens of organizations focused on improving the common good, from the Carnegie Foundation and the Carnegie Endowment for International Peace to Carnegie Mellon University and Carnegie Hall. Countless people have benefited from his philanthropic endeavors over the past century. However, Carnegie's legacy is complicated. Though he gave away vast amounts of money, based on his belief that the wealthy have a "moral obligation to reinvest" their money to "promote the welfare and happiness of the common man," he amassed that wealth by doing the opposite.[4] Building the level of wealth Carnegie achieved—about $300 million at the beginning of the twentieth century, the equivalent of $300 billion in 2020 dollars, making him (as of this writing) the third wealthiest person in the history of the world—was possible only because he was perfectly happy to exploit workers.

Carnegie's wealth came from making the steel that built most of modern America and cities around the world. It's nearly impossible to overstate how callously he exploited the workers in his steel mills, paying them unlivable wages, often only in company currency that had no value outside of the company store and company housing, and creating such inhumane conditions that many workers died. Those who didn't die on the job still died young as a direct result of the atrocious labor conditions. The rise of labor unions was driven by industrial conditions like those Carnegie created. Workers had no choice but to band together to demand better treatment.[5] And while Carnegie publicly claimed to support labor unions,[6] his company was responsible for the Homestead Massacre, one of the largest and most deadly strike-busting operations in US history, which set the labor union movement back decades. Carnegie believed fervently in the American "bootstraps" myth, the idea that you could elevate your position in life if you only worked harder, and thus he seemed to believe that it was okay to treat workers so poorly because they were complicit in their own exploitation and abuse; if they wanted to get a better job, they could simply read some books at one of his (future) libraries and move up to something better.

Though labor laws now prevent the types of abuses that happened during Carnegie's day, his beliefs are still common among corporate leaders. It's virtually impossible to amass extreme wealth without directly engaging in worker exploitation or looking the other way and pretending not to notice it. As Dan Riffle, policy adviser to Congresswoman Alexandria Ocasio-Cortez, says, "Every billionaire is a policy failure."[7] And corporate leaders go to great lengths to get you to focus on the "good" they are doing, either real or imagined—both for their personal vanity and to provide the company with a veneer of goodness. Mark Zuckerberg, founder and CEO of Facebook, would much rather you pay attention to the billions of dollars he's pledged to give away through the Chan Zuckerberg Initiative than to the damage Facebook is doing to democracy by letting disinformation run rampant on its platform and making its customers' private data available to bad actors like Cambridge Analytica. He may go down in history as a great philanthropist, as Carnegie did, but that won't erase the enormous harm for which he's responsible.

As companies and wealthy individuals seek to gloss over their misdeeds with large-scale philanthropic endeavors and the veneer of supporting good causes, or as they create campaigns with the outright goal of distracting us from what's really going on, how do we as wallet activists figure out who the good guys and bad guys really are? And who, then, is worthy of our financial backing? That's our mission in this chapter.

THE CAMPAIGN TO GET YOU TO TAKE THE BLAME

If you care about making ethical choices as a consumer, you're probably already familiar with the term *greenwashing*, meaning attempts by marketers and PR staff to make a company or product seem more environmentally friendly than it is. As we discussed in the previous chapter, making claims that rely on offsets is one example (these claims often use terms like *net zero* and *carbon-neutral*), and there are countless others: claiming that something is "sustainably sourced," "Earth-friendly," or "chemical-free" without defining what that means. ("Chemical-free" is impossible, as even pure water, H_2O, is a chemical, just not a harmful one in reasonable doses.) Claiming something is 100 percent recyclable when most municipal recycling systems can't process it. Touting something as "plant-based" when it's full of polluting chemicals that just happen to be derived from plants. Throwing out unregulated buzzwords like *natural, herbal, pure,* or *green.* Even making a product's package literally green to exploit our associations with the color. These companies know consumers will spend more on products that appear to be environmentally responsible, and they want to cash in.

Besides being manipulative and deceptive, these greenwashing efforts are harmful because they waste consumers' good intentions. Consumers believe they are doing something good by choosing a greenwashed product over another when, in fact, they are funding the same old destructive and exploitative practices. And yet, if we find out that something is greenwashed, we tend to blame ourselves for falling for it, which is exactly what the company wants us to feel. This pattern of getting us as individual consumers to blame ourselves and feel responsible has been repeated time and time again.

Perhaps the most iconic environmental TV commercial in history is the "Crying Indian" ad from 1971, which featured an Italian American actor pretending to be Indigenous American, paddling a canoe in full stereotypical costume, complete with braids and feather. He comes ashore on a litter-strewn beach and looks up to see a passing motorist toss a huge bag of trash out of their car window. The bag lands at his feet, and we pan up to see him shed a single stoic tear. The ad concludes with the words, "People start pollution. People can stop it." The last thing we see is the logo for Keep America Beautiful, an organization whose credibility we have no reason to doubt. Keep America Beautiful was founded in 1953, when littering was a far worse problem than it is today. Their campaigns over the decades have undoubtedly changed public opinion about litter, and, paired with anti-littering fines, they've significantly reduced littering. So who is behind this organization? Keep America Beautiful was founded not by concerned environmentalists, but by the makers of much of that new litter, which proliferated as America shifted from reusable packaging, like sturdy glass milk bottles, to single-use disposables, like plastic milk cartons and beer and soda cans.[8] Their message was not a broad entreaty to pay more attention to the environment writ large, but instead a narrow push to focus on the individual's blame for our litter problem. They actually produced all that litter, sure, but the fact that it's out in the world is *your* fault. (If these facts sound familiar, you may have heard them on *Last Week Tonight*. While this book was being edited, John Oliver devoted an episode of his show to this very issue. If you would like to see many of this chapter's points made by a British comedian, with a bit more swearing, I encourage you to check it out.)

The recycling myth we discussed in the preceding chapter has similar origins. The push to recycle plastic was funded not by environmentalists, but by the plastics and petroleum industry, even though records show that they knew most plastic could not and would not be recycled. A National Public Radio (NPR) and *Frontline* investigation found that, as early as the 1970s, plastic and petroleum executives acknowledged in speeches and in writing that recycling would not keep plastics out of landfills, and recycling was unlikely ever to be economically viable for manufacturers of plastic products. Yet they poured millions of dollars into campaigns to urge consumers to recycle, because convincing people that their plastic was *being* recycled made them feel good about buying more of it. As reporter Laura Sullivan wrote,[9] "Selling recycling sold plastic."

One of the largest carbon emitters in the world telling us to focus on our infinitesimally smaller individual emissions. The makers of litter shaming us for the litter problem. The plastic producers lying to us about what happens to our plastic so we won't hesitate to buy more. These are examples of the lengths bad guy companies will go to in their efforts to convince us that we as individuals are to blame for problems they created. Capitalism is filled with examples of guilting us for our choices while offering us absolution through actions that serve only capitalism. So, with bad guys almost everywhere we look, which companies *can* we trust?

WHAT MAKES A GOOD GUY?

As with all our choices, it's virtually impossible to identify a perfect good guy company that is large enough to serve everyone. But let's imagine what such a company might look like:

❏ **Mission-driven:**[10] A good guy company is mission-driven, meaning that they care about something other than (or in addition to) maximizing profit, whether it's a concurrent social or environmental goal or a commitment to conducting business with a stringent code of ethics.

❏ **Diverse:** Leadership is as diverse as the junior ranks, both demographically and in world view, because the company recognizes that more diverse teams make better decisions. Hiring managers do the work to employ diverse staff, rather than falling back on the old line that there just weren't enough qualified applicants of diverse backgrounds despite their total lack of effort to find any. They invest in training and promotion of traditionally oppressed demographics such as women, people of color, LGBTQ+ people, veterans, disabled workers, workers reentering the workforce after time away to raise kids or care for loved ones, and others, recognizing that there's not a level playing field, and those folks are more likely to have been overlooked for opportunities before.

❑ **Treats employees well:** A good guy company pays workers fairly and provides benefits like comprehensive health insurance and paid sick time and family leave (at least in countries where these are not government-guaranteed rights). Employees stick around for several years, because they feel they are being treated with respect and trust.

❑ **Invests in the community:** The company invests in the local community rather than hoarding profits to serve only their top brass.

❑ **Protects customers:** The company commits to not exploiting customers' private data for gain, maintaining high security standards so they aren't vulnerable to data breaches.

❑ **Follows good labor practices:** The company isn't constantly looking to shift manufacturing to cheaper and cheaper countries. All workers in the world receive a living wage, one that allows someone to cover basic living expenses without a second job or government assistance. The company doesn't use forced labor or child labor. It has verified that its entire supply chain is free of human trafficking and forced labor, committing to supply chain transparency or, even better, traceability. It provides workers with safety equipment and compensates those who are injured on the job. Workers get reasonable breaks and time off.

❑ **Environmentally conscious:** A good guy company makes a sincere effort to minimize environmental harm, looking for ways to decrease energy consumption, source less harmfully produced materials, decrease waste, reduce packaging, and ensure it's not polluting where it operates. The company uses recycled materials when possible and commits to a circular life cycle for products, meaning there's a plan for what happens when a product is no longer useful, so it can be refurbished into something of value rather than going to the landfill.

❏ **Offers quality products:** The company maintains a high quality standard so that customers don't need to replace their products often. It firmly opposes making anything that could pose harm to the health of its customers.

❏ **Accessible and inclusive:** Products are priced to be accessible to as many people as possible. The products themselves are suitable for as many people as possible (clothing sizes for all body types, for example, or makeup in a broad range of skin tones). Advertising and marketing campaigns are inclusive, featuring diverse models of all shapes, sizes, ages, disability status, skin colors, genders, and family compositions.

If we as consumers had a lot of companies to choose from that could check every box on the list we just ran through, we probably wouldn't need this book. Nearly everyone out there will tell you that they're a good guy company, whether they are or not. Your real work is less to recognize the good ones than it is to see through the marketing to recognize and avoid the bad ones.

BAD GUYS WHO KNOW THEY'RE BAD GUYS

Most large corporations know deep down that they are bad guys—they just hope you won't notice. Some of them go to great lengths, like the recycling and carbon footprint campaigns, to convince you that they are entirely different than they truly are. Others barely try to hide their bad actions, using a singular idea as justification for a broad range of misdeeds.

The ubiquitous mega-retailer Walmart is a textbook example of a company doing the latter, using its promise of low prices to get you to excuse its multitude of bad guy practices. By asserting that offering products at the lowest possible price is a social good, because it makes those things accessible to more people, they justify underpaying employees, aggressively fighting unionization, and mercilessly squeezing suppliers on price so that many are forced to move manufacturing overseas and to rely on underpaid or even forced labor from human trafficking victims.[11]

Walmart has made no apologies for being the world leader in the cheapification of the stuff we buy. Before retailers like Walmart, US consumers had access to well-made products that would last. In our current economy, finding anything that's not cheaply made is increasingly difficult, especially at a price that most people can afford. Everything from clothing to electronics has become all but disposable. Walmart has made no efforts to clean up the communities harmed by the barely regulated factories that make the products its stores sell.[12] It doesn't report any of the climate pollution that its oceanic shipping generates (a massive total considering that Walmart is the world's largest mover of stuff across our oceans).[13] Even the company's pledge to go carbon-neutral by 2040 without the use of offsets only counts the emissions of its stores and offices, not its manufacturing and transport, accounting for only about 5 percent of Walmart's total climate impact.[14]

Though Walmart goes to great lengths not to be transparent about such facts, analysts believe that Walmart's employee attrition, the number of employees who quit each year, is somewhere in the range of 50 to 70 percent, attributable to low pay and poor working conditions.[15] (The industry average is 30 percent.) It has vehemently fought gender discrimination lawsuits and has lobbied against federal pay equity laws but has apparently done little to correct its gender pay gap or the massive imbalance between the 56 percent of women who make up its total workforce and the very few women in its senior ranks and on its board of directors.[16] Perhaps most damning of all, a huge number of full-time Walmart employees earn so little that they are eligible for SNAP benefits (Supplemental Nutrition Assistance Program, formerly called food stamps) and Medicaid health insurance, the two most restrictive public assistance programs for the poorest Americans.[17] Despite being a hugely profitable company, Walmart's business is essentially subsidized by taxpayers, whose dollars paid to Walmart employees as public assistance make it possible for Walmart to get away with not paying employees more or allowing them to get on the company health-care plan. The true cost of anything you buy at Walmart is much higher than that low price suggests. And in a perverse twist, Walmart is also the retailer where the largest share of SNAP dollars are spent, so it's even double-dipping on the taxpayer-funded benefit.[18]

A hallmark of a bad guy company is a lack of transparency about things like employee pay and benefits, energy usage and total environmental footprint, what the company does to ensure that workers in its factories or suppliers' factories aren't being abused or exploited, the causes it lobbies for, and even the ingredients its products contain. Bad guy companies will try to draw your attention instead to claims of being a good "corporate citizen" without actually addressing the things that make them bad in the first place, showing off the community programs they support while doing nothing to make their stores or offices more energy-efficient and refusing to increase their employees' pay. The idea of paying workers as little as possible has not always predominated (for instance, Henry Ford understood long ago that he would sell many more cars if he paid workers in his auto plants enough that they could buy a Ford automobile). But today, the workers in many US factories are getting paid barely above minimum wage, with few to no benefits (we'll delve deeper into this trend in chapter nine). Companies that pay employees as little as they can get away with are bad guys, pure and simple.

Another telltale sign of a bad guy company is a firmly anti-union stance. Employees wanting to unionize is a sign that they have significant grievances against the company that aren't being addressed. While it's understandable that companies may not be eager to unionize, there's a big difference between trying to work with employees so that they don't feel they need a union and engaging in union-busting or spreading anti-union propaganda. Unionized companies aren't perfect. But supporting them by buying union-made products ensures that workers may bargain collectively for their pay, benefits, and working conditions. On average, union workers earn almost 25 percent more than nonunion workers of the same demographics in similar jobs.[19] The modern anti-union movement began in 1981 under President Reagan, with the air traffic controllers strike. The air traffic controllers asked for more pay from the federal government, their employer, in recognition of the extreme stress of the job. After promising he'd back them, Reagan turned on them and fired 11,000 striking controllers, banning them from holding similar jobs for life. (President Clinton later lifted that ban.) Reagan's action flipped the prevailing narrative at the time: strikers had held public sympathy prior to this event, but for the first time the strikebreaker became the hero and the strikers the villains.[20] Since then, union membership has declined as manufacturing companies have relocated either out of the country or to so-called right-to-work (meaning anti-union) states.[21] Much of what was recently manufactured in the Midwest and northeastern US is now manufactured in the more conservative southeastern US, where right-to-work is the norm and where average wages are lower as a result. Analysis by Elise Gould and Will Kimball of the Economic Policy Institute found that full-time, year-round workers in right-to-work states earn on average $1,558 less per year than workers in the same jobs in union states, regardless of whether they themselves are union members, after correcting for other factors like cost of living.[22] Unions bargaining on behalf of workers in one workplace has the effect of raising wages in that whole region, and taking that bargaining ability away depresses wages across the board. This shift away from union manufacturing is a big part of why *Made in the USA* is no longer the marker of quality and good worker treatment that it once was.

Though we could discuss a virtually infinite list of bad guy company traits, one final red flag worth discussing here is the production of low-quality products. Just as we ask *Is it too cheap?* before buying something, we can conclude that companies selling low-quality items are cutting corners, likely in many ways. Low-quality products are likely made as cheaply as possible, which means companies paying workers as little as they can get away with, doing as little as possible to ensure those workers' safety, and taking no care to responsibly source materials. It's possible that many of these companies used to take more care and exploit their workers less before being squeezed by corporate behemoths like Walmart, but we must look at their practices now. Companies that produce low-quality products demonstrate no concern for the fact that the things they make will soon end up in the landfill. And because they are probably selling their low-quality products cheaply, they don't have the financial resources to invest in their employees or reinvest in their communities. More than likely, they check almost no boxes on our good guy list.

BAD GUYS WHO THINK THEY'RE GOOD GUYS

While bad guys who know they're bad guys are fairly obvious to spot, the trickier thing is recognizing a company that truly thinks it's a good guy when it's actually a bad guy, or it has worrisome bad guy tendencies. This could be something that seems small, like a vendor on Instagram or Etsy selling a "Black Lives Matter" T-shirt, or a shirt with a specific person's face on it like George Floyd or Breonna Taylor, pushing a good message of racial justice, but profiting from and ultimately commodifying the oppression and even violent death of someone else. (If they donate all the proceeds to an organization like Black Lives Matter, that could be another story.) Or it could be someone who is not of Indian heritage offering classes in a style of yoga that feels really good to do but that doesn't acknowledge or provide any benefit to the people in India who originated yoga as part of Hindu religious tradition.[23] Examples like this—of cultural appropriation and commodification of oppression, often from well-meaning people who care about these issues—are all around us. Let's focus, though, on the big companies who think they're good guys.

The company Johnson & Johnson has for decades been a household name around the world, trusted for its sterling reputation of product safety. They make a wide range of products meant for newborns and babies, for whom product safety is critical, and they've made safety their core brand promise. However, in recent years, it has come out that they knew about safety concerns for their talc baby powder for decades and went to great lengths to cover them up.[24] Though it's not clear whether the issues are a result of talc itself being a carcinogen or of their talc sometimes being contaminated with the known carcinogen asbestos, Johnson & Johnson's talc baby powder has been linked to so many cases of ovarian cancer that they've pulled the product from shelves in the US, replacing it instead with cornstarch-based baby powder, though the talc version is still available in other countries.[25] Covering up the knowledge that a product of yours causes a deadly cancer is one thing, but refusing to stop selling it is quite another. It forces customers to question whether any of their products are actually as safe as they say they are. Though Johnson & Johnson would surely disagree, that's not the behavior of a good guy.

Before it was purchased by Amazon, Whole Foods Market was another example of a company working hard to be seen as a good guy company. For two decades, they ranked on *Fortune*'s list of the hundred best companies to work for. Whole Foods stores always paid well above minimum wage and above what other grocery chains paid, even for brand-new employees. They were a leader in pay transparency, which economists believe leads to better pay equity among demographic groups. In 1986, when the company was only a few years old, CEO and founder John Mackey opened up the company's books so any employee could see what any other employee earned and how profitable every single store was in a given month, giving employees an unparalleled look at, and a sense of personal investment in, the company's fortunes. In 2007, Mackey announced that he would no longer draw a salary or take any other pay from the company, but he has stayed on as its leader to this day. Though Whole Foods is often nicknamed Whole Paycheck for its high prices, it has convinced customers over the years that it puts the money customers spend in stores to good use, offering its frontline workers better pay and benefits than they'd receive elsewhere and investing in local and sustainable food production that benefits even those who can't afford to shop at Whole Foods. Mackey has called this approach "conscious capitalism" (also the name of his 2013 book), aiming for the "win, win, win" of balancing the needs of shareholders (profits), customers, and employees, not preferencing one over the other.

It all makes for a convincing narrative. And certainly, if you are choosing among several large chain grocery stores, you can do far worse in terms of what you're supporting than to shop at Whole Foods. But even before the Amazon takeover, Whole Foods was one of the largest nonunion grocers in the country after Walmart, quite a feat considering that it's only the tenth largest chain by revenue.[26] The company would argue that it has treated employees well enough that they have not felt the need to unionize. But in an industry in which unionization is the norm, resisting employee attempts to do so for as long as Whole Foods has shows a high level of sustained anti-union efforts.[27] Now, under Amazon, known for its aggressive anti-union tactics, these efforts have apparently stepped up.[28]

Employers who actively fight unionization generally demonstrate through plenty of other actions that they are not looking out for their employees. Other recent evidence of this came when Amazon noted that it was raising its minimum pay to $15 an hour in the US, a move that impacted the lowest-paid Whole Foods employees, too. It's absolutely a move we should applaud broadly, as retail and grocery workers, along with frontline service workers like those in fast food, are extremely likely to live below the poverty level. But working full-time at $15 an hour still puts your total annual earnings only in the range of $30,000 a year, not enough to get by in most American cities. What's more, Whole Foods employees reported that after the raise was announced, hours were widely cut, which Whole Foods denies.[29] Employees might have been earning more for each hour worked, but they were earning less overall—a cruel move by the company on its own, but all the crueler and more hypocritical when paired with the big PR push to get credit for the "good guy" change of bumping up low-level pay across the board.[30]

On balance, Whole Foods Market still checks many more of the good guy boxes than the majority of big retailers out there, and if you can afford to buy your groceries there, it's not a clearly bad option. But it shows that a good guy narrative is often not the whole story and that a company that once was a good guy can quickly get on the road toward becoming a bad guy.

The more challenging cases to identify are bad guy or borderline bad guy companies in which the company genuinely seems to be trying to be a good guy, and the company itself clearly believes it is doing the right things. You've certainly seen scores of products claiming to be "green" or "cruelty-free," perhaps offering a "more sustainable" pair of shoes, a "better" water bottle, or recycled clothing. A growing number of companies do seem to be making genuine efforts to create less pollution than their conventional peers produce, to pay their workers better, or to use transparent supply chains. The problem is that, like capitalism itself, the question of whether they are good or not centers on whether you think it's inevitable that we will all continually buy, buy, buy. If you believe capitalism and consumer overconsumption are inevitable, then attempts to make things better around the margins are good and worth applauding. But if you look at whether these greener or more ethical companies are actually doing more harm or good, in most cases you see that they're ultimately creating more demand for more stuff, often encouraging us to toss out our worse stuff that's still perfectly usable, generating lots of waste and a still-sizable impact.

Seventh Generation, a company that makes a wide range of cleaning and personal care products, is one such example. From its inception three decades ago, Seventh Generation has had a mission to produce products that are healthier than conventional equivalents and require fewer of the earth's resources to produce. It has also tried, unlike many self-professed "green" brands, to price products as close as possible to its competitors', so there's not a big barrier to getting consumers to make better choices. While its products are almost certainly better options than the conventional counterparts, if you do a little digging, you see that many of the things it promises are more aspiration than reality. Its website, for example, touts that its plastic bottles for laundry detergent, dish liquid, and toilet bowl cleaner are now 100 percent post-consumer content. These bottles, however, represent only a small portion of their product line, and there's no disclosure about the recycled content in their other packaging, only a vague statement that "by 2025, we aspire to reach our goal that 100% of packaging will be reusable and reused, recyclable and recycled, or biodegradable and degraded."[31] Though it does a lot to provide ingredient and supply chain transparency, Seventh Generation is also not innocent when it comes to greenwashing. It has sold for years now a concentrated laundry detergent in what appears to be a cardboard bottle, stating that it's 100 percent compostable or recyclable. However, logic tells us that something that's purely paper or cardboard couldn't securely hold a liquid, and that logic is correct. Inside the cardboard is a thinner plastic bottle that contains the liquid, and while they claim that portion is recyclable (and in many places it likely is if you do the work to separate the two) the cardboard outer bottle is a clever bit of marketing to convince you that you're not buying plastic, when you are, in fact, buying plastic. Contrast this with the home product brand Method, which packages refills for products like hand soap in plastic that more closely resembles a bag than a bottle, stating that these bags use less plastic than the much thicker bottles they replace. While Method is also still selling you plastic, the difference is that it doesn't hide it in a cardboard shell to convince you that it's completely "green."

While Seventh Generation is not a clear-cut bad guy, some of their greenwashing work and their vague promises make sense when you consider that the company is part of Unilever, the massive multinational corporation behind more than four hundred brands, including Axe body spray, Vaseline, Knorr soups, and Sunlight detergents (also the "green" brands Organics and Love Beauty and Planet). Knowing that consumers value brands seen as responsible, multinational corporations are eager to gobble up virtuous brands, and the typical pattern when this happens is for that brand to become less virtuous. Corporations do not acquire subsidiaries without expecting those brands to be profitable, and often the deal includes installing more profit-minded leadership into the acquired company. This pressure inevitably changes the virtuous company's offerings and practices, rarely for the better. Burt's Bees' founder was a true believer in the environmental movement and limited the company's product offerings to essential products. However, after the company was acquired by the Clorox Company, the Burt's Bees product line expanded dramatically. Though the company states it's still committed to the same quality and environmental standards, it now works to create demand for a wide range of nonessential products, most of which come packaged in plastic or stainless steel, a material that should never be considered disposable thanks to how resource-intensive it is to produce. And, of course, Burt's Bees feeds profits up to a much larger company that is responsible for putting products out into the world like disposable Glad ClingWrap and Glad sandwich bags, as well as a wide range of harmful cleaning products, from Clorox bleach itself to Pine-Sol and Liquid-Plumr. While buying laundry detergent carrying the Seventh Generation brand is certainly preferable to buying one made by a brand that makes no effort to be a good guy, you're right to be skeptical of any brand purporting to be green or socially conscious that is a subsidiary of a massive corporation.

Another good tip-off that a company is playing the part of a good guy without actually being one is when a product is loaded up with bogus certifications and seals of approval. That said, there are plenty of good and valid certifications and seals that can help you navigate your buying choices.

THE VALUE OF THIRD-PARTY CERTIFICATIONS

Though they don't remove the necessity of doing some of your own research, third-party certifications can be helpful to consumers trying to make better choices when shopping.

However, like so much of what we're talking about, the bad guy corporations know this, too, and they go to great lengths to muddy the waters by creating and using various seals of approval and certifications that are all but meaningless in hopes that you'll be swayed by them. Even without bad guy actors in the mix, it's important to know that certifications are still subject to human nature, meaning that most businesses will do the bare minimum necessary to achieve a certification, not work to exceed it if they perceive no additional benefit to doing so. And many companies will use certifications as an excuse for refusing to be transparent in their practices, using the certification as a shield instead of a commitment to be accountable. These factors mean that a certification should be viewed not as the pinnacle achievement but as the baseline standard a product should meet to be considered in the first place.

There are three main types of seals:

1. those conferred by a governmental body, such as the USDA organic seal managed by the US Department of Agriculture or the ENERGY STAR seal run by the US Environmental Protection Agency.
2. those conferred by a third-party organization that has no financial interest in the companies it assesses.
3. those conferred by a third-party organization formed by the very companies to whom it grants its seal of approval.

It's not hard to figure out which one of those three is not like the others. And really, there's a fourth type of seal: one that's entirely made up by a company to make it look like their product has been deemed virtuous in some way that's not actually true. Your task is to learn which seals are meaningful and which are not, so that you don't get tricked into making a financial choice that goes counter to your values.

Government-Issued Seals

A seal issued by a government body is the most likely to hold a product or service to a real standard, with no wiggle room, though that's not the same thing as saying that it represents a rigorous standard. The ENERGY STAR rating, for example, simply lets you know that a particular appliance meets a certain threshold of energy efficiency. If you look around a home improvement store, you'll see ENERGY STAR everywhere you look, including on some inexpensive products, which tells you that the threshold is not especially high. An ENERGY STAR seal also doesn't tell you whether the product is well made and will last decades, or whether you'll be having to repair it constantly or replace it within a few years. But the absence of the seal would be a big red flag against purchasing a product you would expect to carry it. Other similar government-issued seals in the US are the EPA WaterSense seal, signifying that a product is at least 20 percent more water-efficient than similar products within its category, issued for things like showerheads, faucets, and toilets, and the EPA Safer Choice label, which is an indication that the product contains fewer hazardous ingredients than other products like it, that it performs as well as conventional products, and that its manufacturer is at least working toward more sustainable packaging. The major benefit of government-issued seals is that they are legally enforceable. Companies are far less likely to stretch the truth on an application for a seal if they fear prosecution or fines, which makes the seals something you can trust. However, it's still important to find out if the seal in question represents a high bar or a low one.

Third-Party Certifications

Some of the most meaningful seals are those offered by third-party certification bodies that were set up to encourage the good behaviors we wish to see more of. The best ones not only require producers to meet high standards but they also audit producers regularly to ensure that what they say is true and that it stays true over time. The most commonly known seal of this type is Fair Trade Certified, which is meant to signal to consumers that the product bearing the seal has been produced by someone in the developing world who has been paid an above-market price for it, and it has been produced with high worker-safety and environmental standards. Researchers have criticized the fair-trade system for not monitoring how much of the extra money consumers pay for Fair Trade Certified products actually reaches poor farmers and producers. Others have said that most of the benefit of fair trade goes to large farmers rather than small ones, and additional criticism has come from the system's structure of requiring farmers to sell through a single cooperative, introducing opportunities for inefficiency and corruption.[32] So the Fair Trade Certified seal alone is certainly not a perfect indicator that a product is funding what the consumer might expect it to, but the seal in concert with others can still be meaningful. Another widely recognized seal is the Forest Stewardship Council's FSC certification for products like wood and paper that are derived from trees. The seal tells a potential buyer that the wood in the product was harvested from a sustainably managed forest. For a company or product to keep the seal, independent auditors vet the company at least once a year, affirming that its practices continue to be sustainable and ensuring that the chain of custody between harvest and final product is intact. The seal itself does not tell you if the company that turned that wood into paper used good environmental practices in the papermaking process, or if the furniture maker that turned the wood into a table engages in sustainable and nonexploitative practices, but it tells you that the wood did not come from clear-cutting an old-growth forest or from deforesting the Amazon.

Just because a seal comes from a third-party organization does not mean that the seal is meaningful, so it's always important to be skeptical. Researchers have found, for example, that the Marine Stewardship Council's seafood certification was relaxed repeatedly to suit the demands of Walmart and other large retailers, so much so that it's not a good indicator that fish were caught sustainably and that bycatch, like dolphins caught in tuna nets, was stringently avoided.[33] Likewise, researchers say that the Rainforest Alliance and other groups that certify palm oil have not effectively prevented deforestation in Malaysia or Indonesia, the countries where most palm oil was originally grown, or in the Latin American and African countries where production has shifted, and that policing of farming practices is not happening as promised.[34] The Rainforest Alliance seal also doesn't certify that a product contains entirely certified content. An item can still carry the seal if it contains only 30 percent content that meets the Rainforest Alliance's standard. Other seals are credible, but don't paint a full picture. Accreditation from the Better Business Bureau tells you that the company is committed to resolving customer complaints, but it tells you nothing about their business and environmental practices. A certifying body being independent is not enough to ensure a certification actually means something.

In-House and Industry Certifications

In the final category are certifications that are either completely in-house within the company they are certifying or granted by a "third-party" group set up by a company or an industry group. These certifications are unlikely to be meaningful.

Examples of in-house seals are the Whole Foods Market Whole Trade seal and The Body Shop's Community Fair Trade, both meant to be similar to Fair Trade in terms of guaranteeing that suppliers in poorer countries were paid a fair wage or price for their products or labor. While it seems true that both companies make sincere efforts to pay suppliers a living wage, because they regulate these efforts themselves, we have no third-party verification of what's happening. Rather, these seals encourage us to ask why all their products do not carry them if their commitment to fair pay and poverty alleviation are as defining as they say.

An example of a seal created by an industry trade group is the Sustainable Forestry Initiative, meant to be associated with the FSC certification, which was developed by the forestry industry and allows unsustainable practices like clear-cutting and using pesticides. The Federal Trade Commission (FTC) in the US provides guidance in its Green Guides for making environmental claims, including specific standards around using a seal that isn't clear in what it signifies or making a broad environmental claim without qualification or caveats, but that doesn't mean these standards are always applied. For example, the FTC states that "marketers should qualify recyclable claims when recycling facilities [that can handle a given product] are not available to at least 60 percent of consumers or communities where the product is sold," but seeing the statement they suggest—"This product is recyclable only in the few communities that have appropriate recycling programs"—is exceedingly rare.

Though the list of certifications available to companies and products is long, knowing a few of the most trusted seals available can help you identify responsible sources. Check the list on page 297. Other than the organic certifications offered by various governments, there are also a broad range of food certifications, which we'll discuss in chapter seven. Unfortunately, good certifications do not exist for all industries, but that could change in the future. A 2018 report by the Changing Markets Foundation assessed certifications broadly, calling out the problems with fishery and palm oil certifications in particular, and stated that there is not a single satisfactory certification available for the textile and garment industry.[35] Their recommendation: abolish the weakest standards and reform the stronger ones to hold producers to higher account. It's another reminder that a certification itself should never be the sole metric you use in making a financial decision.

THE GOOD IN THE BAD

In general, being skeptical of anything made or sold by massive corporations is a good practice. Any company with shareholders will be under enormous pressure to maximize short-term profits over other interests, and that's generally bad for its employees and the planet. But just as we need both widespread systemic change and individual action, we can't shift our entire economy to be more ethical and sustainable if we don't also push big corporate actors to do better through consumer action.

Sometimes you're forced to do business with big corporations because you don't have a lot of choices nearby other than chain and big-box stores, and sometimes it's because your budget is limited and big-box stores tend to be a whole lot cheaper than the little guys. Sometimes it's because that's the only way to get a particular thing you need. If you need to buy a car, for instance, there's no way to "shop small" or "buy organic" or do really any of the things that ethical consumers are often encouraged to do. You have a choice of a few dozen automakers in the world, most of which operate similarly, as well as whether to buy new or used and how big and gas-guzzling a vehicle to drive home. But you as a buyer can use your purchase to create demand for what you want to see more of and shrink demand for the most harmful stuff. As one notable example, in the early 2000s—the era of Don't Ask, Don't Tell in the military and the Defense of Marriage Act that outlawed same-sex marriage—automaker Subaru made the deliberate choice to market directly to lesbians. At the time, almost no major brands were even willing to acknowledge the existence of LGBTQ+ customers, so Subaru's choice was considered radical by many. But lesbians loved it, not only buying enough Subarus to help set the brand on a path of growth in the US but also signaling to other brands that acknowledging and marketing to audiences other than heterosexual, cisgendered white men or white housewives could pay off.[36] Marketing includes not only spending ad dollars to reach a particular audience segment but also research, listening to them in the first place about what they'd like to see in a product or in a company. While we can't credit Subaru with causing the change in attitudes around LGBTQ+ rights and same-sex marriage, the company certainly helped chip away at the problem, in large part because consumers rewarded it for its allyship. Sometimes there can be a real positive impact from doing business with the big guys if they are doing something especially progressive. So there's no shame in shopping with them if you think of your purchases as a way to push them in a better direction.

WHAT AM I FUNDING?

A scene in the sitcom *The Good Place* provides a perfect illustration of the challenge we face as consumers who wish to be ethical in our complex economy. "There's this chicken sandwich that, if you eat it, it means you hate gay people," explains Eleanor. "And it's delicious!" As consumers, we are often caught between a product we really want and our displeasure at what that choice either signifies or directly funds. The show was alluding to the fast-food chain Chick-fil-A and its support of antigay causes, a stance that inspired many people to boycott the chain, despite how delicious those sandwiches truly are. But to complicate matters further, the chain later announced that it would no longer support those causes and would stay out of politics entirely moving forward. Setting aside animal rights, environmental impacts of fast food, and worker issues, does its course correction mean Chick-fil-A is no longer a bad guy?

The final guiding question we should ask to help us make a financial choice is: *What am I funding?* Because that's truly what your dollars are doing. They are going into someone else's hands, a good guy or a bad guy who is then paying workers fairly or underpaying them, sourcing materials from responsible producers or not, making choices to reduce its environmental impact or just not worrying about it, contributing to causes you support or vehemently disagree with, and lobbying for things you'd like to see change or fighting back against any changes to the status quo. Before that transaction happens, you get to decide if you want to fund that company's efforts, or if you'd like to put your dollars into the hands of someone else who will use them in a way that better aligns with your values.

Virtually all corporations make political contributions, as do plenty of smaller businesses, so this fact alone doesn't mean a company has nefarious intent. However, knowing where those contributions are going can tell you a lot about a company's priorities. The Center for Responsive Politics' OpenSecrets site draws from required public disclosures to compile companies' political spending, from how much they spend on lobbying to how much they spend on political candidates on both sides of the aisle, even tracking the difference in party giving over time. Through OpenSecrets, for example, we can see that Amazon spent nearly $17 million on lobbying in 2019, the ninth largest sum of any company in America that year, and it spent $2.3 million on political contributions in the 2020 cycle, with the largest contributions going to Joe Biden and various Democratic committees.[37] That would suggest that Amazon supports more progressive policies. But looking more closely, we can see that the bulk of the contributions to Democratic campaigns came from individual employees of Amazon.

Election law requires you to report your employer when making a political contribution, and the company itself split its contributions evenly, giving $30,000 each to two Democratic committees and two Republican committees, and giving $10,000 to a broad range of House and Senate candidates in both parties. Facebook's donations the same year look virtually identical, as do scores of other tech companies'.[38]

That type of political giving, trying to ensure that a company can get meetings with whoever wins, regardless of party, is common, so your choice is whether that's what you want your money, in part, to fund. But it's also to assess whether a company's political giving backs up its cause promises or actively undermines them. For example, AT&T, which says it's a champion of LGBTQ+ rights, has funded the Republican Attorneys General Association, a group that has helped elect a broad range of Republicans with an anti-LGBTQ+ agenda (including Pat McCrory, who signed into law North Carolina's so-called bathroom bill, banning transgender people from using the public restroom aligning to their gender identity and promoting the false and harmful notions that it's okay to discriminate against trans people and that many trans people are sexual predators).[39] Going back to Amazon, though it has been remarkably devoid of any positions on social or environmental issues from its inception, its political action shows us what the company truly values. In 2018, the city council of Seattle, where Amazon is based, passed a small payroll tax of $275 per employee per year to fund services for those experiencing homelessness[40]—a problem that exploded in lockstep with Amazon's growing presence in the city. Amazon in turn threatened to stop all construction in Seattle, putting enormous pressure on city leaders, and led an effort to repeal the law, forcing the council to reverse course and repeal the bill itself only weeks later. That apparently was not enough, however, and Amazon spent $1.5 million in the next election to try to defeat six out of the seven council members up for reelection.[41] Given that Amazon is notorious for paying almost no corporate income tax, its willingness to spend millions of dollars on political action and lobbying but next to nothing for the public good reveals much about its priorities.

Outside of politics, we can dig into the causes that companies support and determine whether a company has signed a pledge of corporate social responsibility (CSR). Though CSR is far from perfect, and it will always be limited to more token efforts if the company is focused on profits above other goals, the causes outlined in the CSR pledge will give you a sense of what the company claims, which you can then compare to its political giving to help determine if the pledge is sincere. You can also compare things like the company's statements on social media to the reviews its employees leave on sites like Glassdoor and Indeed. For example, during the social unrest around the police killings of Black Americans in the summer of 2020, many companies stated their public support for Black Lives Matter, but few backed it up with internal policy changes or financial donations. The site Refinery29, for example, was called out for building its brand around the idea of inclusivity but treating employees of color poorly.[42] You as a consumer get to decide what you want to fund. (And remember that visiting a website with ads is funding that site.)

Though you can quickly determine whether a company's core product is something you want to fund—for example, you don't have to do any digging to figure out if a tobacco company or gun manufacturer is providing social or environmental good in the world— you can't necessarily tell what's going on behind the curtain, among all the various suppliers that feed the company's business. You don't know if a pair of shoes you want to buy that claims to be carbon-neutral is manufactured with child labor, or if the owner of the factory has been charged with human rights abuses. That's when it makes sense to investigate a company's supply chain. Many companies don't even know everything about their own supply chains, so this isn't necessarily an easy task, combined with the fact that *supply chain transparency* is still a fairly new concept and thus a poorly defined term. But it's an area of growing interest among consumers and governments alike, and the tools to get this information continue to improve. In 2010, California passed the California Transparency in Supply Chains Act, which requires all large companies and manufacturers doing business in the state to disclose whether they actively work to identify and eliminate human trafficking and slave labor in their supply chains around the globe. Because California represents one of the largest economies in the world, the law requires a large percentage of multinational corporations to make this information available. Though the law does not require that companies actually address problems in their supply chains, only disclose them, you can easily search for any company's statement and decide for yourself whether the actions it is taking are sufficient to address your concerns. Various other laws force companies to disclose other aspects of their supply chains, like the Dodd-Frank Act, which requires companies to disclose conflict minerals (those minerals like gold and tin mined in areas with armed conflict and whose illegal sales finance the fighting) in their supply chains, and a law in France that requires companies to report on their carbon emissions. Searching a company's name along with the phrase *supply chain disclosure* will give you a range of information to assess. If you can't find anything from your favorite company, write to them directly and ask what they're doing to ensure supply chain transparency, specifically around the issues you care most about. And if they won't share anything, that's a sign that you should take your business elsewhere.

Putting all of this together—the political contributions, the support for causes, the supply chain oversight, the corporate practices, the demand a company generates, the pursuit of meaningful certifications—we get a pretty clear sense of who is at least making a sincere effort to be a good guy, and who is just a bad guy through and through. In the case of Chick-fil-A, the company we discussed at the beginning of this section, it has done nothing to right its past wrongs—it pays just as little to workers as other fast-food chains, and we don't know a lot about where its chicken comes from. It's pretty safe to say Chick-fil-A is a bad guy. But that said, giving the company a few dollars for a chicken sandwich every once in a while does a lot less damage than spending thousands of dollars on cheap merchandise with a bad guy retailer. A useful exercise is to ask yourself if you'd give the amount of money you're considering spending with a bad guy company to a politician who espouses views you find abhorrent. Would you be okay giving that politician $5? $50? $500? Make your financial choice accordingly.

TOOLS AT YOUR DISPOSAL

Keeping up with which certifications are meaningful and which are not can be tough. Knowing what you're funding with a purchase may not be apparent to you. Knowing that some product claim is greenwashing is not something every consumer can be expected to sniff out. Fortunately, a range of resources exist online to help you make sense of things.

Researching Certifications

If you see a certification you're not familiar with, searching for that certification name and the word *bogus* or *credible* will return research others have done on whether its claims are to be trusted. The Ecolabel Index maintains a list of the more than four hundred environmental certifications offered around the world, and though the tool is not especially user-friendly, it can help you determine whether a certification is legitimate. Searching for a company or product name and the term *greenwashing* will give you a sense of whether the company is in the habit of misleading consumers to sell more product. And searching for a company name along with *political contributions* or *causes supported* will help you better understand what you're funding outside of that company's business practices. Of course, as with all of the internet, be wary of "sources" that consist of unqualified opinions on disreputable sites. Look for information coming from government bodies, credible nongovernmental organizations, nonpartisan think tanks, and mainstream media sources.

Many of the third-party certifying organizations maintain a registry on their sites of all of the products and companies they've certified, making it easy to find products that meet their standards. For example, the Cradle to Cradle certification site, C2CCertified.org, has a Find Products tab that lets you search by product category. Or you can simply search for *Cradle to Cradle certified clothing*, swapping in your chosen certification and the product or business category you're interested in.

Researching Violations

Searching a company's name alongside *FTC* or *Federal Trade Commission* will bring you results for cases when the company has misrepresented its products in some way, often with regard to environmentally friendly claims. There are big-name paint companies who've claimed their paints contained few or no volatile organic compounds (VOCs) when that wasn't true. There are food producers who've used the USDA organic seal when the products didn't actually meet those standards.

There are a slew of big retailers who falsely labeled products made of rayon, which can be made from a wide variety of sources, as being made of bamboo, which made the products sound more environmentally friendly than they were. There's the sunscreen that purported to be "all natural," and charged a premium for that, but wasn't.[43] All of those cases were resolved, and companies were forced to make their labels accurate, but searching before making a purchase could show you if a company you wish to buy from is involved in current charges of misrepresentation. The FTC can't police every product, and it focuses solely on products sold in the US, but it tends to catch the most egregious cases of misrepresentation.

Assessing a company's privacy practices is virtually impossible for a layperson to do, so rather than trying to make sense of a long privacy policy full of legalese, search a company's name and the terms *privacy violation* and *data breach*. If the results that come back include FTC fines for violations, that's an extremely bad sign, as are results for large-scale or repeated data breaches. In general, it's good to assume that every company you interact with online is tracking you, but it's wise to be careful about who sees your personal information.

Researching What a Company Funds

To find out what a company supports, search for it on OpenSecrets to see political contributions and lobbying spending. Look it up on Progressive Shopper to see its proportion of spending to each party—though this includes giving by employees, which often skews the figure—as well as its list of issues that go against progressive principles. For example, we can see there that Home Depot gives the bulk of its contributions to Republicans, so in turn it enables the gun industry, it pinkwashes LGBTQ+ rights, and it funds climate deniers.

LEGO, on the other hand, gives all of its contributions to Democrats and has no serious issues. (This is not to say that giving to Democrats is inherently good, but it tends to correlate to fewer worker abuses and support of other bad guy causes.) The site Goods Unite Us provides much the same information as OpenSecrets but without separating corporate from individual giving, which skews its figures, but it offers the feature of suggesting alternative brands that rate better on its scale for each category. And InfluenceMap's company profiles let you specifically see how a company scores in working toward climate goals aligned to the Paris Agreement.

See the Research Tools section at the back of this book for many more tools you can use to research companies and products before making decisions.

REVISITING THE FOUR QUESTIONS

We've now covered the overarching ways that companies and capitalism conspire to convince you not to dig too deeply or interrogate their motives and instead just go through life as a mindless consumer. But as a wallet activist, you know better than to fall for it, and you're now equipped with the four main questions you can use to guide you in any financial decision you're making, in concert with your financial values:

For whom? Does the action proposed serve those who truly need the change, because they have the most disadvantages, or does it largely serve those who already have lots of advantages?

Can everyone do this? Is this choice that I'm considering something everyone can do? And, if everyone did it, would that be sustainable? If everyone can't do it, what does that tell me?

Is it too cheap? Is something priced so low that it could not possibly have been produced or couldn't be offered without exploitation of people, the planet, or both?

What am I funding? What type of world am I helping create if I contribute profits to the entity offering something?

As we move now into the part of the book discussing specific areas of your financial life, keep these questions in mind.

PART TWO

Practicing Wallet Activism in Every Aspect of Your Life

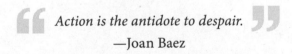 *Action is the antidote to despair.*
—Joan Baez

CHAPTER 6

What You Buy

In the Languedoc region of France, known especially for gravelly wines that pair well with the local cassoulet and the Mediterranean's seafood bounty, lies the town of Carcassonne. Renowned for its exceptionally well preserved medieval walled city, a UNESCO World Heritage site, and by some for the board game named after it, Carcassonne is a place where it's easy to feel like you've gone back in time. The view from the fortress towers reaches all the way to the Pyrenees, with only farms and vineyards between the old city walls and the mountains far in the distance. Even outside its namesake citadel, modernity feels far away, whether you're looking up at the old stone houses, stumbling over uneven cobblestone streets, or passing by Gallo-Roman sites.

One recent November, Mark and I found ourselves in Carcassonne on a rainy night. As we hurried down a street so narrow it felt like an alleyway, trying not to get drenched as we made our way to dinner, I happened to glance up at a store window. After nearly a month in

France—a country that works assiduously to maintain the purity of its language, rejecting most attempts to normalize words borrowed from others—my brain had adapted, and anything not in French felt jarring. But there it was, big and bold in the window: BLACK FRIDAY.

How odd, I thought. Any American phrase felt out of place here, in this ancient little town, but especially that one. We continued on, had an unforgettable dinner, and promptly stopped thinking about those unexpected English words. A few days later, however, we rolled into Aix-en-Provence, a bigger town with medieval origins that practically punches you in the face with its charm. We arrived in the dark, and in the morning we set out to explore. Gradually, it dawned on me. There were "Black Friday" signs everywhere. Some said Black Vendredi, the French word for Friday, but most said the whole phrase in English, or even the broader term Black Days.

In the US, the last Thursday in November is Thanksgiving, the holiday meant to celebrate the feast between Pilgrims from England, who were starving, and the Indigenous tribes who shared their food with them, saving their lives. The day after Thanksgiving has long been considered the first day of the Christmas shopping season, and as such, it took on the name Black Friday, the day when stores and retailers went into the black, accounting slang for going from a negative (or red) balance on the ledger sheet to a positive (or black) one. The day should not have much significance outside of the US, because no one else celebrates Thanksgiving on the last Thursday in November. And yet, here we were, walking around towns and cities in France advertising their massive Black Friday sales, despite that day holding no special cultural meaning for the French people.

The idea of overconsumption feels, in many ways, quintessentially American. America is the birthplace, after all, of widespread car ownership and big gas guzzlers, of oversized single-family homes behind sprawling lawns, of walk-in closets to hold an enormous collection of clothes and shoes. Except rampant consumerism is no longer confined to the United States.

Before the Industrial Revolution, Christmas was not universally associated with the giving of gifts, and any gifts given were likely to be modest.[1] It was a day to drink with family and friends, more akin to a calm, wintry Saint Patrick's Day than the months-long capitalist orgy that now marks the holiday season. Like every other religious holiday in Christianity, it involved perhaps going to church and then spending time with loved ones, and giving lots of gifts would have felt as ridiculous as it would feel now to give gifts on the Fourth of July or Labor Day. But in the mid-nineteenth century, as goods began to be produced more affordably, marketers needed to convince people to buy all these things they'd never bought before.[2] Prior to the Industrial Revolution, the average person would not even consider purchasing clothing. That was something made by someone in your household. You might buy certain items like leather gloves from a craftsperson who specialized in making them, but you did not go shopping. Shopping simply was not a thing. It was during the Industrial Revolution that we saw the advent of fashion outside of the aristocracy, the idea that you needed to buy something to keep up with the times and that something bought last year would become unfashionable and require replacement.

That marketing of seasonal items and manufacturing reasons for people to give lots of presents, all in an effort to drive up demand and make more money, has continued unabated to the present day. Frankincense and a PlayStation are basically the same thing, right? We now have not only an entire season devoted to shopping for Christmas gifts, something in which many non-Christians participate, but the day that kicks it off has spread around the world, too. But then, we've manufactured plenty of other consumer occasions, from Valentine's Day to Amazon's invented Prime Day, which typically happens each summer. And that phenomenon is no longer limited to America, either. A few years before France, we were in London for Christmas and were surprised to learn that Boxing Day, December 26, a holiday that originated as a time to box up your excess and share it with those less fortunate, is now purely about consumerism. The crowds we saw on the streets and in the shops for Boxing Day sales rivaled any Black Friday crowds we'd ever seen in the States.

Today, the whole of our capitalist society is geared toward convincing you to consume, consume, consume. Shopping is tied to our most cherished family celebrations. It's become how we send our congratulations, our condolences. Because of that, rejecting a lot of this consumerist messaging and consciously right-sizing your consumption can feel like a subversive or revolutionary act. A big part of wallet activism is learning to be okay with that. And the point warrants a quick reminder: this is *not* "conscious consumerism." Consumerism assumes that the point is *to consume*, even if you're doing so more thoughtfully. Consuming at the same level, but with slightly better options, won't get us where we need to go. We're not asking *what* to consume, we're asking *whether* to consume. Often, the best answer is not to consume at all.

HOW MUCH CONSUMPTION IS SUSTAINABLE?

If we manage the earth's resources responsibly, the truth is that it can support a great many of us with an excellent quality of life. But unfortunately, we're not being the least bit responsible in our stewardship of those resources. It's why the billionaires are funding spaceship companies, instead of investing in renewable energy infrastructure, so that they'll be able to blast off to Mars when we've finally sucked the earth dry. And that's really a perfect metaphor for the central problem: those with the most money consume the most, and they're least concerned about their role in our collective problems, because they can afford to escape them. People living on a few dollars a day in the developing world aren't burning through our petroleum reserves, filling the air with methane and CO_2, eating far more meat than they require, buying multiple homes on grand plots of land that sit empty most of the year, watering big lawns of inedible grass despite frequent droughts, or committing the environmental or social sins that have gotten us to where we are today. The problem is rich people.

Of course billionaires consume more than the rest of us, multi-millionaires consume plenty, and those earning six figures a year live much larger than the average person. But when I say the problem is rich people, I probably mean you, too. Earning $58,000 a year puts you in the top 1 percent of earners on the planet. Earning only $20,000 a year, a sum that makes it tough to scrape by in a wealthy country, still puts you among the top 10 percent of earners in the entire world. Though we know those earning $20,000 a year in the US aren't consuming at unchecked levels, because they simply can't afford to, the point is that more than half of Americans, and an even larger share of people in other wealthy nations, are rich in a global sense.

Those of us who have more money consume more. It's as simple as that, and it's true around the world. And in countries where it's never been true before, it becomes true as they move out of poverty. Their citizens begin driving cars instead of taking the bus or riding a bike, they eat more meat, they buy more stuff.[3] We can't blame people for wanting to improve their standard of living. Being able to afford shelter, healthy food, enough clothes that you don't have to wash them every day, a bed and chairs that don't hurt your back, appliances that let you cook for yourself, an occasional adventure to experience something outside the ordinary—all of these are consumption that objectively makes life better. And it's a level of consumption that the earth can easily sustain if we manage our resource extraction thoughtfully and transition to less polluting energy sources. But we've blown way past that. The average person in a wealthy country lives surrounded by stuff, the ghosts of online shopping sessions past, of trying to fill a hole that it turned out could not be filled by a physical object. This is not an argument to get rid of all that stuff but rather to take a different approach to everything you consume moving forward.

OUR TOP PRIORITY: DECARBONIZE

On every level—as consumers, as citizens, as influencers in our own circles of friends and family—our most urgent priority must be to do everything we can to head off the worst effects of climate change. The UN's Intergovernmental Panel on Climate Change says that we must make rapid adjustments to the status quo now, because by 2030, it will be too late to head off catastrophic impacts. By far the most impactful thing we can do is to decarbonize our lives. The single biggest cause of global warming is carbon dioxide, and it's released through a great many activities, including manufacturing, food production, deforestation, and construction, but none more so than when we burn fossil fuels. Fossil fuels, namely petroleum and coal, power nearly everything—running our factories, powering our cars, heating and cooling our homes, and more. Fossil fuels have made possible our journey from an agrarian planet to an industrial one to the post-industrial society we're heading toward. But it's time to change that.

If we're serious about preventing as many effects of global warming as possible, we must leave fossil fuels in the ground. The dense concentration of carbon within fossil fuels must never find its way into our atmosphere. Doing that means converting most of our power infrastructure from fossil fuels like coal, oil, and natural gas to renewables like solar and wind power (and nuclear power—which is controversial, but the topic should be on the table if we're serious about addressing climate change[4]). The cost of solar and wind power is now on par with the price of generating electricity from fossil fuels. Electricity storage that makes renewables work, storing power while it's being generated when the sun is up so it can be fed into the grid at night, is continually getting cheaper and better. We have the technology today to convert everything we do to renewable electric except for air travel, and research is happening to make that a reality, too. All we need is the initial investment to make the switch, and then we'll save money in the long run because we won't need to keep feeding fossil fuels into the system. We must demand action at the policy level by writing to our state and federal leaders, because we as individuals alone cannot fund the necessary investments in research and infrastructure this effort requires. But we can make choices as consumers to help drive the right kind of demand.

On a day-to-day level, that means doing what you can to reduce your fossil fuel consumption. The UN's *Emissions Gap Report* states that two-thirds of global emissions[5] are linked to households, and that the richest 1 percent of the population globally accounts for more emissions than the poorest 50 percent.[6] To stay on track with the targets set in the Paris Agreement, the richest 1 percent need to reduce their greenhouse gas emissions by a factor of thirty, others in wealthy nations need cut their emissions multiple times over, and the poorest half of the world can increase its emissions slightly.[7] Energy use plays a big role in this. Because we don't pay for the energy we use right at the moment we use it, unlike purchasing a physical object, using energy doesn't feel like consumption in the same way. But it's essential that we view energy as equivalent to any other purchase and cut back accordingly. If you have a car, drive as little as you can. Gradually adjust the thermostat warmer in the summer and colder in the winter, giving yourself time to adjust and remembering that there's no carbon cost to putting on another sweater or changing into shorts. Turn lights off when you leave the room. Take shorter hot showers. Look at your power bills and commit to decreasing your total usage each month. About two-thirds of our electricity still comes from fossil fuels, even if it's "clean natural gas" rather than coal,[8] so reducing the total amount of power you're pulling out of the grid will result in less CO_2 released into the atmosphere.

Then, just as what you do most of the time is more important than what you do rarely, focus on the big choices you make that have an outsize impact. If you're a car owner, commit to never purchasing another petroleum-powered one, switching to electric when your current vehicle dies. (And then demand that your federal representatives change how we pay for road maintenance, so it's not only from gas taxes, making sure electric car owners aren't getting a free ride on the backs of those who can't afford to make the switch.) Better yet, try living without a car or with fewer in your household. If you need to put heating or cooling equipment into your home, choose electric options over heating oil, natural gas, or propane. Choose an electric, on-demand water heater over a big tank powered by natural gas. Choose the electric range and stove. (Need more convincing? After decades of overlooking the health hazards of cooking and heating homes with natural gas, experts now say the risks are too great to overlook. Cooking with gas introduces particulate matter, nitrogen dioxide, carbon monoxide, and formaldehyde, resulting in levels of indoor air pollution that are illegal outdoors. Gas use is linked to significantly higher rates of asthma and worse outcomes for respiratory disease.[9] *The New England Journal of Medicine* recently recommended that gas appliances be removed from the market entirely because of their health effects.[10])

It sounds odd to say that we need to reduce our electricity use and also switch over to electric. It's about doing two things at once: reducing our reliance on fossil fuels right away by pulling less energy out of a grid that still largely depends on them, and setting ourselves up to transition smoothly into an all-renewable, all-electric power grid in the near future. Though it is currently a big source of carbon emissions, electricity is source-agnostic, unlike a gasoline-powered car. A car needs a specific kind of petroleum-based fuel to run, but we can get electricity from anything that generates heat or motion. The planet is covered with such sources, which we can tap into without pulling fossil fuels out of the ground. Buying an electric car signals that we need more electric car charging stations, which tend to go hand-in-hand with investments in renewable energy. Avoiding anchoring yourself to dirty energy is an important approach to take for the climate and a good choice financially for you. At some point you'll be forced to make the switch, and it's better not to have spent money in the meantime on devices that burned more fossil fuels, only to see these purchases become obsolete. Think of it as future-proofing your energy reliance.

Perhaps most importantly, speak up to your electric utility as a customer, a person who pays its bills. Tell it you want a more renewable energy supply. If your utility doesn't offer you the option first, investigate if it has a program that lets you opt in to renewables, perhaps for a surcharge that goes to fund more investment in new infrastructure. If you can afford to spend a few extra dollars on your monthly utility bills, do it. The more people who opt in, the more reasonable the cost becomes. Ask if your utility provider has a program to install solar panels where you live, using your home as a power plant, and give it permission to do so if that's a decision you can make. (Putting solar panels on your roof is great if that's something you can afford, but reduce your total electricity usage first. Solar panels are energy-intensive to produce, they don't last forever, and having "free energy" on the roof can make it feel like it's not important to conserve. We aren't going to meet our climate goals with rooftop residential solar, but if you're committed to pairing solar with conservation, and you can feed a significant amount of electricity back into the grid, then go for it.)

If we can switch energy use in the US to 100 percent electric, driven by renewable energy sources, we can eliminate most of our carbon emissions. That's huge. It's a reason to have hope. As wallet activists, we can play a big part in shifting demand in the right direction, driving us toward that decarbonized future.

RECONSIDER MATERIALS

Aside from powering our world, fossil fuels also go into a huge number of the products we buy. The quartz countertops we discussed back in chapter four contain plastic binders, derived from petroleum. Our paper cups at Starbucks are coated with plastic on the inside. There's plastic in our chewing gum, in our tea bags, in our cigarette butts, in the disposable wipes that claim to be flushable but aren't.[11] And most clothing manufactured today is made entirely from or includes some fibers from petroleum-based plastics. The result is that our waterways are filled with microplastic particles from washing our clothes, both contributing to the plastic pollution in the oceans and bringing microplastic into our bodies as those particles make their way into the water supply that we drink and use to grow our food. Researchers in South Korea found microplastics in the vast majority of sea salt brands from around the world, meaning when you're sprinkling salt onto your meal, you're also sprinkling on plastic.[12]

As we discussed in chapter four, most plastics are never recycled. When we do make the effort to recycle plastic, it often results in other forms of harm we may not anticipate. For example, as William McDonough and Michael Braungart write in their seminal book *Cradle to Cradle*, which drove the circular life cycle movement, "The creative use of downcycled materials for new products can be misguided, despite good intentions. For example, people may feel they are making an ecologically sound choice by buying and wearing clothing made from fibers of plastic water bottles. But the fibers from plastic bottles contain toxins such as antimony, catalytic residues, ultraviolet stabilizers, plasticizers, and antioxidants, which were never designed to lie next to human skin." ("Antioxidants" are substances that prevent oxidation, and in this case, they are different than the good-for-you antioxidants found in foods and nutritional supplements.) Just because something is recycled doesn't make it good.

What's more, the production process for most plastics is hazardous to the workers who produce them, exposing them constantly to potential harm, and creating toxic by-products that pollute the environment. This is just as true for plastic recycling as it is for virgin plastic production. Even in wealthy countries, researchers don't track rates of sex-specific cancers like breast cancer among plastic workers, even though some plastics are known to impact sex hormones specifically, so we don't even know the full impact of plastic manufacturing and recycling on workers.[13] The existence of workplace safety laws does not guarantee that workers are truly safe if those laws are incomplete or if constant monitoring by regulators doesn't happen. (It doesn't.) Our top priority when we do need to consume things should be to avoid creating demand for more plastic.

That's not to say plastic has no utility ever. If I need to go to the hospital and have an IV line put in, I absolutely want to know that there's brand-new, sanitary plastic tubing available for that line, even if it's a single-use plastic. And I want to know that disabled people who need plastic straws will always have access to them. But we must make those the exceptions, not the rule. If you find that you have no choice but to buy plastic, seek out products with recycled content to boost demand for recycled plastics and reduce demand for new plastics. *Can everyone do this?* Can everyone stop buying plastic completely? No. But we can all buy a lot less.

I am not saying that you should run around your home, collect everything made of plastic, and throw it away. The movement to reject plastic entirely may very well have caused a huge volume of still-usable plastic to go into landfills and the ocean while also creating more demand for resource-intensive products made from things like stainless steel—a far larger environmental and climate impact than just continuing to use the plastic you already have. If you have health concerns about plastic, try to repurpose plastic from the kitchen else-where in your home. As we'll discuss later in this chapter, how we dis-card things is just as important as what we consume in the first place. But our focus here is to avoid buying and creating demand for new plastics, not to rid our lives of them. The one exception is polyvinyl chloride, or PVC, which can still be found in shower curtains, kids' toys, pet toys, plastic wrap, raincoats, and a whole range of flexible materials, as well as the white pipes you might use in home improve-ment or gardening projects. PVC plastic contains phthalates, which are added to make the plastic flexible, and the by-product dioxin results from its manufacture. Phthalates are linked to a wide range of health concerns, from asthma, to breast cancer, to impacts on the reproductive system.[14] Dioxin is a potent carcinogen, one that persists in the environment and in our bodies for years. PVC is not recyclable, and it doesn't biodegrade in the landfill, instead leaching dioxin and other hazardous substances into the ground and water. You should dispose of PVC products via your local area's hazardous-waste collec-tion process.

Drastically reducing your purchasing of plastics will go a long way toward reducing harm to both the environment and manufac-turing workers. It's the only broad category that you should focus on eliminating as much as you can. For everything else, the key is less the material itself and more the sourcing and usage of it.

When you have a choice, the best material options you can choose, ranked with the best choices at the top of the list, are:

- anything you already own or can acquire secondhand.
- natural fibers like hemp, bamboo, and cotton, especially if they are organic.
- wood that has been forested sustainably (or, in the case of paper, if it contains as much recycled content as possible).
- glass, especially if it's recycled.
- metal, especially if it's recycled, only for things you'll keep for the long term.
- compostable products when disposables are necessary.
- recycled plastic, when there's no way around plastic.

That said, each of these materials comes with its own set of considerations.

Natural fibers: Natural fibers are the best choice you can make, especially if you can find products made out of fast-growing bamboo or extra durable hemp. (Though beware that bamboo is often mixed with plastics, especially when it's used in fabric form, so you'll want to look at the fine print of the item's contents.) Usually, your most common option for natural fiber will be cotton. There's still an environmental and social cost to cotton, from the large amount of water it requires to grow (which is problematic because it's grown largely in desert areas like Egypt) and because farm and garment workers could still have been exploited at many points along the way. But cotton, like other natural fibers, can be repaired, it will biodegrade, and it won't leach harmful substances into your body or into the ground or water when it's discarded. All the better if you can choose unbleached cotton.

Wood: With wood, the source is extremely important, as old-growth forests are still being clear-cut around the world, and many stylish woods like teak are virtually impossible to find in sustainable versions. Environmentalists have also programmed us for decades to believe that it's bad to cut down a tree, no matter what. In fact, many of our most catastrophic wildfires grew out of control because we've for too long tried to preserve trees at all costs, allowing forests to become overgrown rather than letting naturally occurring wildfires thin out the forests to keep them healthy. And how many people have disliked the idea of a tree being cut down to serve for a few weeks as a Christmas tree so much that they've instead purchased a fake tree made of plastic and metal that's almost impossible to recycle because of how the materials are interwoven? It's hard to imagine making this same choice, and believing it's the more environmentally responsible one, for any other product. If the tradition was to celebrate around a broccoli stalk, no one would think twice about it or consider buying a fake version, because we know that broccoli grows back, and it will biodegrade into valuable compost when we're done with it. The fact is that Christmas trees are farmed like any other crop, just on a longer growth cycle, and that's true for much of the wood and wood-based products we might buy.

Make a point of seeking out the Forest Stewardship Council (FSC) seal on both wood products and paper products, so that you know the trees weren't old-growth or the result of clear-cutting, and make sure you check out what happened to the tree after it was cut down, like whether the papermaking process it went into was an old-school toxic process or a more responsibly conducted process (you may be able to find this information on the manufacturer's website). Ideally, a product that isn't pure wood should contain both FSC-certified lumber and post-consumer recycled content. If you take those steps, you can absolve yourself of any guilt about cutting down a tree. And, if you've been wondering since chapter four about what type of countertop you should buy if you simply can't use the one you have, knowing all the downsides of engineered stone, the answer is FSC-certified wood. (Bamboo may also be available in wood form, though watch out for harmful glues and resins used to turn it from stalks into boards.)

Glass: Glass does have the issue of exposing workers to silica dust, but if you can find mostly recycled glass, which is widely available and may not even be marked as recycled, you'll know that much less harm was done to workers, because new silica dust is not released in the glass-recycling process.

Metal: Stainless steel, the pinnacle of "eco chic," is now used to make a wide range of consumer goods, from water bottles to lip balm tins to food containers. Unfortunately, the process of making stainless steel is not remotely humane or eco-friendly. As we discussed in chapter four, making steel requires mine workers to subject themselves to hazardous conditions and substances, it requires burning coal at several stages to refine the iron ore, and the production requires both inputs of hazardous metals and chemicals and creates hazardous by-products. Moreover, stainless steel is rarely recycled because it doesn't fit the mold of the standard metal objects we recycle, like aluminum soda cans and steel ("tin") food cans. That said, if you can find something made from *recycled* stainless steel, that can be a good choice, because it diverted good-quality material from going to the landfill, and it takes much less energy and extraction to recycle steel than to create new material. The exception is if the stainless steel is meant to be disposable, containing something that you'll use up in a short time. A troubling trend has been for retailers to greenwash products that once would have been packaged in plastic by packaging them in stainless steel or other similar metals, like the lip balm tin example, even though it will only be used for a short time before being discarded. A good general rule is: if you must buy metal, buy recycled. But never buy it for disposable products, and if you can avoid it altogether, do.

Compostable products: Compostable products sound good, but they are better in theory than in practice. Made of bioplastics, derived from plants instead of fossil fuels, compostable products are designed to break down in a matter of months or years, rather than staying intact for centuries like other plastics, but studies have found that not all actually break down as claimed, and worse, most are compostable only in industrial settings, not at home. Some experts have also speculated that the existence of compostable food take-out containers alongside traditional plastic products will create confusion, with plastics ending up in the compost bin and compostable (but not recyclable) products ending up in the recycling bin, contaminating both processes.[15] Still, compostable products are almost certainly better than regular plastic products, and if you have no choice but to use disposables, they are a better alternative. Just do your best to get them into a municipal compost bin rather than the trash.

Finally, for things with a lot of contents or ingredients, get to know those that are harmful for you, which also likely means they were harmful for the workers who made them. Avoid Teflon-treated pans, which off-gas harmful chemicals as you cook. Choose cleaning products with ingredients you recognize over those with a bunch of chemicals with numbers in their names. As much as you can, avoid these chemicals, all of which are banned in the European Union but widely available elsewhere:

- formaldehyde (and any substance that includes formaldehyde in the name like paraformaldehyde)
- methylene glycol

- quaternium-15
- mercury
- any phthalates
- any parabens
- polyfluoroalkyl substances (PFAS)
- p-phenylenediamines

Keep in mind that many chemicals do not have to be disclosed, hiding within the blanket term *fragrance*, for example, so you can use a resource like the Environmental Working Group's Skin Deep database, their Healthy Living app, or the Think Dirty app that lets you scan products in the store to check on their ingredients. While these chemicals are used because they add desirable qualities, like making cleaning easier, ask *For whom?* If they're harmful to your health, or to the health of those who make the products, they're not really serving you.

REJECT DISPOSABILITY

The invention of fashion marked a crucial turning point in our consumption patterns. For the first time in human history, it was conceivable that you'd replace something that was still completely usable, solely because it was no longer cool. Prior to that, most people did not have much discretionary income and would therefore work to extend the life of their belongings, repairing them when necessary and replacing them only when repairs were no longer practical.[16] Consumer culture has moved about as far away from that thinking as possible, instead convincing us that the right way to do it is to acquire more simply because we can. That attitude has, in turn, made so many of our possessions essentially disposable. To reduce our impact on the planet and climate, and to avoid the exploitation of workers that goes into making the stuff we buy, we must wholly reject this culture of disposability.

To give a sense of scale, more than 13 million tons of recyclable textiles, mostly clothing, linens, and shoes, go to landfills every year.[17] That's 26 billion pounds of content that could be recycled—or better, could simply continue to be worn, especially if we can make minor repairs. And that's true for an enormous share of what we buy: it leaves our possession well before it's reached the end of its useful life. But things going to the landfill, while the stats are horrifying, is not the real problem. The real problem is that disposal tends to be paired with new consumption. We don't just throw out a shirt we don't like anymore, we buy a new one. When we treat things we buy as disposable, we create more demand for more disposable stuff. Everything we throw away is lost potential.

What if, instead, we only bought things that we expected to use for ten or twenty years and were committed to repairing instead of replacing? That can be a tough stance when it's cheaper to buy a new toaster than to fix the one we have, shoe repair shops are increasingly rare, and so many products are built around planned obsolescence, but it's one we must take. *Can everyone do this?* Can everyone learn to make minor repairs? Absolutely. As much as you can, reject anything that's meant to be disposable, or anything that you know will only be used for a short time. For example, I am chronically unable to keep from spilling food on myself, so for me, white clothing might as well be disposable. The production of white clothes and textiles requires toxic bleach to produce, and then requires more bleach to maintain that bright white color and treat the inevitable stains. However, wearing a darker color wardrobe has none of these problems, and a black shirt is unlikely to become unwearable because it's stained.

It won't work for everything. For example, there's not currently a responsibly produced and durable cell phone that we can keep for twenty years. And sometimes, we simply need to buy things with short-term value, like baby clothes. But we can commit to finding them secondhand and then passing them on to someone else when we're done with them. If we would approach as many of our purchasing decisions as possible this way, we'd buy far less, and in turn create far less demand for the things we must see much less of in the world.

We sometimes face a choice that would be different if the world were different, and we're stuck with imperfect options. If your old refrigerator dies, for example, and the repairs on it will cost almost as much as the price to buy a brand-new, ENERGY STAR–rated fridge, it can feel like the right choice to buy the new one, especially if you live in a state where most electricity comes from burning coal and the new fridge will pull much less electricity out of the grid. In your case, that might be the right choice. But the specifics matter. If your state is producing mostly renewable electricity when you're faced with the choice, then fixing your old fridge, though it needs more electricity, will have an overall smaller impact, because you aren't creating demand for a newly manufactured, complex machine, and you aren't dealing with appliance disposal problems—safely getting rid of the climate-decimating coolants within it, as well as all the transportation and overseas shipping that would be involved. *Can everyone do this*, spending less to repair big items than it would cost to replace them? Of course.

An emerging trend in the garment industry is to offer to take back clothing and recycle it into new clothing, a promise made by fast-fashion retailer H&M, among others. While these intentions may be sincere, be wary of claims like these, and remember the strategy of the plastic bottle industry to sell you on recycling is to get you to buy more plastic. *For whom?* It's not for the underpaid garment workers or plastic recyclers, it's to allay your guilt so you'll buy more clothes. If it's a choice between recycling something perfectly wearable that you already own and buying something new, or buying nothing at all, you'll do less harm buying nothing every single time.

Finally, we can't talk about disposability without talking about packaging. What we buy is more packaged now than ever before, so much so that a full third of everything in today's landfills is packaging material.[18] Some of that is hard to avoid, especially without better recycling programs for things like milk cartons or the bag inside the cereal box. But if we're as deliberate about avoiding unnecessary packaging as we are about our actual purchases, we can meaningfully reduce the global demand for plastic. Here are some steps you can take:

- **Do your best to avoid products that are overpackaged for no good reason,** especially things like makeup and personal care items, foods that could easily be sold loose, and multi-packs of items that result in more packaging, like twelve-packs of paper towels in which each roll is individually wrapped. (Better yet, stop buying paper towels and tissues altogether, and instead buy a stack of cotton dish towels that you use to clean up messes and then wash. Cotton cloths sold as washable baby wipes are nicer on noses anyway. Old T-shirts are even better, and you probably have some of those already. If you buy new, avoid microfiber, which is plastic.)
- **Avoid packaging that requires you to use more packaging when you get home.** The typical packaging for bacon is a good example of this: it does not close on its own, and often, people will put the opened bacon package inside another plastic zipper bag that will get tossed when the bacon runs out.
- **Avoid products packaged in plastic when there are similar options packaged in more easily recyclable glass or paper.**
- **Look for ways to buy in bulk that result in less packaging total,** but only if you know you'll use all of something before

it goes bad, so you aren't generating food waste. That may be using the zero-waste approach to grocery shopping when and to the extent you're able, filling your own bags or jars out of the bulk bins, or it might be simply buying the largest quantity you can of something that doesn't contain individually wrapped portions within it. For example, if you color your hair at home, as I do, instead of buying a new box of hair color each time that contains within it several single-use plastic bottles, consider switching to coloring products designed for professional stylists that you can buy from a beauty supply store in larger quantities, so you end up with only two plastic bottles for every ten times you color, rather than two to four bottles every single time.

When buying online, you don't know what packaging something will arrive in. We've all had the experience of buying one tiny thing that arrives in a needlessly giant box, perhaps filled with plastic materials to cushion it. There's no way to manage it perfectly, but remember that just because something arrives packaged doesn't mean it's necessarily worse than buying it at the store. If you order toilet paper online, for example, it usually ships in just the box containing your paper rolls. If you buy that same toilet paper at the store, it also arrived in a box, but you don't see the box because the stockers removed it before putting the package on the shelf. While the shipping from the fulfillment center counts in the impact of getting that box to you, by not driving to the store and back, and instead letting the mail carrier who drives by your house every day anyway bring it to you, you might do less harm to the climate.

For things that don't come already boxed, choose whenever you can to have things shipped together, even if it means they get to you more slowly, and express your desire not to receive things packed in plastic. For example, you can do an online chat with Amazon customer service and register that request, and they'll put a note in your customer profile that warehouse workers will see when they ship your orders. You can also look at the time given for placing an order ("Delivery Thursday, order within 3 hrs and 10 mins") as a clue that different items in your order will be sent from the same fulfillment center, cutting down on how many different packages arrive.

For retailers with whom you shop regularly who ship things only in plastic, message them to tell them you won't shop with them anymore until they convert to less harmful packaging. And while it's important to be discerning about packaging, it's also important to view it in the proper context. If buying something online, which means it will come in additional packaging, gets you to buy less than you would at the store because you can avoid impulse buys, then look at the big picture. The extra packaging required to buy the one thing might be saving all the packaging and contents of the things you would have bought at the store but didn't. We're trying to reduce our overall impacts, not keep score on who can avoid online shopping.

SHOP LIKE YOU GIVE A SHIT

If you begin to focus on avoiding plastics and harmful materials, and you stop viewing things as disposable, all of that is a good start. But to truly become a wallet activist, you need to take one more step: shopping like you give a shit, not just about the planet, but also about all the people impacted by our consumption. With the things you buy, it's looking at who makes it, how they make it, and what other hands it passes through on its way to you, and choosing what practices you're comfortable supporting.

For example, though a *Made in the USA* label doesn't mean what it once did, that label on an article of clothing tells you that it *wasn't* made by trafficked children in an overcrowded and unsafe sweatshop in Bangladesh, or at least the finished garment wasn't sewn there (the fabric still could have been, so it's important to look into sourcing and the supply chain). Garment workers are among the most exploited in the world, especially in poor countries like Bangladesh, the Philippines, Turkey, and Vietnam, where most textile factories operate, and the abuses affect mostly women, who are already more vulnerable economically virtually everywhere. According to the Clean Clothes Campaign, which promotes rights for garment workers, the problems within the fashion industry include poverty wages, hazardous workplaces that have killed thousands from fires and collapsed buildings, wasteful practices and pollution, gender discrimination, active union-busting, no job security, and token claims of responsibility that are ultimately meaningless.[19] That's why we see this shocking and stark fact: globally, only 2 percent of fashion workers earn a living wage.[20] Many garment manufacturers say their supply chains are transparent, and they say they audit factories within the supply chain, but without an independent third-party conducting those audits, there's no reason to believe they actually happen.

Making active use of the question *Is it too cheap?* goes a long way here. If a new article of clothing is priced cheaply, you can virtually guarantee it was made under conditions that would horrify you. (You're also much more likely to treat it badly if it's cheap, shortening its useful life.) The US Department of Labor has an app called Sweat & Toil that lets you look up specific goods or specific countries to see where exploitative practices are happening. For example, if you are considering purchasing something made from copper, and you can determine that that copper came from the Democratic Republic of the Congo, you can use the app to learn that copper from the DRC is produced using forced child labor. Armed with that information, you can either find copper from another source that's less exploitative or you can opt not to buy it altogether. Even just searching for the product name, company name, country of origin, and the word *exploitation* can yield a lot of helpful information.

Thinking about the hands it will pass through is important, too. Whether you're buying online or buying from a large chain store, everything that ultimately reached you has passed through many hands in the distribution and warehouse process. And warehouse jobs can be just as exploitative as manufacturing jobs, both because they tend not to be well paid and because they can involve hazardous conditions in which injuries happen frequently. For example, a review of records by The Center for Investigative Reporting (CIR) revealed that Amazon has what CIR terms a "safety crisis" in its fulfillment centers, with injuries happening regularly and rates of injury increasing around peak periods like the holiday shopping season and the company's invented Prime Day.[21] If you have no choice but to shop with Amazon or another big online retailer, whether because you can't afford other options, it's hard for you to shop in person, or you don't have good local options, you can lessen the potential for your purchase to do harm by avoiding shopping during peak periods. As much as you can, avoid Prime Day and the period from Black Friday through Cyber Monday. If you must shop during those times, select no-rush shipping so that your order will go to the back of the line to be fulfilled when things are a bit less harried.

Making a point not to shop around peak periods is a good practice generally. The vast majority of roses and other cut flowers offered for sale in the US and Canada come from South America, primarily Colombia and Ecuador, which are now the world's largest flower producers after the Netherlands.[22] In an effort to get farmers in the region to stop growing the coca leaves that become cocaine, the US instituted the Andean Trade Preference Act and later the Andean Trade Promotion and Drug Eradication Act, for the region's other agricultural products, removing tariffs on crops deemed more desirable and giving farmers in the Andes region a financial incentive to grow things for export to America. This created the South American flower boom that continues to this day, injecting capital into the region and boosting local economies. Most of the year, flowers are flown north on commercial airline flights, filling otherwise empty space, and contributing relatively few carbon emissions on their own. (Growing roses and other cut flowers in South America is also less carbon-intensive than growing them in greenhouses in North America, for example, because of the ideal climate near the equator.) However, around peak periods like Valentine's Day and Mother's Day, flowers are in such high demand that they travel north on specially hired cargo jets.[23] As a result, not only are flowers more expensive during these peak periods but they also generate dramatically higher carbon emissions to get to your door. There's no reason to stop buying flowers altogether, but if you must buy them at peak periods, try to source flowers grown locally.

Fundamentally, learning to consume less starts with learning to know the difference between a want and a need. What counts as a need for you is not for anyone else to say, but consumer culture trains us to say "need" reflexively when what we really mean is "want." Needs are things we can't live without, that make it possible to go about the necessary activities of life. For example, for some, makeup may feel like an unnecessary want, while for others who work in settings that expect it, makeup is a need. Outside of food, shelter, health care, and clothing, most things are up for debate about whether they're necessary. But the debate is a distraction. What matters is training yourself out of viewing everything as a need and instead recognizing wants for what they are. That's not the same as saying that you're not allowed to consume anything that's a want, but by properly categorizing things, it's easier to choose not to consume at least some of the time, and over time, to make not buying something the reflex and buying the exception, instead of vice versa.

When buying something, give as much of your demand as possible to good guy companies, and look for products that also do social good. But remember that doing so does not give us a free pass to avoid pushing for policy action or rejecting consumerism as much we can. So much of the "social good" economy is still built on capitalist principles of trying to get us to spend as much as possible on things we don't truly need, while making us feel like we're doing something good so that we don't ask too many questions. The work of wallet activism is to see through that marketing and stick to your values.

DECLUTTER REALISTICALLY

The existence of secondhand thrift stores is a good thing for those who wish to shop secondhand, those with a limited budget, and the nonprofit organizations that use proceeds from the thrift shops to fund their programs. But the existence of thrift shops tricks us into believing that getting rid of things is not wasteful but generous. You're not throwing away those pants or relegating that blender to the landfill, you're donating them to Goodwill and creating jobs!

Elizabeth Cline, author of *Overdressed: The Shockingly High Cost of Cheap Fashion*, coined the phrase "clothing deficit myth," the notion that somewhere out there are a bunch of people who don't have enough clothing, and thus our castoffs will go to those who need them more than we do. We can expand this to all the things we might get rid of and call it the "stuff deficit myth." People who are struggling aren't struggling for lack of clothes or stuff. People are struggling because we don't have enough affordable housing, jobs don't pay enough, and we punish people for being sick, Black, an immigrant, or any number of other traits that deviate from the cisgendered, able-bodied, white male supremacy built into the fabric of our society. In short, people don't need your stuff.

As for the thrift stores themselves, most of their job is not selling the things you donate, it's throwing those things away. Only about 20 percent of clothing donated to secondhand stores is ever sold, with the vast majority either ending up as trash or getting shipped to developing countries like Guatemala, India, Tanzania, and Angola, which are now inundated with our castoff garments. A third of all clothes donated globally end up in sub-Saharan Africa, and the result is that local textile industries have been harmed by the influx of cheap clothing, with Ghana's shrinking by 80 percent between 1975 and 2000 and Nigeria's being almost entirely wiped out.[24] For the large share of that clothing that doesn't sell in the countries to which it's exported, those countries are now stuck figuring out what to do with it, and plenty still ends up in the trash, but only after having traveled thousands of miles and consuming loads of fossil fuels along the way. For the things that don't get shipped abroad, Goodwill or whoever you donated to has to pay to dispose of them, because they're trashing large quantities of unsellable goods. *What am I funding?* When we donate items indiscriminately, we're funding more trash disposal and the expensive offloading of our excess onto others. Despite good intentions, we might be doing far more harm than good. It's time to reckon with that fact, and to stop thinking of the possibility of donating things as an excuse to buy more stuff we don't need.

Having the option to declutter encourages us to see more of what we possess as disposable. As we've seen, the entire disposal system is built to make us feel good about buying more. Landfills are hidden away out of view so we don't have to confront our trash. Plastic makers convince us they're recycling much more than they really are so we'll buy more plastic. While the intention behind thrift stores and other intermediate stops for our discarded items is certainly different, its impact on our thinking can operate the same way. Feeling like a thing we're tossing is going somewhere good absolves us of feeling responsible for where it ends up. Asking *For whom?* will often show we're discarding selfishly, not to help others. If we look at where our stuff is going, it's a lot harder to justify discarding it.

Of course, there's no value to keeping something around that you truly won't ever use again. Many of us who grew up with parents or grandparents who lived through the Great Depression can recount seeing cabinets full of margarine and Cool Whip containers they just couldn't bear to throw out, or closets full of clothes that hadn't fit anyone in thirty years. I'm not suggesting anyone develop hoarding tendencies, but rather that you need to approach the decluttering process just as mindfully as you would the process of bringing something into your life, focusing not on whether something "sparks joy," to use the phrase coined by Marie Kondo, but whether you can easily derive more use out of it. I admire Kondo and her messages of minimizing what you buy and taking care of what you own, but measuring decluttering success by number of trash bags is problematic if our goal is to stop viewing things as disposable.

While it's still better to donate things that are in good condition rather than trash them, don't view donating as your first option, because that gives you 80 percent odds of those things going to the landfill or being shipped overseas. Instead, do some reflecting first. Ask yourself what your motivations are for discarding it. Are you discarding something that's still perfectly useful so that you can replace it with a newer version? If you're freeing up space in a drawer or closet by discarding things, will you truly keep that space empty, or will it become an invitation to fill it with new stuff? Does the promise of finding a good home for something in the future justify buying it in the first place? Thrift stores are currently overrun with fancy china dinnerware sets their original owners assumed they could pass off to kids or grandkids one day as heirlooms, but those folks ultimately didn't want them. If the idea of filling your home with things that used to belong to your parents or grandparents doesn't appeal to you, don't assume others will one day value anything you wish to pass down.

As much as possible, shift your view of donating to an option of last resort. Then, do what you can to ensure your castoffs find a use somewhere:

- Host a garage sale or a swap with friends where everyone brings the things they don't wear anymore.
- List items on Craigslist, eBay, Poshmark, or your local Buy Nothing group on Facebook.
- Announce on social media the things you want to get rid of and see if anyone wants them.

If you can get your things into someone's hands directly, there's a far greater chance they'll actually be used. For items that no one wants, or that aren't in great condition, consider ways you can repurpose them. Free T-shirts are so ubiquitous that most of us have more of them lying around than we'll ever wear. And sure, some could become sleep shirts, but none of us need ten sleep shirts. However, if you're looking to reduce your usage of disposable paper products, cotton and cotton blend T-shirts are great to cut into squares to use instead of paper towels, and the more synthetic-based T-shirts that tend to be extra soft are great replacements for tissues. Every home should have a rag box where worn-out clothes go so that anytime you need a cleaning cloth, you've got a ready supply.

For things you wish to get rid of that seem like they should be recyclable but aren't allowed in your curbside bins, contact your local recycler to find out if you could drop them off. Or research other recycling options like TerraCycle, a company that sends out mailers so you can ship back harder-to-recycle items that they'll take care of for you.

Paying for this yourself can be costly, so ask the brands you shop with if they'll commit to a circular life cycle for their products, including paying to ensure their packaging gets recycled. For example, skincare brand Josie Maran lets customers print a free return shipping label with TerraCycle to return empty containers.

Talking about decluttering ultimately brings us back to purchasing things in the first place. Thinking in terms of a circular life cycle, before you buy something, ask yourself how you'll discard it when you've derived all the value from it that you can get. Do you realistically expect to keep it for your whole life? Are you willing to do the work to find it a new home when you're done with it, rather than simply donating it? Can you envision repurposing it when it's no longer in style? If all of that seems like too much work, it's a good indication that you might not need it in the first place.

JOIN THE TRUE SHARING ECONOMY

If every single one of us having something is wasteful, then it makes sense to reduce the number of a given object that must be produced without requiring anyone to go without it. Sharing more of our collective possessions is how we do that. The term *sharing economy* has become confused with the relatively new practice of using technology to connect those with something to share with those who need that thing, namely transportation and lodging, as we'll discuss in chapter eight. But the true notion of sharing is one we can and should employ much more to reduce consumption.

Whether it's splitting a lawnmower between several neighbors, because you don't need to mow your lawn every day, or opening up a local tool library so that people can do home improvement projects without having to buy a bunch of tools they'll use only rarely, any effort to get more usefulness out of things and to reduce demand for those resource-intensive products is good. The rise of Little Free Libraries, glass-fronted boxes people are installing in their front yards to encourage book sharing among neighbors, is a familiar example of the sharing economy. (Though some critics have argued that Little Free Libraries can draw interest away from public libraries, which are a critical public service, and push gentrification of urban neighborhoods, so it's not necessarily something we should all rush to implement.[25])

For things you may use only once or twice, the best form of sharing might be simply to rent rather than buy. Numerous options exist now for renting all types of clothing, and tool and equipment rental is available in most local communities. As power tools especially have decreased in price, equipment rental has become less popular—but before buying a tool, assess how often you'll truly use it. The cost of buying something might be only three or four times the cost of renting it for your project, but if you aren't certain you'll use it often, renting can still make the most sense, both for your own finances and to preserve resources. Also consider "sharing" with local businesses for occasional needs. For example, while a few cents a page may sound expensive for printing, it's much cheaper and less wasteful than owning a printer and buying new ink or toner regularly.

In a way, buying secondhand is a form of sharing, as it's about ensuring that more than one person gets use out of something before it goes to the landfill. Just as you can use the numerous online tools to declutter things you no longer need—from Poshmark and Craigslist to Buy Nothing Facebook groups and Freecycle—you can also use them to find things you would rather not buy new. And of course, old-fashioned thrift stores are a great option if you have the time to sort through the inventory to find what you need. Most thrift stores are run by nonprofit social service organizations, with proceeds funding their services, and most also employ people affected by homelessness, incarceration, or some other oppressive socioeconomic circumstances.

Consignment stores, while less often philanthropic in nature, provide another brick-and-mortar option for buying secondhand.

There's a virtually endless list of possible ways to share resources within a community or among neighbors, and if you're motivated to start something, you'll almost certainly find people interested in joining you. Some communities have started bicycle libraries, giving neighbors a place to repair their bike without needing to own all the tools. Community gardens or allotments are another growing source of resource sharing. Community gardens allow residents to claim a plot that they plant and maintain, but often with access to shared tools like shovels and hoses, reducing the need for everyone to own their own set of tools, while providing access to garden space to those who may not have a yard or outdoor space of their own.

PURCHASES YOU CAN FEEL GOOD ABOUT

Talking about what to buy or not can feel like a long list of no-no's. While that's not my intention, it is worth discussing purchases that you can universally feel good about. A good place to start is to look back at your financial values statement in chapter three and to consider what types of purchases align with your values.

For example, while my top priorities are around climate and inequality, I also value the arts and humanities, which I believe enrich our lives immeasurably. Therefore, I prioritize purchases that align with those areas. I spend money without question on dance performances, art museums, credible news media organizations, and so on. As an author who recognizes that publishers only want to publish your books if you demonstrate that you can sell them, I always buy books written by friends and people I wish to support. If I plan to keep the book forever, I will buy a physical copy, and otherwise, I buy the e-book or audiobook, so that nothing has to be manufactured or shipped for me to enjoy it. I wish to see more demand for books in the world, and the information and imagination contained within them, so I use my money to create that demand. (I still use the library plenty, especially for older books, and for best sellers that are doing just fine without my support.) Along similar lines, I happily pay to see movies in the theater that reflect things I want to see more of in the world, rather than waiting for them to come out on a streaming service: movies centered on people of color or LGBTQ+ people, women super-heroes, and social justice story lines that aren't about white saviors. You certainly have things you wish to support without question, so give yourself that permission. Expecting yourself to labor over every potential purchase will quickly lead to burnout, and so in addition to adding things to the "never buy" list, it's good to give yourself a few categories to spend without guilt.

Secondhand purchases are something you can almost always feel good about, unless the item you're buying is simply irredeemable from a climate or social perspective. Just consider before you buy whether your purchase could, in fact, create demand for new products, even indirectly. For example, while it's hard to quantify, we can imagine that the value of used cars would go down if fewer people were inter-ested in buying them, which would remove much of the incentive for people to trade in slightly used cars to buy new ones. If you're buying a newer used car when you still have a perfectly good car, your taking a slightly used car off someone's hands could be freeing them up to buy a new one . . . meaning you're still contributing to demand. Cars, how-ever, are the only major area where you need to consider this. Other-wise, buying secondhand is generally positive.

Anything handmade or homegrown is also something you can generally feel good about buying, as are most gifts of experience, assuming it's not an experience with an outsized impact on the cli-mate or other people. I don't assume this applies to anyone reading this book, but we're at the dawn of the age of space tourism, and aside from the astronomical monetary cost, the rocket fuel required to get someone up to the zero-gravity zone for a few minutes is all but impossible to justify. So long as the experience you're considering isn't exploitative, doesn't consume a massive amount of energy, or generate a lot of waste, you're probably safe.

A wonderful resource to use when giving or receiving gifts is the SoKind registry. SoKind allows anyone to register for things like gifts of experience, gifts of time and skill, secondhand gifts, gifts of philanthropy, day-of-event help, and a range of other options that still allow everyone to enjoy gift-giving traditions, but in ways that are less focused on consumerism and overconsumption.

———

There are a lot of people out there pushing messages about living with less, some guaranteeing instant happiness if you can pare down your possessions to the absolute minimum. If that's your cup of tea, great. So long as you're careful about how you declutter and discard, I will never try to push you to buy more. But fortunately, doing right by the planet and our fellow humans doesn't require us to sit in near-empty rooms, owning as little as possible. So long as your focus is on reducing your future consumption, especially of energy and of newly manufactured goods, you can rest secure in the knowledge that you're doing just fine.

CHAPTER 7

The Food You Eat

Garlic is the rare vegetable that's planted in the fall. A grower breaks apart the garlic bulbs and sinks individual cloves into the earth, pointy side up. The cloves sleep through the winter, emerging with green shoots in the spring and maturing into a full bulb underground in the early summer. The bulb is then plucked out of the ground and allowed to dry to extend its shelf life. The humble garlic bulb isn't something that most consumers who aren't also gardeners pay much attention to. It doesn't need refrigeration, and it sits out on the counter until either we're ready to use a clove or two, making a mess of its papery covering as we break into it, or we let it stick around too long until it sprouts new garlic, and then into the trash or compost it goes. Or we buy garlic powder instead, never interacting with the bulb itself, letting someone else make that mess so we can get the flavor with just a few taps on the bottle. It's doubtful that we think of what garlic truly is: the most commonly consumed vegetable in the US, as well as in many countries around the world. It's a central component of our diets, yet it rarely warrants discussion of any sort. But here's another fact about it: 90 percent of the garlic sold in the US[1] (and 80 percent of global supply[2]) is grown in China. Despite being an incredibly easy crop to grow, requiring less work than almost any food we eat, and one with varieties adapted to virtually every climate zone on Earth, it also has a shockingly high carbon impact relative to its nutrition because it's needlessly grown oceans away from billions of the people who eat it.

Capitalism dictates that producers will always look for ways to increase their profit margins, so we shouldn't be surprised when production of something moves to the place in the world where it can be produced most cheaply. We expect that for bigger-ticket items, but not for something as small and inexpensive as garlic. Because garlic is something we just don't think about that much, it's likely that few of us would pay a premium for garlic just to be sure it was grown nearby. We have bigger things to worry about. But unlike with consumer goods, the homes we live in, and the financial institutions we bank with, we aren't limited to thinking about food in terms of what we are or aren't willing to pay for. We can also ask whether it's something we could grow ourselves. Given its adaptability and its virtually no-maintenance growing habit, every one of us with a pot of dirt and a sunny windowsill could realistically and inexpensively grow all the garlic we need, and we could cut off a needlessly wasteful supply chain.

In a perfect world, we'd all be able to eat cheap, fresh, local, organic produce all the time, broccoli would taste better than bacon, and the animals we choose to eat would emit only oxygen and rainbows, not methane and ammonia. Of course, this is not that world. This chapter discusses how we can operate ethically and healthily in a deeply flawed food economy, taking into account where our food comes from, the true importance of organic, the controversy around GMOs, and—the key question—how much we eat of certain foods.

WHERE OUR FOOD COMES FROM

We can't talk about food without talking about industrialization. Since World War II, the industrialization and mechanization of agriculture has accelerated, practiced on a far larger scale than previous generations could have imagined. It has also become heavily reliant on synthetic nitrogen fertilizers, toxic pesticides and herbicides, and heavy irrigation, a trend that has escalated in recent decades.[3] The promise of industrialized agriculture was that it would increase crop yields and feed more of us more efficiently, but that has not happened, at least not without lots of externalities.[4] Instead, we have massive negative impacts from our modern food production system—on humans, animals, and the environment—hidden within a huge portion of the food available for us to buy. The food that lines store shelves also looks much different than in the past, with so much processing and packaging that many foods are unrecognizable from the form they take as they come out of the ground or graze the land. That has enormous health consequences.

At the same time, we've seen a split within the food system, not unlike the ever-widening gulf between rich and poor. The Harvard T.H. Chan School of Public Health found that the cost difference between a healthy diet of largely unprocessed, nutrient-dense food and an unhealthy one of mostly processed, nutrient-poor food is at least $1.50 per person, per day, or $2,190 a year for a family of four (and that was in 2013 dollars, so the total is certainly higher now).[5] Researchers at the University of Washington Center for Public Health Nutrition found that ultra-processed foods cost on average $.55 per

100 calories, while unprocessed foods cost $1.45, a nearly three-fold difference, and that unprocessed foods also increase in price over time much faster than ultra-processed foods do.[6] At a time when a person earning the median income cannot afford a one-bedroom apartment in a single US city, and 20 million schoolchildren, more than a third, receive free lunch at school every day because their families can't afford to feed them, asking everyone to pay potentially thousands of dollars a year more for their food is simply not an option.[7] *Can everyone do this*, switch to a fully unprocessed diet? No.

Research by the US Centers for Disease Control and Prevention (CDC) found that, on average, 56 percent of our calories come from subsidized foods like wheat, corn, soybeans, the dairy and livestock that feed on those subsidized grains, and, increasingly, the wide array of processed foods sweetened with the corn derivative high-fructose corn syrup.[8] The subsidies paid to farmers for growing these crops, along with subsidized water, make the prices for processed foods lower than they would be without them, helping explain why Americans consume more meat and dairy than residents of any other country.[9] If everyone in the world ate as much meat as Americans do, humans would need to use every square foot of habitable land for grazing livestock and growing grain for feed, and we would have run out of fresh water back around the turn of the millennium.[10] The artificially low prices for processed foods especially mean that those who can't afford to buy healthier food are paying the price with their health: eating more subsidized foods is linked with higher rates of diabetes, heart disease, and obesity, including childhood obesity, which is most closely linked, paradoxically, to food insecurity and poverty.[11]

Because the problems of our food system are so closely linked to food subsidies, stemming from the outdated 1973 Farm Bill, only policymakers can spur the widespread change that's needed, which means pushing your federal elected officials to reform that legislation. But reducing demand for subsidized foods can help make the case.

Most people today have some concept that the meat that ends up on a plate probably did not come from an animal that spent its life in an idyllic pasture setting, surrounded by fresh air, green grass, and clean water. But given that consuming meat isn't just driven by nutrient density, it's driven by taste and dietary preferences, we have a built-in bias not to look too closely at where our animal products come from. The truth is, unless you're going out of your way and paying a lot more, every animal product you eat comes from a process that's just as mechanized and industrialized as the processes for plant-based foods. Ranchers rely on lots of synthetic inputs to help their animals grow bigger and faster, altering their food and what's added to that food, and deciding how much sunlight animals are exposed to a day. For example, most pork in the US, Canada, Japan, South Korea, and New Zealand is raised with growth-inducing drugs that encourage the pigs to put on lean muscle mass quickly and with less food, most frequently the chemical ractopamine, a substance that's banned in 160 countries, including the European Union, mainland China, and Russia. There's now a movement among pork producers to move away from ractopamine, but interestingly, it was not driven by US consumer outrage, but rather by China banning the chemical and producers not wanting to miss out on that massive market.[12] There's no reason to think that those phasing out ractopamine won't jump at the chance to use the next growth-inducing pharmaceutical that comes along if they can get away with it.

With beef cattle, the big growth spurt comes not from pharmaceutical products, but from the widely used practice of "finishing" cows on a feed lot, known technically as a concentrated animal feeding operation, or CAFO. Most cattle spend the last four to six months of their lives packed together, standing around in their own waste, gorging themselves on corn and other grain-based agricultural by-products, getting ready to go to slaughter between the ages of fourteen and twenty-two months.[13] In general, the animals that we eat today live short lives in confined quarters, with every day they live and every calorie they eat engineered to maximize profit. That's even true for much of the fish we eat, with densely packed fish farms popping up all over the world. Conventionally raised chickens live in cages and are routinely fed antibiotics, because otherwise diseases can rapidly spread within the crowded conditions in which they're raised.

Animal rights groups talk frequently about the horrific conditions for animals in meat processing facilities. The musician Paul McCartney famously said, "If slaughterhouses had glass walls, everyone would be vegetarian," but the truth is that the conditions for humans in these facilities are not much better. While most factories today barely resemble the factories in our imaginations, with far fewer people in them than you'd expect for their size, mostly handing off tasks between giant robots and automated systems, food production—most especially slaughterhouses and meat processing plants—is where you still see workers packed shoulder-to-shoulder in inhospitable conditions. The 500,000 people who work in American meat processing facilities are among the least empowered workers in the country, with virtually no union representation and largely "at will" employment, meaning a worker can be fired at any time without cause. The bulk of workers are Black and brown people in low-income communities, and 51 percent of frontline meatpacking workers were born outside the US.[14] In fact, agriculture is more reliant on the labor of undocumented immigrants than any other industry, and bosses use that fact to their advantage, threatening workers who speak up about the working conditions with deportation.[15] So many workers are afraid to lose their jobs that many workplace injuries are never reported, meaning we don't even know the true figures, though meat processing is among the most dangerous jobs in America even with that massive underreporting.[16] During the COVID-19 pandemic, very little changed about meat processing practices, and the virus ripped through numerous Tyson Foods, Smithfield Foods, and JBS USA facilities in the Midwest and southeastern US, as workers who get no paid sick leave were forced to work sick or lose their jobs.[17] *Is it too cheap?* Undoubtedly yes. Our meat is cheap not only because the livestock eat subsidized food but also because we underpay our meat processing workers for their labor, and don't pay their bills when they get sick or injured.[18]

Although fast food is not so hazardous for workers, similar issues are at play: low pay and lack of paid sick leave and union representation, despite workers asking for both for years. If fast food were not almost entirely made of subsidized foods and brought to us by underpaid workers, it would cost significantly more. Under pressure from unions and workers' rights groups, fast-food behemoth McDonald's announced it would no longer lobby against raising the federal minimum wage, which represents progress. But fast-food workers are still nowhere near the $15 an hour that many economists and activists say is the minimum required to scrape by in America.[19] The average fast-food worker currently earns $19,000 a year, barely above the federal poverty level for a family of two, and fast-food workers are likely to rely on government assistance programs to get by, in effect subsidizing fast-food company profits with taxpayers' money, similar to what we see with Walmart workers.[20] And though some chains like Burger King are beginning to experiment with reusable packaging—really just dishes shaped like fast-food boxes—fast food is also a major contributor to litter and is one of the top sources of single-use plastics. Whether or not Chick-fil-A still donates to anti-LGBTQ+ causes, it's hard to argue that any fast-food chain is a good guy company. (In-N-Out Burger, a West Coast fast-food chain, probably comes the closest, with pay well above minimum wage and consistently high marks from employees. However, it sources most of its beef from Harris Ranch,[21] the largest feedlot on the West Coast, notorious for cows packed in tightly atop mounds of their own waste, with a smell that no one who has driven Interstate 5 between Los Angeles and the Bay Area can ever forget. In-N-Out has also made no efforts to date to cut down on its disposable packaging.)

Though subsidized crops like grains and soy harm our entire food system, the process of growing them harms relatively few people directly. Most of the process is mechanized, from planting to harvest to processing, and fewer people can work many more acres of land than was true a few decades ago. But in the fields where our fruits and vegetables grow, it's a different story. An estimated 2 million people work on farms across the United States, most of them from among our poorest workers.[22] Most fruits and vegetables are picked by hand, labor that usually involves stooping and carrying heavy loads long distances. Workers are subjected to the hazards of high heat, lack of shade and water, as well as exposure to pesticides and other toxic substances sprayed on plants, and they rarely receive workers' compensation if they get sick or injured on the job. Even more so than meat processing plants, farms rely on immigrant labor, and 53 percent of farmworkers were born outside the country, many of them undocumented or on seasonal work visas that make them extremely hesitant to speak up about mistreatment.[23]

Interestingly, counter to our notions that big equals bad, workers on small farms have the fewest protections. The Fair Labor Standards Act requires that farmworkers who are paid on a piecework basis, say by bunches of spinach or bushels of apples picked, are entitled to at least the minimum wage for their time. Small farms, however, are exempt from these rules and can pay workers as little as they want. Small farms are also exempt from the Migrant and Seasonal Agricultural Worker Protection Act, the main employment law for farms, which sets minimum standards around the treatment of farmworkers.[24] Finally, farmwork has the most lax rules around child labor, letting kids as young as twelve work long hours in the fields, and allowing sixteen-year-olds to perform tasks deemed hazardous.[25] In California, one of the most progressive states where the bulk of unsubsidized foods are grown, farmworkers are granted additional protections above federal minimums, but they still aren't granted overtime until they work seven days a week, or more than ten hours a day, sixty hours a week, and twelve-year-old kids are allowed to work eight hours a day and forty hours a week on nonschool days.[26] If you have the opportunity to talk to farmers, especially at the local farmers market, ask them about their labor practices. What you learn might shock you.

In addition to these serious human impacts associated with agriculture, the production of the food we eat comes with major drivers of climate change. What was once driven largely by nature, with few things added to the soil other than animal manure and rainfall, has become a massive source of fossil fuel usage and greenhouse gas emissions—the leading cause of pollution and algae blooms in our waterways—and the culprit behind deforestation and desertification. Since 1960, humankind has rapidly shrunk our standing forests to make way for cities, harvest the wood for construction or papermaking, and create pastures for raising cattle and other agriculture. Especially in the Amazon, we're losing thousands of square miles of rainforest a year, much of it Indigenous land that's supposed to be protected. Deforestation also leads to desertification, increasing the temperature swings in a region because the trees no longer help maintain a more constant temperature, making it inhospitable to wildlife and thus robbing them of habitat, and accelerating the loss of fertile topsoil. Bare dirt is itself a driver of climate change, and deforestation creates a lot of that. And around the world, we're losing topsoil and soil fertility rapidly through modern agricultural practices that strip nutrients out of the soil and allow soil to be lost to erosion, without regenerating those resources.[27] Areas that lose their topsoil can't absorb water readily, leading to more flooding and loss of groundwater that would otherwise be absorbed from the surface. And they can no longer absorb and store carbon, instead releasing it into the atmosphere. They are also less able to harbor future plant life, making reforestation more difficult.

Deforestation also has a multiplier effect: not only are we losing the carbon storage of the trees that are cut down and the soil that's lost, but the land is then used to increase the number of grazing cattle, which are among the most efficient emitters of greenhouse gases thanks to the methane they release through rumination—methane is a gas that's twenty times more potent than carbon dioxide in its ability to trap heat in the earth's atmosphere. Across the globe, it's estimated that meat production is responsible for more greenhouse gas emissions than all industrial processes and transportation combined. *What am I funding?* If we eat beef of unknown origin, we might be directly funding the decimation of the rainforest and all the negative impacts that cascade from that.

If you're a human and you eat food, unless you live entirely off the land without purchasing fertilizer or seed from someone else, you are a part of this system. We can't opt out of eating. Nor can we expect to go back to some imaginary prior era that likely never existed in which everyone tried to grow their own food and be self-sufficient. Industrialized agriculture is highly flawed and in need of change, but it's less destructive than billions of people in the world trying to farm, not the least because plenty of us would fail at it and starve. The solution isn't to scrap the system, it's to reform it. And you have a big role to play in that.

HOW IMPORTANT IS ORGANIC?

Technically, *organic* simply means that something contains carbon and was derived from a life-form, but the word has come to mean that, in the case of crops, a food or agriculturally derived product like cotton has been produced without the use of synthetic fertilizers or pesticides. In the case of animals, it means they were raised on organic feed and not given antibiotics or growth hormones.

While many organic farmers focus on being good stewards of the land, most organic agriculture today is practiced at an industrial scale, as an extractive practice, looking to pull as much value out of the ground as possible without giving anything back, leaving behind soil with no nutrients or microscopic life due to the practice of mono-cropping, growing only one type of crop in a large area.[28] A plant crop being certified organic doesn't mean that *no* chemicals were sprayed on it. In fact, plenty of perfectly allowable organic pesticides will wipe out honeybees, on which we rely to pollinate our food and which are disappearing at an alarming rate from colony collapse disorder, almost as fast as conventional bug killers. Organic fertilizers can also get into waterways, causing algae blooms that suck up the oxygen in a body of water, killing all the fish in it, though not quite as powerfully as synthetic nitrogen fertilizers. The all-or-nothing organic standard that forbids anything synthetic going onto plants or soil makes no distinction between the extremely harmful synthetic pesticides and herbicides and the mostly beneficial synthetic fertilizers, the latter of which are indistinguishable from a plant's perspective. (What's more, without the synthetic nitrogen fertilizers in use today, billions of people around the world would be at constant risk of starvation.) All of which is to say: there's nothing inherently magical about a food being organic. You can be a responsible farmer growing conventional crops, and you can be an irresponsible farmer growing organics.

Commonly, articles debating whether organic is better focus solely on whether organic fruits and vegetables have higher vitamin and mineral levels than conventionally grown produce. Based on that research alone, they conclude that organic is no better. However, that research (which is often funded by conventional food producers) exists to distract us from what's actually important in the question of organic versus conventional. When we eat food, we expect it to contain some level of nutrition, but we also expect it not to make us sick. According to the EPA, certain pesticides cause cancer, some affect the nervous system, and others affect our hormones and the endocrine system.[29] While the EPA sets limits of what dose of each pesticide it considers safe, no one monitors the farmers when they spray their fields, and research has shown that pesticide levels on fruit and vegetables can sometimes exceed safe and legal limits.[30]

Then there are the farms. Farms that use organic methods help maintain biodiversity, improve soil quality in general, and cause far less runoff pollution than do conventional farms.[31] For farmworkers, the difference is even more pronounced. Both organic and conventional farmers spray pesticides, herbicides, and fungicides on their crops, just derived from different sources, and farmworkers are exposed to those substances, impacting their health in both cases. Though it hasn't been studied extensively, there's evidence to suggest that farmworkers exposed to the conventional sprays are more likely to have a weakened immune system, to have chronic respiratory irritation, and to have a much higher risk of certain cancers.[32]

That said, there are upsides to conventional farming. Conventional farming methods allow for more intensive agriculture in a smaller area and higher crop yields, concentrating the environmental impact and, many growers say, reducing the amounts of water and fertilizer required because conventional farming uses less space overall. In arid and semi-arid areas like the Great Plains, conventional farming can do a better job of retaining soil and preventing desertification because organic methods must often rely on tilling for weed control, which leads to dust storms and soil loss.[33] Conventional farming also requires less grueling labor from workers, because chemicals do the job of weeding and harvesting is generally easier when there's more food growing on each plant. One thing we can do to ensure that farmworkers aren't being exploited to bring us our organic produce is to push lawmakers to change the organic certification to include a social commitment to worker well-being, as well as to tell the farmers we interact with through farmers markets and community-supported agriculture (CSA) that we expect them to consider their workers as thoughtfully as they consider what they're growing.

All of this adds up to organically grown vegetables having a larger climate impact and a greater toll on workers (in terms of effort, not toxin exposure) than their conventional counterparts.[34] In general, the less land we as humans can devote to creating food, and the more land we can leave alone to sequester carbon, the better. And while most nitrogen fertilizers are currently derived from fossil fuels, we could shift to other sources with less of a climate impact, like fertilizers derived from antibiotic production by-products or from the more deliberate use of animal manures. We should push for less total nitrogen fertilizer use, as studies show it is routinely overapplied, causing runoffs and dead zones in bodies of water, and work to ban the most harmful herbicides and pesticides.[35] But simply expanding the amount of organic food we grow without addressing our demand within other parts of the food system would actually result in more harm to the climate and to people, not less.

So when *does* organic make a distinct difference for the better? A sizable benefit of organic meat, dairy, and egg production is that organic certification mandates that animals cannot be fed or given antibiotics, a practice that is routine in some parts of the industry. Though the farm lobby has fought to block direct study of the issue, scientists believe that the overuse of antibiotics in livestock is a major contributor to the rise of antibiotic-resistant superbugs in humans.[36] Eliminating the use of antibiotics among livestock would undoubtedly slow the rise of these deadly pathogens. It would be possible to ban or majorly curtail antibiotic use in food animals without forcing all farmers and ranchers to go organic. But right now, as a consumer, your only guarantee to avoid contributing to antibiotic resistance via the food supply is to buy only organic meat, dairy, and eggs. *Can everyone do this?* Probably not all the time. While the price difference between organically and conventionally produced foods is shrinking in most places, with organic foods costing on average only 7.5 percent more (though it varies enormously between stores[37]), the difference is still massive for some key staples: for milk, eggs, and bread, the cost is nearly double for organic.[38] But if you can afford to buy organic animal products, you help make them more affordable so that, one day, everyone can.

So, where does that leave us in the organic-versus-conventional debate? If you're determined to eat only or mostly organic food, regardless of the evidence on organic fruits and vegetables, you're likely not doing significant harm, simply because organics are a tiny slice of all agriculture, and because most organic produce has pros and cons that more or less balance out (though some exceptions are coming up). Likewise, if you make your choice of when to buy organic produce based on a tool like the Dirty Dozen and Clean Fifteen, created by the Environmental Working Group to tell shoppers which produce items are most likely to have high levels of pesticide on them when grown conventionally (the Dirty Dozen) and which have the lowest and are okay to buy conventionally grown (the Clean Fifteen), that's fine. Creating more demand for organics overall is generally good. (Even better would be for a new standard to exist that allows synthetic fertilizers but outlaws harmful pesticides and herbicides, sort of a conventional-organic hybrid.) But if we're talking about what most of us should do, when weighing these factors, conventional wins out for most plant foods, and organic wins for all animal products. It's fairly straightforward, until we consider one more thing.

WILL GMOS SAVE US OR KILL US?

Genetically modified organisms, shorthanded as GMOs, are the result of breakthroughs in genetic research that allow scientists to select a specific trait from one organism and insert that trait into the genome of another. This is a far cry from natural plant breeding methods, and thus GMOs cannot be present in foods that are certified organic.

GMOs are either our savior or our downfall, depending on who you talk to. Proponents say we cannot feed the world's growing population without them because we need the higher yields that GMOs promise (but which they have, so far, not delivered[39]). Opponents say that GMOs are inherently unhealthy for us and many will go on to cite unscientific claims that really boil down to "they seem icky." And sure, hearing that a frog gene has been spliced into a tomato makes it a little tough not to picture a frog as you're biting through the gelatinous tomato flesh. But neutral experts tell us that GMOs are not inherently good or bad. If GMOs did deliver dramatically improved crop yields, those of us who purport to care about global poverty should be in favor of their use, as they could help avoid widespread famine and could be created to thrive in the drought conditions that are becoming more common as the planet heats up. Those results have not yet come to fruition, but that's not to say they never will.

The problem with GMOs is not really about GMOs themselves, but rather the practices that they make possible. The bulk of the GMOs in our food today are engineered not to grow differently from their unaltered cousins, but to survive the onslaught of one particular and especially toxic herbicide: glyphosate, which goes by the brand name Roundup. "Roundup-ready" seeds grow into grain crops—mostly GMO corn, soybeans, and canola—that thrive even when doused with massive amounts of this potent weed killer. The herbicide is also widely used to kill and dry out non-GMO crops like beans, barley, oats, and wheat so that they can be harvested faster instead of being allowed to dry out at nature's pace in the field. The World Health Organization's International Agency for Research on Cancer lists glyphosate as a probable human carcinogen, and indeed, Roundup's maker, Monsanto, has had to pay more than $10 billion to settle tens of thousands of cancer claims.[40] Other studies have shown that it regularly causes health problems such as respiratory irritation and acute myeloid leukemia in those who work around it, and it has been linked to a wide range of effects, from hormone disruption and reproductive toxicity to liver and kidney damage, DNA damage, and neurotoxicity among those who consume it or even just live near fields where it's used.[41] Glyphosate also harms wildlife, soil biology, and whole ecosystems, and it has a range of unexpected harmful impacts.[42] One study found that the presence of glyphosate increases the risk of humans in the area contracting Lyme disease, because the glyphosate dramatically reduced the population of local lizards that eat the ticks that carry the disease, allowing the pests to multiply rapidly.[43]

Organizations like Human Rights Watch, the US Public Interest Research Group, and hundreds of nongovernmental organizations and grassroots groups have asked world governments to ban glyphosate outright. Glyphosate is banned in the European Union, but it remains perfectly legal in most of the world, and it's the most used weed killer in the US.[44] It's virtually impossible to avoid being exposed to glyphosate, because it's now so prevalent in our environment. US Geological Survey research found glyphosate in 40 percent of the stream samples it tested, and in 70 percent of rainwater samples.[45] A study that was concluded in 2017 by researchers at the University of California, San Diego, monitored the urine of older adults between 1993 and 2016—the period during which glyphosate use exploded in the US as GMO crops became widespread—and found that those with glyphosate in their urine increased by 500 percent during the study period.[46] An analysis by consumer watchdog the Environmental Working Group of a wide range of oat-based breakfast cereals and snack products marketed to children found levels of glyphosate on all but one of them in excess of its children's health benchmark, with one of the highest levels in Cheerios, which had a prevalence of 729 parts per billion (ppb), more than four times higher than the 160 ppb the organization recommends as the upper limit for children's safety.[47]

Because glyphosate is used on both GMO and non-GMO crops for different purposes, only policy action can ban it altogether, requiring us to speak up and demand change from our elected leaders. We can also refuse to buy oat-based products from companies like General Mills and Quaker, who use oats from farmers who spray glyphosate on their crops. But given the current inextricable link between GMOs and glyphosate, the best course of action right now is to avoid GMOs as much as you can so as not to contribute to demand and to support the continued ban on GMOs in organic certifications. In the future, this could change if specific GMOs show that they offer more benefit than harm, but that's certainly not true today. The only sure-fire way to avoid these specific GMOs known to cause harm is to buy organic when it comes to those plant foods known to be associated with glyphosate use (oats, corn, soybeans, lentils, flax, rye, buckwheat, millet, potatoes, and sugar beets that become sugar), and processed foods that contain grain-based by-products (cereals, pasta, breads, and crackers), as well as the meat, dairy, and eggs discussed in the last section. If your budget doesn't allow you to buy those things organic, another solution is to reduce your consumption of them and focus on foods that are safer in their conventional form.

WHAT YOU EAT AND DON'T EAT

It might feel like all of this has been a lead-up to me telling you that you can't eat meat anymore. Or cheese. Or ice cream. Or Egg McMuffins. It hasn't been. We absolutely need to be more deliberate in our food choices, but there is plenty of good evidence to suggest that we can achieve the necessary changes in our food system's climate and environmental impacts, and in its treatment of humans, without having to give anything up entirely. But we do need to change how much we eat of certain foods. According to the United Nations, 24 percent of global greenhouse gas emissions are from agriculture and land use—twice as much climate pollution as all the cars in the world.[48] What we eat, and how much of it we eat, matters.

The debate over nondairy milk alternatives is a good example of how easy it is to tie ourselves up in knots over a choice and lose sight of the big picture. A few years ago, as almond milk was becoming more widely available and popular, it came out that it takes more than three hundred liters of water to make one liter of almond milk.[49] Suddenly, the product that had been the darling of eco-minded consumers was an outcast, unthinkable to drink by anyone who cares about the planet and our limited resources. But that one statistic didn't give us the whole picture. It's true that it takes more water to grow almonds and make almond milk than it does to make soy milk, rice milk, oat milk, or the other alternatives. But if you look at where the almond orchards are, you'll see that they're predominantly in the southern portion of California's Central Valley, and these orchards were planted mostly on land where cotton used to be farmed.[50] Cotton is one of the most water-intensive crops there is, and almond trees require less water than farmers used to put on that very same land. In addition, planting almond orchards is reforesting the land, making it in part actually beneficial to the climate. And every nondairy milk alternative has issues of its own: rice also requires a lot of water, and the growing process is fossil fuel–intensive; soy is a subsidized commodity crop grown in vast monoculture plots devoid of biodiversity, and it's heavily sprayed with glyphosate if it's not organic; oats, too, are sprayed with glyphosate, and because they're frequently cross-contaminated with wheat, most oat products are not suitable for consumption by those with gluten allergy or sensitivity. We can find something to gripe about with any option, but the important fact is that choosing *any* nondairy milk alternative is a better environmental choice than cow's milk. You might decide that the best choice for you is produced closest to where you live, so you're not creating demand for a product that travels a long distance. And all of that still leaves packaging out of the equation. If you're at the store, choosing between nondairy milks, and one choice is in a plastic bottle while the other is in a paper carton? Go for whatever is in the carton: even though it's coated with plastic, it's still much less plastic than the bottle, and cartons can be shipped more efficiently.[51]

There are four primary factors to keep in mind when making choices about what foods to eat regularly, and which to consider the exceptions:

1. the greenhouse gases involved in producing it
2. the land use involved
3. the distance it has traveled to reach you
4. how it's packaged

If we don't consider all of these things, we can end up making choices that mean well but don't have the intended impact. For example, a vegan diet containing no animal products is widely considered to be the most climate-friendly diet. But a person who eats a vegan diet high in fresh berries, which are flown in from overseas much of the year because they are too perishable to be shipped by slower and less carbon-intensive methods, actually has a more carbon-intensive diet than an omnivore who eats a moderate amount of poultry and very few berries. A vegan diet isn't necessarily a low-emissions diet, and a diet including animal products isn't necessarily high in emissions. It all comes down to the details.

In terms of both greenhouse gas emissions and land use, the worst foods we can eat are the ruminants: cows and sheep. They require a significant amount of land for grazing, and they are one of our biggest emitters of that potent greenhouse gas methane.[52] They also require the additional land, water, and fossil fuels to grow the food they eat in addition to the grass they graze, making them an incredibly inefficient way to get our calories and nutrition. This is not to say you can't eat red meat, but that you should move toward minimizing its presence in your diet. And though it's certainly better for animal welfare to let cows spend their whole lives at pasture eating grass, a surprising fact is that grain-finished beef actually has a smaller carbon impact than grass-finished beef does.[53] Cows produce more methane when they eat grass than they do when eating grain and by-products, and cows fed only grass get to full size much more slowly, requiring them to stick around and emit all that methane for longer to end up as the same amount of food. Grass-finished beef does have the important benefit of not producing a massive amount of cow waste that must be trucked off and dealt with, unlike the waste produced at CAFOs or feedlots, with the manure serving to fertilize and regenerate the grass in the pasture. So both options have big negatives associated with them, and it's all the more reason to make beef a minimal part of your diet. That said, some promising bits of news have emerged recently. Farmers developing better regenerative farming methods have found that it's possible to reverse some of the climate impacts caused by beef and dairy cattle by taking advantage of bacteria in the manure that absorb methane.[54] Other researchers have found feeding cows seaweed could cut their methane emissions by 82 percent.[55] These practices are still rare exceptions, though. So if we ask the question *Can everyone do this?* the answer is no, not everyone can eat this better, less harmful form of beef. If you can find it and it's within your budget, though, supporting these approaches will bring the price down for others over time.

Pork and dairy are next down the list, and fish and poultry are lowest among animal foods in terms of both emissions and land use,[56] though they each have their own issues. Fish is either farmed, which is a polluting activity that's harmful to the native sea life nearby, or it's caught through industrial-scale fishing operations that have brought many of the earth's fisheries to the brink of collapse, damaged coral reefs around the world, and been responsible for immeasurable quantities of bycatch (the dolphins, sharks, sea turtles, and other aquatic life-forms that die in nets meant for different sea life). Though chicken is not an especially carbon-intensive food to raise, the industrial scale on which most chicken is raised creates serious pollution problems of runoff and waste disposal.

Collectively, we use double the amount of the earth's habitable land for grazing animals that we use for growing crops. By deemphasizing animal products in our diets, we can put a lot of that land to use to feed many more people with plant-based foods. Of course, even that rule about animals is not hard and fast: oysters, for example, are considered by many to be a net-positive food to consume in environmental terms. They don't feel pain, which can assuage concerns of those focused on animal suffering, and they are powerhouses at filtering pollutants out of waterways. Oyster aquaculture (that is, farming in the water) is considered beneficial to the restoration of coastal marine ecosystems.[57]

Despite fruits and vegetables having the lowest greenhouse gas emissions associated with them, that's only true if they were grown fairly close to you. We eat foods grown all over the world without knowing it, and the "food miles" associated with shipping something a long distance, especially if the food was flown in, can dramatically change its environmental impact. The same is true for how something is packaged. A bunch of spinach bound together with a twist tie has a dramatically lower impact than does the same amount of spinach packaged in a plastic bin. Not only is plastic production an energy-intensive process, but because the bin is rigid, much less spinach can be transported on the same truck or train car than if we're transporting bunches of spinach that can be packed together. *What am I funding?* Buying a plastic bin of spinach means funding the shipment of air, from all the empty space in the container, along with the spinach.

We've been trained to expect bananas and avocados and apples on grocery store shelves every day of the year, even though these are all seasonal foods. We don't have to give these things up to reduce the environmental impact of our diets, we just have to pay more attention to where the foods came from. If you live in an area that has productive year-round agriculture, you may be able to eat local, say, only eating foods grown within fifty or one hundred miles. For most of us, that's not realistic. What is realistic is to read the little stickers stuck to things, see where they were grown, and make an effort to eat only things grown within your own country. (For example, quinoa grown near you does less environmental and human harm than quinoa that uproots the lives of Bolivian farmers.) *Can everyone do this?* Yes. It will mean no avocados in January, and the apples you eat in the summer have been in dry storage since the prior autumn, but you'll be making a meaningful difference. And if you want spinach, but it's only available in a bin? Then buy an unpackaged head of lettuce or bunch of kale instead.

In terms of overall diet, the climate impacts of a vegan diet and a Mediterranean-style diet are close, and the latter gives you a lot more flexibility. It's mostly vegetarian with fish and poultry a few times a week, and red meat like beef maybe once a month. According to Conservation International, if we all ate a Mediterranean-style diet, and brought down the portion sizes of the meat and dairy we eat so they're no longer supersized, it would eliminate 15 percent of all global greenhouse gas emissions by 2050, the equivalent of taking a billion cars off the road. That should give us all hope. Without giving anything up, and by just changing how much of certain things we eat and the timing of when we eat other things, we can make a real dent in global warming. For the average meat eater in a wealthy country, eliminating high-emissions foods like beef and flown-in berries can reduce your individual climate impact by 28 percent. If you feel inspired to cut those things out altogether, that's terrific. But if you can't imagine it for yourself, or know you'd have a tough time persuading others in your family, then just focus on what you eat most of the time.

Of course, affordability remains an important piece of this discussion, and not everyone will be able to make the same choices. Data show that prices for many types of organic foods have come down over time, with greater demand and supply, with almost no premium for getting the organic version of things like spinach, soy milk, and baby food. There are some items for which the premium for organic is high. Let's take milk as an example. If you can't afford to buy organic, focus instead on reducing how much milk you consume and how quickly, or consider switching even some of the time to a nondairy alternative like low-priced organic soy milk. And, if you can afford to buy organic and ethically raised animal products, do that. *What am I funding* with organics? In part, you're funding more affordable organics. As for fast food, we know from the data that it's folks in the middle class and above who eat the most meat (and consume the most of everything), so if you can afford to make it a once-in-a-while splurge (or cut it out entirely), do that, but don't judge those who can't afford other options.

While shopping for food, it can be helpful to know which seals and certifications are meaningful and which are just marketing. Be wary of unqualified usage of terms like *natural, no additives, made with organic ingredients, hormone-free, cruelty-free, ethically raised, free-range, pasture-raised, vegetarian-fed*, and *grass-fed*. None of them are regulated or have a set definition, and a cow could be labeled hormone-free even if it was injected with testosterone.[58] The labels that are meaningful are these:

- USDA organic (or the national government seal for the country you're in)
- Fair Food Program
- Certified Humane Raised & Handled
- Food Alliance Certified
- Global Animal Partnership (look for ratings four and higher)

The Fair Food Program certification tells you that workers were treated fairly. The latter three signal that animals were treated humanely, which is important. Even if their lives are short, we owe it to them not to make them miserable. Despite issues with the Marine Stewardship Council seal and the Fair Trade Certified seal, it's still likely better to buy food with one of those seals than without. An especially dubious seal to be wary of is the Non-GMO Project Verified certification. While its intentions are good and its standards are high, it does not do any independent verification that what's in a product is what the producer reports. And given the nature of food manufacturing, in which suppliers regularly shift and change, something that was GMO-free not long ago could contain GMOs and lots of glyphosate now. Look instead for an official organic certification if you're trying to avoid GMOs in that particular product.

FOOD WASTE

We can't talk about reducing the environmental impact of our food choices without talking about food waste. This one broken aspect of our food system has an outsized impact. If we took all the food wasted around the world every year and tallied up the energy it took to produce, transport, and store it—all for naught—and then compared that sum against the total emissions of entire countries, food waste would be the third-largest emitter of greenhouse gases in the world.[59] In the US, 40 percent of the food we produce never gets eaten. And yet, one in eight Americans is hungry and doesn't know where their next meal is coming from. Food waste is not only an environmental issue, it's a social justice issue. Our household food waste alone makes up 43 percent of that total, or 17 percent of all food we produce, more than enough to feed everyone who is hungry. The average American household throws away 32 percent of its food a year, worth $1,866.[60]

A large portion of food waste happens before individual consumers get their groceries home, from products that stores don't consider pretty enough to put out on shelves, because customers have shown them through their choices that they expect a carrot to look a certain way and a butternut squash to be a certain size. Many fruits and vegetables that are "off spec" never even leave the fields, rotting in place or feeding the scavenger animals. Some stores have begun selling these "ugly foods," but it's rare for shoppers to have the chance to buy them. But you can ask your local stores and farmers markets to stock ugly produce. Some companies now operate delivery services to find homes for this otherwise wasted food, offering consumers willing to deal with imperfections a chance to be a part of reducing food waste. Imperfect Foods is one such company, and their offerings include everything from misshapen produce to oddly shaped end pieces of bacon. Services like Imperfect Foods, however, still ship foods long distances, and incorporate a significant amount of packaging into their offerings, so this approach is not a cure-all. As much as you can, try to buy not only ugly foods but also those produced as close to you as possible, with minimal packaging. Most of all, we all must get over the notion of what food is supposed to look like if we care about reducing food waste.

The greatest bit of food waste that you have control over is the food waste in your own home. So make a commitment to combat that. Here are some ideas:

- Try not shopping for a few weeks to eat down what's already in your fridge and freezer (and repeat this regularly as needed).
- Make a meal plan before shopping so you know how you'll use everything on your list.
- If impulse buys at the store are a problem for you, then place your order online, where you have more self-control, and either have your groceries delivered or pick them up curbside.
- Keep a bucket in the fridge or freezer where you put all of your family's food waste for a week or two, so everyone can see how much there is.

- Designate a spot in the refrigerator for "use first" items, things that are close to spoiling.
- Trust your nose and eyes to tell you if something has spoiled rather than relying solely on "best if used by" or expiration dates.
- Get in the habit of serving smaller portions and letting people take seconds if they want them rather than serving big portions right off the bat.
- Don't buy a new ingredient aspirationally, because you saw someone else cook it, unless you already have the recipe in hand and know exactly when you'll make it.

Some or all of these approaches might work for you, or you might need to figure out a different approach. Start by paying attention to the food you're wasting and then get to work eliminating it at the source.

———

A whole range of factors may go into your choices about what foods to eat or avoid, from ethical or moral views about what's right and religious considerations, to food allergies and intolerances, as well as your cultural background and simply what you like best. The choices you make around food have big impacts in the world, both on our fellow humans and the climate. The more intentional you can be with these choices, the better for all of us.

CHAPTER 8

Being a Good Neighbor

In the southeast corner of Washington, DC, far from the towering marble landmarks and monuments to heroes of war, lies the historic neighborhood of Anacostia, named after the river that separates it from the rest of the District of Columbia. Anacostia was home to mostly residents of European descent until the 1960s, when white residents fled the city for the newly constructed suburbs in Maryland and Virginia, ensuring that Anacostia, like many of the predominantly Black neighborhoods in DC, would be neglected by leaders and investors for decades. The construction of an interstate spur between the neighborhood and river during this era created a barrier both physical and psychological between Anacostia and the rest of the city. Rates of poverty increased, and development in the neighborhood all but dried up. As DC began to see new investment in the late 1990s and 2000s, Anacostia was left out of that growth, even though it has its own Metro stop, something that drove economic activity in other parts of the city.

Like many US cities, DC has a history of de facto segregation, with white residents residing largely in the more upscale northwest quadrant and right around Capitol Hill—or moving out of the District entirely and heading for the suburbs—and poorer Black folks living in the neighborhoods everywhere else that saw the least investment. Given that, you might expect that the revitalization of Anacostia would look a lot like what's happened in other historically Black neighborhoods in DC: white residents come in and push Black residents out, forcing long-standing local stores and restaurants to close because their customers have moved away, chain coffee shops and yoga studios popping up to replace them. But instead, Anacostia is rapidly becoming a model of how to be a good neighbor, from revitalizing an area without harming the existing residents, to creating more transit-friendly development, to keeping more people in the city instead of the suburbs.

In 2014, the nonprofit organization Building Bridges Across the River announced an ambitious plan to link Anacostia to the rest of the District via a river-spanning park built on the bones of an old bridge—DC's answer to Manhattan's High Line—calling it the 11th Street Bridge Park. Rather than simply announcing the revitalization plans to residents, the organizers of the park worked closely with community stakeholders over the course of many years to ensure that the park, as well as the accompanying investments in the surrounding communities on both sides of the river, would provide benefit to those who've long called the neighborhood home, not just the new, higher-income people who will likely be attracted to the area after the project's completion. The concept is called inclusive recovery or inclusive development, and its aim is to ensure that the growth (both what's planned and what will inevitably happen if the investments are successful) ultimately results in more opportunity for the existing residents and business owners, not just a newly spiffed-up neighborhood that white folks can move into as people of color get forced to move elsewhere.[1] The project calls its central document not an economic development plan, but an equitable development plan. Even though as of this writing the bridge is not yet built, the organization leading the effort is already investing significantly in the community in ways that lift up those who are typically least likely to factor into development plans. The park organizers partnered with the community and other organizations to develop community garden plots, put on arts and culture festivals, train residents in the neighborhood in construction and OSHA-certification and help many of them find full-time jobs, provide small-business assistance and pro bono accounting services to local business owners, help low- and moderate-income residents of the neighborhood purchase homes, and educate local renters about their rights as tenants. The goal at every turn is to help those who already live there stay there, while investing more and improving quality of life in the neighborhood and its surrounding areas.

The Anacostia example is wallet activism at a community and government level, not an individual level, making a concerted effort to channel large-scale financial resources toward improving a neighborhood for those who already live there, which is far from the norm. But its example provides a helpful model when thinking about our own individual choices and the types of change our choices drive, so we can all be good neighbors.

———

Historically, neighborhoods have been built not to include, but to exclude. American suburbs sprung up as cities diversified, and white flight from the urban core led to predominantly Black cities surrounded by rings of white. You may have heard of redlining, the discriminatory practice that systematically denied investment and lending in areas deemed "undesirable" or "high risk" (typically older districts in cities, which tended to be predominantly Black communities; they were outlined in red on so-called residential security maps, hence the name) and sought to price everyone but white families out of newer and more affluent areas. Such policies denied homeownership opportunities to Black, Latino, Asian American, and Indigenous families—opportunities that white families easily accessed, setting them on a path to building generational wealth that most people of color were robbed of. It also ensured that de facto segregation would persist long after laws upholding it were struck down. Though the practice was technically outlawed in the Fair Housing Act of 1968, given the huge amount of personal discretion involved in making investments or granting loans, the practice continues in many ways to this day.

Redlining meant that families of color couldn't live near the better-funded schools that white students had access to. It meant that families of color were relegated into neighborhoods that were allowed to crumble, as investment dollars poured into the whiter parts of town. While many neighborhoods in highly segregated cities have already received new economic development investments, many of these disinvested, low-income neighborhoods remain within our cities.

In addition, though redlining is technically gone, virtually all US cities are shaped extensively by exclusionary zoning, policies that restrict what can be built and where, effectively shutting most people out of living close to desirable jobs and affluent schools. The book *Dream Hoarders: How the American Upper Middle Class Is Leaving Everyone Else in the Dust, Why That Is a Problem, and What to Do About It* by Richard Reeves of the Brookings Institution is a must-read for those who want to understand this concept, as well as all forms of *opportunity hoarding*, a term coined by sociologist Charles Tilly. Reeves defines opportunity hoarding this way: "When valuable, scarce opportunities are allocated in an anticompetitive manner: that is, influenced by factors unrelated to an individual's performance." In talking about the distorted value of land and housing in cities with exclusionary zoning, Reeves writes, "Land in the more prosperous cities where the upper middle class lives is also valuable, not least because it eases access to the local labor market and often to good public schools." He continues, "And the many local ordinances, especially those containing strict rules on density, are anticompetitive barriers around the borders of upper middle class neighborhoods. Exclusionary zoning is opportunity hoarding." Rules that restrict multifamily housing like duplexes, town houses, apartment buildings, and high-rises are common in cities, and even more so in cities that have reputations as especially liberal or progressive, like New York City and San Francisco. This means that for everyone except the top earners, moving into the neighborhoods—those that have the highest property values, which are a powerful driver of wealth accumulation and which feed into the richest schools, which tend to provide more opportunities for children—is simply not an option. Back in chapter four, we talked about the benefits that the mortgage interest deduction confers on wealthier people who can afford to buy homes, and homeowners also get to deduct from their income tax the property taxes they paid, something renters cannot do even though their rent pays the landlord's property taxes. According to Reeves, "We are using the tax system to help richer people buy bigger houses near the best [funded] schools."[2]

Though the tax system is a large, systemic force that can be changed only through policy action, that doesn't mean that individuals with financial power are off the hook. In his book *Durable Inequality*, Charles Tilly writes that there are two main drivers of inequality: (1) exploitation, which we've discussed a great deal and which we tend to view as something done by someone else over there, and

(2) opportunity hoarding, which is aided by policy and systemic barriers, but which people also commit on an individual level and which you may have benefited from directly.[3] According to both Reeves and Tilly, exploitation is what you take from others, and opportunity hoarding is what you keep for yourself. While many economists have written a great deal about the ways that the policies and behaviors in cities feed inequality, I believe that the opportunity hoarding framework is the most useful for thinking about the role we play as individuals in perpetuating or tearing down that system. It's essential to understand our history, our present, and the forces at play as we talk about how to be a good neighbor in the physical places where we live.

WHERE YOU LIVE

The choice of where to live is one of the largest and most impactful economic decisions you will make, whether you make it once or many times over the course of your life. Most people pay more for housing, whether through rent or a mortgage, than for any other expense. A whole slew of environmental choices are involved as well, from whether to live in an existing home that's full of energy leaks or a newly constructed home that's more efficient, to whether to try to live as close to the city core as possible or to move farther out, costing less and giving you more space but also increasing the energy it takes to get back and forth to the city.

The population of the US increases by 1.7 million a year, split evenly between births and immigration, and those folks need somewhere to live. However, given the average US household size, we should need only about 650,000 new housing units each year to keep up. We're building double that just in new single-family homes (more than 1.3 million of them a year), not counting new apartments and condos—and even if we presume that many of these homes are replacing older homes that were demolished, the rate is hard to justify. At the same time, we have more than 1.5 million homes sitting vacant across the country and an additional 7.4 million that are second (or third) homes that sit empty most of the time. All this while housing shortages and affordability crises grip cities, and more than half a million people a year experience homelessness. This tells us that we're building new homes not because there's urgent demand for them among people who need a place to live, but because there's money to be made.

At the same time, much has been written about the ever-expanding size of the American home, which is now, on average, 600 to 800 square feet (approximately 55 to 75 square meters) larger than the average in other countries.[4] We're fed a steady diet of messages meant to keep us striving for more: homeownership is the American dream, your first home is a "starter" home, you "need" a bathroom for each person, and on and on. The real estate industry is heavily invested in getting you into the home of your dreams but also in reminding you that it's not your forever home, it's just where you start out. Entire cable TV networks exist to remind us that where we live isn't good enough, and we either need to move or to invest big bucks in improving it, whether or not it is even the right decision for you. And the real estate industry is greenwashing itself these days, marketing brand-new homes as energy-efficient and "green," touting their triple-paned windows, their airtight seals that don't let cold leak in or out, and maybe even their rooftop solar panels. They neglect to mention all of the energy and raw materials that go into constructing a brand-new home, how much waste an average residential construction project generates, or how long and carbon-intensive a commute often comes with buying new construction. Don't buy it. Refusing to be a part of creating demand for more new construction is a powerful act.

Environmentalists have long told us that the best thing for the planet is for as many of us as possible to live in dense cities, concentrating our climate impacts but minimizing the distance we have to travel to get to work or other services and reducing our overall energy needs, leaving as much of the area outside of cities as possible untouched. And despite all the efforts by the so-called green building sector to sell us on their innovations, the best thing we can do is find ways to reuse housing that already exists. "The greenest building is . . . one that is already built," said Carl Elefante, former president of the American Institute of Architects.[5] Ideally, environmentalists say, we should also try to live near a public transit hub and to get only as much space as we truly need. In a perfect world, that's good advice. But housing tends to be unaffordable near city centers, especially around transit hubs. If cities don't maintain a sizable stock of affordable housing in the walkable urban core, the outcome may be a city that's *less* climate-friendly, not more. A 2019 analysis published in the *International Journal of Urban and Regional Research* found that simply making a city or neighborhood more walkable didn't result in a reduction in climate impacts. That's because making an area more walkable often creates greater displacement, with more affluent residents who tend to consume more energy and buy more manufactured stuff moving in, and lower-income residents who consume less getting pushed out.[6] And as many learned during the COVID-19 pandemic that began in 2020, having only as much space as you truly need can lead to unhappiness if you need to spend any significant amount of time at home. Many who could afford it moved out of the big cities during that time in search of more space, though it's not yet clear if that will be a permanent change.

But it's still important to factor transportation into the equation. The transportation sector is the largest emitter of greenhouse gases in the world, accounting for more than a quarter of all CO_2 emissions,[7] most of that coming from regular passenger cars, and commuting is the largest share of most people's driving. You can see the climate impact of your commute at MapMyEmissions.com to help put things in real terms. If you're able, both logistically and physically, to commute via public transportation, or, best of all, to walk or bike to work, to stores, to kids' schools, and to most of the services you use, you can drop the climate impacts of your commute dramatically. But public transportation, especially in the US, is not nearly as useful as it could be. Most commutes today are suburb to suburb, while transit systems are built around the assumption that everyone is trying to get downtown, with system maps resembling the hub and spokes of a bicycle wheel. That's part of why three-quarters of people drive to work—public transportation doesn't suit their needs. But it's not all-or-nothing in terms of commuting by car. The difference of living only two and a half miles closer to work than you otherwise might, and driving that shorter distance twice a day, two hundred days a year, is a difference of a thousand miles. That's enough of a difference for your car insurance to cost less, for gas to cost significantly less, and to make a meaningful difference in your commute's climate impacts.

When it comes to choosing where to live, you're not likely to encounter the perfect option. Only so many homes are available to buy or rent at a given time. You're constrained by how much you can or want to pay. Outside of New York and Boston, US cities have only a limited number of locations where public transportation options are plentiful, and living in those areas might be cost-prohibitive. Perhaps you want something specific in your home to make it work for you, like room for a home office, or some outdoor space, which will rule out many of the available properties. When making the choice, do your best to find a home that will allow you to consume as little energy as possible, both from transportation and from home utilities like heating and cooling. Then, fight through your local political process for more buses, which can expand public transportation to more areas almost instantly, with no new infrastructure required, along with more transit-oriented development, creating more affordable housing options near transportation hubs.

If you can afford to buy a home rather than rent, there's a final factor worth consideration. Virtually all land in North America, and much of it on other continents, was stolen from the Indigenous peoples who inhabited it before colonizers from Europe arrived. You can use the Native Land app or visit Native-Land.ca to find out which Indigenous peoples' land you're on. (I live on land stolen from the Washoe Tribe of Nevada and California.) Though most owned residential property is passed down to descendants when its owners die, anyone can choose instead to leave their property to the land's rightful owners and encourage neighbors to do the same. The NDN Collective, an Indigenous-led organization focused on building Indigenous power, launched the LANDBACK Campaign, an effort to get lands returned to tribes and groups that were stolen in violation of treaties signed with the US and Canadian governments. Bequeathing land to the local tribe or group is a way to support reparations for past wrongs using individual financial power.

ACCOUNTING FOR CLIMATE CHANGE

Of course, if you're choosing a home in a coastal or low-lying area, it's important to be realistic about how rapidly our sea levels are rising. People are still buying million-dollar condos in Miami despite "sunny day flooding" being a regular occurrence, when seawater flows into streets without any hurricanes or storms to push it there, and despite regular incursions of salty seawater into the region's fresh drinking water. More than any other big city in America, Miami is already experiencing the effects of global warming's sea-level rise, and the problems there are only going to get worse. To ignore the realities of climate change, or to just blindly trust that someone will take care of the problem before it gets too bad, is to live in a fantasy world. In the real world we need to make long-term housing decisions that won't get us into trouble.

When choosing where to live in a low-lying or hurricane-prone area, there are several important things to know. First, several states along the Gulf Coast have tax structures that provide all the wrong incentives for climate resiliency. In both Texas and Florida, the primary source of revenue for the state is property tax, not income tax, and this creates incentives for local governments to approve as many developments as possible to boost tax revenues, including in areas where building clearly should not happen. Recent hurricanes have been so much more destructive not just because they are stronger due to global warming but also because we have a lot more houses built in floodplains than we used to. Buyers have likely assumed—wrongly— that no one would build a house where it's so likely to flood. But that ignores capitalism. The point is always to make more money, not to think about people's long-term health and safety.

Second, virtually every homeowner's insurance policy you can buy, whether it's federally backed flood insurance, regular homeowner's insurance, or an earthquake policy in more seismically active areas, will pay to rebuild your home only in the exact same spot where it was before, often only in the very same footprint. After every major hurricane, we see the same news stories about those "fools" who choose to rebuild after their home was destroyed again, but those stories never mention that they likely have no other choice. A home in an area that floods often or is hit frequently by hurricanes is incredibly difficult to sell, and because you can't take the insurance money and buy a house farther inland, you're stuck. Much of homeowners' wealth is tied up in their home equity, so the choice is either to rebuild in a spot where they know they probably shouldn't or to lose everything. Of course they rebuild.

Third, we can't bank on government buyouts. Beach communities in Southern California that are already seeing regular low-level flooding have begun to contemplate a concept called managed retreat, in which you move the town inland and to higher ground so that it's better situated to handle sea-level rise. The only problem is that managed retreat requires an enormous amount of money, either to buy coastal property owners out of their homes, or to create a scheme of transferring everyone's ownership to an equivalent parcel inland and then assisting them in rebuilding. Given how concentrated our population is near the coasts, the cost of widely implementing managed retreat would be astronomical, and we can't assume there's anyone to foot the bill. We already have a federal program to buy people out of their homes in hurricane-prone areas, but few have benefited from it, and they've mostly been white residents with more resources.[8]

So when choosing a home in an area vulnerable to sea-level rise, you need to decide with the understanding that you're likely on your own. Do your own research to determine if the spot you hope to live is likely safe enough. While you do that, keep in mind that major floods now happen every few years, and consult maps generated by climate scientists about projected sea-level rise. Depending how old you are and how much longer you expect to be around, you could need to choose a spot quite far inland or consider moving to a different area entirely so your financial well-being does not hinge on how seriously local leaders take climate change.

For those living in wildfire-prone areas, the same considerations apply. We should expect fire seasons to get longer and more destructive and avoid buying homes in the most wildfire-prone areas, both for our own safety and to avoid creating demand for new homes in those areas. If you drive through an area after a wildfire has passed through, it's striking how many of the homes that were destroyed are up on ridgelines, and right against the forest, what land-use experts call the wildland urban interface (WUI), the zone where houses are in or around undeveloped natural terrain and flammable vegetation. The nearness of all that fuel to houses means that communities in the WUI are more susceptible to wildfires, and fires are harder to fight there. Consult fire-risk maps for your area, and then add an additional margin of safety knowing that things will worsen. In general, fire tends to travel uphill, and it can pass faster through more densely built neighborhoods, where residents don't have enough space to create a fire buffer between each property.

BE THE BEST (OR THE LEAST BAD) KIND OF GENTRIFIER

As we've touched upon, the reality is that housing in the US and many developed nations not only has a racist history, it's still racist to this day. Even in liberal bastions like San Francisco and Portland, exclusionary zoning makes it incredibly difficult to build new housing in the city or near transit, and residents tend to fight all new building proposals, regardless of the specifics. As a result, most cities still have high rates of de facto segregation, with higher-income, predominantly white residents living in the parts of town with the most services, and lower-income, less white residents living in disinvested areas or getting pushed out of the city altogether. In places like Denver, historically far less segregated than older cities in the eastern half of the country, the segregation is actually getting worse. Because of exclusionary zoning, most lower-income people in cities have few choices about where to live. That's why, unlike in the rest of the book, this section and the two that follow speak specifically to those who are affluent and largely white, the people who have more choices about where to live, and those most likely to engage in or benefit from opportunity hoarding.

It's fashionable among progressives to decry gentrification (often without stopping to realize that they themselves are gentrifiers—not unlike bemoaning all the traffic when you're contributing to it). But the alternative is to leave all neighborhoods historically populated by people of color, immigrants, and low-income people in a state of disinvestment, which is neither just nor sustainable. We should be able to invest public dollars in a disinvested neighborhood without displacing anyone, but this is capitalism. We see interest in revitalization only when there is big money to be made (the term *public-private partnership* is a big tip-off that capitalism is a driving force). If that revitalization money had existed within the neighborhood to begin with, it would never have become disinvested in the first place. So revitalization almost always means bringing in money from outside, which tends to bring in people from outside who are drawn to the new services and cheaper housing compared to more affluent neighborhoods. And that equals gentrification.

Therefore, those who have benefited from community investment or who have the privilege of being able to choose between multiple places to live, owe it to people who've historically been left behind economically to invest in their communities, too. And they should do it in a way that benefits the residents who already live there, not just the new folks moving in. Gentrification is most often used to mean the revitalization of an area in a way that does not benefit existing residents, which does not pass the *For whom?* test. Gentrification serves rich developers and the affluent people who will move in and then talk about everything in the neighborhood that needs "fixing," even if it suits the old residents just fine. Or new parks and cultural events will come along, but only after the residents who were asking for those things for decades were forced out of the neighborhood. Gentrification is predominantly a negative force for the many residents who will likely be evicted and face homelessness as it drives up rents and home prices, or who will watch their small businesses be forced to close by those same rising rents and by competition from sexier chain stores that move in.

In a choice between neglecting areas and denying those residents economic opportunities, or gentrifying those areas with new investments and opportunities, gentrification is most often the better choice. The key is to do it equitably and in partnership with existing residents, as in the Anacostia example, which is not the way it's generally been done. Most neighborhoods gentrifying now have a history of being redlined, and it's important to recognize that history. Many of the residents who still live there today might have been forced to live there because they had no other options, either financially or legally. It might feel painful to them to see much wealthier people moving in who have no understanding of the neighborhood's history and who view it as a space they can shape to meet their needs without considering longtime residents'.

A common occurrence as neighborhoods attract more affluent residents is for those new residents, especially white residents, to begin calling the police on locals, especially people of color, for things like noise and congregating, without taking the time to get to know the neighborhood. Going into a new neighborhood with a sense of entitlement that it should be exactly what you want and that anyone who doesn't bend to that should be punished, is a surefire way to be the worst kind of gentrifier. But getting to know the neighbors and the community's traditions, and respecting that the neighborhood was theirs first, is a far better approach.

If you're in the position of being able to choose to move into an "up-and-coming" neighborhood, support reuse of housing that retains the character of the community and seeks to displace as few people as possible. "Community character" is often cited in fights to uphold exclusionary zoning, but it's one thing to claim community character when you're talking about a neighborhood populated by the highest earners and entirely another to talk about it in the context of a disinvested neighborhood with economically worse-off residents. The same goes for density: while more density of people near transit, good jobs, and good schools should be the goal, creating it by destroying the character of a historically disinvested community is not a good trade-off, especially if no efforts are happening to increase density in the richer neighborhoods at the same time. New buildings will undoubtedly be less green, no matter what their builders claim. Where a whole bunch of high-rise condos go in, replacing single-family homes, you should be suspicious of how the development is being conducted, and whether the city or the developers are listening at all to local residents' concerns. *For whom?* Swanky new high-rises are rarely for folks who've always lived in the neighborhood. New construction on sites that weren't previously housing, like converting old factories into lofts or constructing new buildings on a patch of previously open land, is least problematic, especially if it helps improve housing affordability around public transit rather than contributing to more sprawl.

If you're renting in an existing building, research the property and landlord beforehand to be sure they aren't involved in unethical or illegal practices like harassing elderly tenants to get them to move out, so that wealthier tenants willing to pay higher rates will move in. Your city and state housing departments may allow you to search the address online for tenant complaints, code violations, and lawsuits.[9]

After you move in, spend money at the existing local stores and restaurants, not the newer and hipper ones, especially family-owned businesses and those owned by people of color. A bunch of affluent people moving into an "up-and-coming" area tends to draw the Whole Foods and Trader Joe's of the world to the area, along with trendy cafés and restaurants, which has a disastrous effect on small businesses that had long served the community. One study found that 90 percent of the bars and restaurants in a heavily gentrified area, Williamsburg,

Brooklyn, New York, had been open less than ten years, while the number of Latino-owned small businesses had decreased by 50 percent.[10] *What am I funding?* Patronizing small, long-standing businesses maintains community, while shopping with chains and new businesses funds displacement. Do what you can to keep the existing folks in business, and encourage your neighbors to do the same.

And finally, if you want to see things change, get involved, but not by forming or joining a new group of concerned citizens. Groups like those tend to steamroll the needs of longtime residents in favor of those of the newer residents who don't know the history or care much about what others might need. Instead, get involved in existing community groups, especially those that have participation from older residents, so that their needs are not left out. If you aren't sure what groups already exist, ask your neighbors who are longtime residents, ask small-business owners in the neighborhood, or search your local newspaper archives for older stories about the neighborhood and residents demanding change. When you join those groups, listen more than you speak, and use your privilege to fight for the things residents have long been asking for, seeking to amplify rather than speak for them.

Even if you do all of these things and take great care not to bring harm to a neighborhood by moving there, if you're white, as many gentrifiers are, or you're higher income than the people who were already living in the neighborhood, you can't help but contribute to the negative aspects of gentrification, even if it's just because you're taking up space that could otherwise be occupied by someone with fewer financial options than you have. So use your privilege for good: fight for more affordable housing and less exclusionary zoning in the area through your local political process, encourage investment from programs that help residents stay in their homes rather than get forced out, and push for development that benefits everyone, not just the developers.

HOW NOT TO BE A NIMBY

In addition to being thoughtful about where we choose to live, it's also critical—if we care about social justice especially—to interrogate the mindset we bring to that place, especially knowing what we know about exclusionary zoning and access to well-funded schools and economic opportunity. Many people, including progressives, approach the neighborhood where they live as something they're entitled to enjoy forever with no changes and no sharing with others who come from a different socioeconomic background (which often also means a different skin color or country of origin). This attitude is summed up in the phrase *not in my backyard*, abbreviated as NIMBY. And there are a lot of ways that a NIMBY attitude can show itself.

Being a NIMBY is fighting affordable housing in your neighborhood because it could "attract the wrong kind of element." It is opposing up-zoning to higher density, when that's the only thing that will make housing, schools, and jobs more equitable and accessible. NIMBY is fighting plans to open a homeless shelter nearby, because it will mean more homeless people hanging around the area. Being a NIMBY is calling the police when your neighbors have too many cars parked in their driveway or on the street, as a sign that many people are living in the house, or when they throw a loud barbecue, or when a child of color sets up a lemonade stand on the corner.

Though awareness is beginning to change among some progressives as antiracism ideas penetrate the public discourse more deeply, many may still feel the knee-jerk reaction of, "Sure, I want those things, I just don't want them in my backyard." *Yes, I support public housing, but does it have to be so close to me? Yes, I agree we need more affordable housing, but why don't we put it across town instead? Yes, I want all kids to have good schools, but not if that means lowering the quality of my kid's school.* This is opportunity hoarding. Many of these ideas are rooted in racist and classist stereotypes that low-income people and people of color are automatically up to no good, or that they bring crime to a neighborhood simply by existing. If we look more closely at the sentiments many progressive NIMBYs express, we see real ugliness in there, whether it's intended or not.

To be good neighbors, we must fight back against any NIMBY instincts we feel arising within ourselves, and to ask ourselves the question, "If not in my backyard, then where?" If you believe a proposal is environmentally irresponsible or unjust, pushing against it on principled grounds is one thing. But expecting someone else to deal with the problem so you won't have to is putting your comfort above the well-being of others with less socioeconomic power than you possess. *Can everyone do this?* Can everyone fight every development and insist that power plants, landfills, affordable housing, and new transportation projects go "somewhere else"? No. We need those things, and we can't assume that everything should be someone else's problem. Being a wallet activist means fighting for our collective good, not just your own.

CHOOSING SCHOOLS FOR YOUR KIDS

Fighting for our collective good also means making sure all children have access to quality educational opportunities. Most people don't have a choice about where to send kids to school. The neighborhood school is the only option. In that case, pushing for change is largely a policy matter at the local or state level. But, if you have the means to choose whether to send children to private school—using your financial power to change their circumstances—or you have a choice between multiple public or charter options that aren't accessible to everyone (even if for a reason as seemingly mundane as being able to drive them to school farther away when other parents can't), then your choice can be a form of wallet activism. Like the prior two sections, this one is specifically addressing parents who have that choice, which disproportionally means those who are more affluent and more likely to be white.

The question of where to put children in school can be stressful, especially in bigger cities where public schools don't always have a great reputation and private or charter options abound. Schools know that. As reporter Chana Joffe-Walt of *This American Life* said in her excellent podcast series *Nice White Parents*, she never felt more powerful as a consumer than when she toured schools near her home in Brooklyn, New York.[11] (When you're being treated as a consumer, that's a big indicator that there's an opportunity for wallet activism.) Public schools work hard to attract students from more affluent and educated homes, because those things are associated with students getting higher test scores, and higher test scores mean more students want to attend that school, which equals more funding. School budgets are determined by schools' daily enrollment, so every child that enrolls at or leaves a school impacts the resources that that school has to work with. Though that may sound awfully like the capitalist drive for greater profits, it's really much closer to desperation. Most public schools operate on such shoestring budgets that being able to get a few more dollars for a few more pupils can help enormously.

Affluent white parents aren't the only parents wrestling with questions of school choice. But the choices those parents make can place actual harm on children whose parents don't have the choice. In their book *Family Values: The Ethics of Parent-Child Relationships*, Harry Brighouse and Adam Swift write, "Whatever parents do to confer a competitive advantage is not neutral in its effects on other

216

children—it does not leave untouched, but rather is detrimental to, those other children's prospects in the competition for jobs and associated rewards."[12]

Many affluent parents can happily send their children to the high-quality local public school made possible by exclusionary zoning. The problem we're addressing here is that, in areas where not all the schools perform well, many affluent parents feel themselves in a conundrum pitting what they perceive as the best interests of their own children against the greater good. Parents can do what they see as best for their own kids, pulling them out of the local public school and moving them to a private school where they are more likely to thrive—but doing so harms the kids who have no choice but to attend the neighborhood school, which now receives less funding because of lower enrollment. Or parents can keep kids in their neighborhood public school. That may be a more challenging environment for their kids or simply provide fewer opportunities like Advanced Placement classes, but it benefits the neighborhood school and has positive effects on the other students, both because it brings additional funding and because more parent involvement is associated with better outcomes, and parents with economic means are statistically much more likely to have time to engage in their kids' schooling.[13] Doing what's best for the individual harms the collective, and doing what's best for the collective may seem like it could hold your child back from future opportunities.

When you talk to parents about education, nearly all will say the same thing: "I'll do whatever I can to help my kid get ahead." As an adult, you know how unforgiving the world can be and how important those little advantages could end up becoming. But an important question that we're not asking enough is: *Ahead of whom?* Privileged parents making choices in what seems like one child's best interest often has the unintended consequence of imposing harm on another child whose parents didn't have the same choice. *Can everyone do this?* Absolutely not. And when we multiply these questions out to all parents and all kids, we repeat the same cycles of economic inequality and social injustice that many of these same affluent parents say they wish to see dismantled.

Research has shown that progressive parents struggle with these choices but still tend to put the interests of their kids ahead of their own values and ideals.[14] Much of that is based on a false choice: that you can be either a good parent or a good citizen. But, as Reeves writes, "Being an opportunity hoarder is not the same thing as being a good parent."[15] That false choice rests on the belief that you can't get a good education in a school that's mostly nonwhite, or that Advanced Placement classes have more value than raising kids in a diverse environment that will help them develop a more complex and empathetic understanding of the world. (College admissions officials know which schools have more Advanced Placement classes and other unequal resources, and they assess students accordingly, rather than penalize students with fewer prestige points on their applications.) In her book *White Kids: Growing Up with Privilege in a Racially Divided America*, sociologist Margaret Hagerman cites research that studied white kids from privileged backgrounds and compared the development of those who attended the local public school to those who attended private school. There were dramatic differences in how those students understand race and privilege. Kids who attended private school were more likely to be oblivious to their own privilege, believing they were better and smarter than kids at public schools and more deserving of better outcomes in life. They were also more likely to make statements reflective of color-blind racism, such as "racism is over." The white kids who attended public school, however, could clearly articulate systemic racism, discrimination, and the racial wealth gap, and they spoke with passion about the necessity of addressing these injustices. They witnessed teachers and school police officers treating their friends of color differently, and they learned how to relate to diverse peers, too. In other words, the parents who chose the privileged perception of what it is to be a good parent over being a good citizen were much more likely to raise kids who are not especially good citizens. As Hagerman wrote in an op-ed for the *Los Angeles Times*, "If progressive white parents are truly committed to the values they profess, they ought to consider how helping one's own child get ahead in society may not be as big a gift as helping create a more just society for them to live in in the future."[16]

Reeves draws a distinction between parental actions that help parents' own children, like reading to them early in life, and actions that are to the detriment of other children, like fighting to uphold exclusionary zoning, putting a child in private school, and paying extra for college counselors that help kids shape their applications to elite higher education institutions. Because the latter actions are anticompetitive and harm other children, they fit squarely in the category of opportunity hoarding. His proposed solution: "A change of heart is needed: a recognition of privilege among the upper middle class."[17] In other words, it's time to focus on what's best for all kids, not just one's own.

SHARING COMMUNITY RESOURCES

We talked in chapter six about the sharing economy in small-scale terms: primarily getting more use out of objects that go to waste when used only by one person or household. But the sharing economy is relevant here, too, especially when talking about bigger things like cars and housing. This sharing happens primarily through the so-called ride-share apps like Uber and Lyft, and with property rental sites like Airbnb and Vrbo, though many other platforms exist and continue to be launched.

The actual idea of ride-sharing is: I'm driving from Chicago to Detroit, and I'd like someone to split the cost of gas with me. You need to get from Chicago to Detroit, but you don't have a car. We find each other, and voilà, everyone gets what they need without creating a demand for more cars or burning two cars' worth of gas. But that's not what Uber and Lyft are. While it's a customer-friendly move to let you choose whether to get a cheaper ride by riding with other strangers or to pay more to ride in a luxury vehicle, it's just taxi service by a different name—except that it's not regulated like taxi service, and it happens to seriously harm taxi drivers.

The system for becoming a taxi driver involves buying what's called a medallion, in essence a license to operate a taxi, and they are costly—often hundreds of thousands of dollars in big cities. Cabbies pay off these medallions over many years, and they made the decision to buy a medallion at a time when they could reasonably expect that people would continue to need cab rides for the foreseeable future. With Uber and Lyft now taking so much business away from taxi drivers, many drivers still owe tens or hundreds of thousands of dollars on their medallion loans, they can't sell the medallion to anyone else because driving a taxi is no longer a good way to make a living, and they have no way to make their payments. (The medallion system itself is also rife with exploitation.[18]) Even in cities that don't charge huge premiums for medallions, drivers still have the cost of buying and maintaining a taxi that's not usable as a personal vehicle. And, because taxis are regulated by local governments, customers have official recourse if an incident should occur in one. Every taxicab commission has a complaint and hearing process, and you can see the drivers' identification from within the vehicle, so you know who to complain about.

Having the option to share a car you own or to get a ride from someone who has a car and the time to take you places is theoretically a positive shift. It could reduce the number of people who feel they need a car and allow those with cars to earn additional income that could change their life circumstances. If this could be done in an equitable way, and while managing the harm done to taxi drivers by the shift, it would be something to celebrate. Unfortunately, despite that promise, we're not there yet. Uber and Lyft, currently the dominant forces in the ride-share industry, have made clear through their practices that they are driven by profits and little else. There's no start-up cost to drive for them (other than having a fairly new car already), which is a big positive for drivers who wish to earn some income from their vehicles. But there's also no official registration process in most cities, and there is little recourse if something happens to make a customer feel unsafe, other than getting back a note that the company "takes your concerns very seriously" and then no follow-up to be assured action was taken. The alarming reports of sexual assaults that have happened to ride-share customers (and to drivers themselves), and the insufficient responses from the companies, demonstrate that accountability has been minimal at best, though Uber has said it is taking steps to address the issue.[19] With any progress comes some pain, as people invested in the old system struggle to adapt. We could say that's what's happening here, if we saw solid evidence that the ride-share companies were doing more good than harm. For example, if we saw fewer cars being purchased, that would be a demonstrable good. And if we saw that ride-share drivers were being fairly compensated for their labor, that would also be a positive indicator. However, neither is true outside of rare examples.

There's no evidence that the widespread presence of Uber, Lyft, and other ride-share companies has changed car-buying behavior, meaning that the very notion of ride-sharing in this sense is false. And research by the Economic Policy Institute has shown that ride-share drivers earn only slightly above minimum wage on average, when you factor in all of their expenses, and even below minimum wage in states that have raised theirs above the federal minimum.[20] Because ride-share drivers are classified as contractors, not employees, they pay a greater share of their earnings in self-employment tax, covering both their own and the employer share of Medicare and Social Security withholdings. They also have to pay for gas and car insurance, and they don't get paid when they're waiting for someone to request a ride. All of this brings their "W-2 equivalent wages," or what their earnings would equate to in a typical job, to $9.21 an hour.[21] Uber and Lyft take a huge cut of what customers pay, essentially just for running an app, while the drivers who do the actual work and make it possible for the companies to exist earn the annual equivalent of $19,157 *before taxes*, in line with fast-food workers who are likely to require government assistance to get by. Driving for the ride-share companies is popular as a side hustle, allowing drivers to supplement another income. But if a worker couldn't get by doing a job full-time, only as something above and beyond another income, that's a dead giveaway that they are being exploited.

It's true that ride-share apps make it awfully convenient to get a ride, but it's worth pausing to consider your options. In cities with high medallion fees, taking a taxi might be best if you can afford it, so you're not getting a deal on your ride at the expense of a highly indebted cabbie while supporting the ride-share companies' exploitation of its drivers. If you do decide to take a ride in an Uber or Lyft, ask the driver how much they're getting paid for the trip, and tip as well as you can to ensure they're fairly compensated for the time spent, including the time getting to you, and factoring in something for the fuel. (Tipping in the app is only allowed in some countries, so you may need to tip in cash.) In some cities, drivers are banding together to form their own cooperative ride-share platforms to compete with Uber and Lyft, like the Drivers Cooperative in New York

City, so investigate if you may have an option that is fairer to drivers (and maybe also cheaper for you).[22] Finally, if you can, engage with your city or state government and push for regulations that force the ride-share companies to treat their drivers better, including fair pay, health insurance, and paid sick leave, so that they can't continue to bring in massive profits at their drivers' expense.

On the property side, Airbnb and other short-term rental sites have made it possible for people to have many more options while traveling than just hotels and hostels, allowing them to rent anything from a spot on the couch in an occupied apartment all the way up to the entire run of a grand chateau. The sharing economy has absolutely given people more choices, and in many cases made travel more affordable while also allowing those listing their property to make a little extra money. But it has come with massive costs, too. Not long ago, cities that tourists love to visit had a pressure-release valve on their visitor capacity in the form of hotel rooms. If the hotels were full, you couldn't easily go there. This helped keep tourists to levels that might still feel crowded, but which the local infrastructure could handle. But with the rise of property "sharing," many tourist cities like Rome and Amsterdam have found themselves so flooded with tourists that city services are failing, and residents are finding the cities unlivable. And it's easy to see why: even if an apartment that would normally house two people is now continually occupied by two travelers, the people who live there and the tourists behave differently in important ways. When you're home, you eat most meals at home, you don't crowd public spaces most days, and you don't ride public transportation many times a day. But the visitors spend most of their time relying on a city's services, whether it's eating most of their meals at restaurants, using public transportation for much more than a commute, or simply standing around the public square, posing for Instagram pictures. Cities all over the world can't cope. The overcrowding has become so severe that Venice has begun charging an entry fee to day-trip visitors to discourage them from coming, because so many more people can now spend the night on the island.

Like ride-share companies, Airbnb and other short-term rental sites let property owners get around the regulations that are supposed to be in place to protect visitors and the city alike. To open a bed-and-breakfast, for example, most local governments charge a hefty registration fee, as well as taking a share of profits as tax and in some cases performing inspections to ensure things are up to code. They may also have an approval process to ensure that tourist capacity doesn't exceed what their local infrastructure can handle. Though it's starting to change bit by bit in a few places, almost none of that happens with short-term rentals, meaning not only that visitors have fewer protections but also that cities lose all say in lodging capacity and can't collect the fees and taxes that help them maintain the services that tourists use. The ease with which anyone can now rent out space has been a big motivator for a lot of investors to buy properties solely to rent them out on Airbnb, which also has negative consequences. Buying a property to use as a short-term rental that could otherwise serve as someone's home reduces the available housing stock. That, in turn, raises rents based on supply and demand, but it does nothing to raise local wages so people can afford the higher rent. In many big cities and tourist destinations, including rural places like ski towns, short-term rentals have contributed enormously to the housing affordability crisis. The proliferation of short-term rentals has benefited travelers and Airbnb "hosts" but has hurt almost everyone else. Before you secure a short-term rental, research the place where you're going. Search whether it's experiencing a housing shortage or affordability crisis, or whether it experiences tourist overcrowding. If the answer is yes to either question, try hard to stay in a hotel instead, or consider skipping it altogether.

TRAVELING WITHOUT EXPLOITATION

In addition to being good neighbors where we live, we should also strive to be good neighbors in a global sense, treating the places we travel the same way we'd want visitors to our towns and cities to behave and considering the impact on both locals and the planet.

Air travel itself is responsible for 5 percent of all global climate emissions, and the volume of airline travelers is expected to double by 2040 as more people in countries rising out of poverty can afford to take to the skies. That said, the bulk of flying volume is consumed by the richest people: 12 percent of adults take 70 percent of flights, mirroring other overconsumption patterns we see. And of all modes of transportation, air travel is the least suited to decarbonization. Some airlines are exploring ways to use recycled fuel that creates fewer emissions, and capturing and storing those emissions instead of putting them into the atmosphere, but no one thinks we'll have large electric passenger planes powered by renewables anytime soon.

Cruise ships are an even bigger environmental disaster, burning enormous amounts of fossil fuels to propel, power, and climate-control the ships, dumping waste in the oceans, and wasting unfathomable amounts of food at their all-you-can-eat buffets. And while most airlines have unionized pilots and flight attendants, cruise lines rely heavily on exploited labor, hiring poor people from developing countries and paying them sub-poverty wages. They also take an extractive attitude to the places they dock, investing little to improve the well-being and living conditions of people in impoverished countries like the Bahamas while profiting wildly from their natural beauty. *Is it too cheap?* While cruises may not exactly be cheap, their cheapness relative to other forms of travel is made possible entirely by labor exploitation and lax environmental practices.

Surprisingly, the best way to travel long distances in terms of minimizing greenhouse gas emissions is by bus. Train travel is the runner-up.[23] Though train service is limited in the US and Canada outside of the northeast corridor, and much of the developing world does not have reliable train service, both buses and trains allow you to reach more places than planes or cruise ships can take you, for less money, and with the smallest environmental impact, assuming you don't need to cross an ocean. It was through bus travel that I visited Ozogoche, Ecuador, a place I otherwise would never have experienced.

To avoid exploiting others while traveling, research whether the places you want to go are already overwhelmed by too many tourists, as you would when deciding whether to book a short-term rental or hotel, and skip those places or travel during the off-season. Look for places that are working hard to attract tourists, and help them grow their local tourist economy. Research whether the service workers you interact with are well compensated in each of your destinations, and tip generously if they're not, especially in poorer countries or regions. (While tipping is not the norm everywhere, especially in countries where service workers are paid fairly, it's rare that tipping will be seen as odd or offensive, with Japan, Hong Kong, and South Korea as notable exceptions. Research your destination before you go.) And skip places that exploit animals for profits, such as those that sell elephant rides or keep large animals in confined spaces where they do not belong.

One especially tricky type of travel is what's known as voluntourism, traveling somewhere specifically to work on a project that will do good in some way. The appeal of this type of travel is obvious: you get to see a new place while feeling like you've contributed or given back to those less fortunate. The problem comes "when you need to be centered as the one solving these problems and when the recipients of your aid/charity are always Black & Brown people," as the No White Saviors team, based in Uganda, puts it.[24] Often, voluntourism efforts that purport to do good merely replicate colonial attitudes, namely that people in poorer countries are unable to help themselves and that people from wealthier and largely white countries know better. Rather than assuming a voluntourism project is automatically good, do some research, and interrogate your own motivations. Lubega Wendy, a human rights activist and part of the No White Saviors team, suggests,

> [Ask yourself] questions like; why are you making these volunteer/tour/mission trips? What are your intentions? Are they egoistic/self-serving, or do you simply want to take cool photos? Do you have the qualifications to solve the problems you're eager to solve? Do you have these problems back home? Or you are simply interested in solving exotic problems? Is your solution to these problems long term and sustainable (handing out a pair of shoes and cleaning drainage tunnels is not long term), does it involve capacity building, does it engage the community? In other words, are you welcome?
>
> Asking these kinds of questions and many more will help ... dismantle the structures of development porn (aka poverty porn) that objectifies and exploits individuals, especially in [places that are] considered developing countries ... As you make those trips we are asking you to keep in mind the cultural and contextual differences that you will encounter, leave room for criticism and be willing to learn.[25]

If you have special qualifications that a local community has specifically requested, and you can help bring about long-term change, then it may be worth considering a voluntourism trip. But otherwise, skip the trip, and donate part of what you would have spent to the community to support their efforts directly.

Though the carbon emissions associated with air travel are dramatic, I'm not here to tell you not to fly. I think travel can make us better people who are more empathetic to the needs of our fellow humans in countries outside our own, and it can give us a better appreciation of this beautiful planet of ours. The key is to do it as responsibly as possible, and if you're a frequent traveler, to do it less, maybe much less. (I've been as guilty of this as anyone, and now make an effort to minimize how much I fly.) To reduce the environmental impact associated with air travel, take planes only for long-distance travel when there are no other options, and then take trains and buses to travel shorter distances, for example between cities in Europe or in the Eastern US or Canada. Consider buying meaningful and permanent offsets for each trip you take, not simply checking the box to buy the unvetted offsets an airline might offer you. As much as you can, try to plan your trips to minimize the total number of flights you take, like taking one big trip less often instead of multiple short trips. And then practice all the same habits abroad as you practice at home, trying to avoid packaging waste and food waste, not purchasing things made through exploitation, and avoiding fast food (trying all the local food is the best part of travel anyway). Above all, focus on minimizing your impact on and disruption to those whose homes you're invading.

———

Perhaps more than in any other area of life, being a good neighbor requires us to question the status quo and to use our financial power differently from how our neighbors may use theirs. Collectively-minded people generally know that it's bad to shop with retailers who exploit their workers or to eat foods covered in pesticides. But when it comes to our behavior as neighbors, both at home and away, the status quo is one of deeply ingrained self-interest rather than a focus on the collective good. If you can retrain your mind and learn to see your choices differently, you can avoid upholding deeply unjust and harmful systems, and perhaps even do some good.

CHAPTER 9

Your Power at Work

Administrators at the Fresno Unified School District (Fresno USD) in California's Central Valley had for years witnessed widespread economic inequality persist in the community, and women and people of color in particular struggle to get ahead or even get by. They decided that they did not want to help perpetuate that problem. They analyzed the research and found that, even though the education field is made up of predominantly women, women consistently earn less than men, much of that attributable to the larger salaries men are offered to take new administration jobs. So, Fresno USD instituted a blanket policy in 2004 designed to remove this bias in hiring and making job offers. Any new management-level hire would receive a 5 percent bump in pay over their prior position, as well as a bonus if they had a master's degree. Believing they'd solved the problem, they turned their attention to the many other pressing issues facing underfunded school districts.[1]

Aileen Rizo was hired by the district as a math consultant, someone who instructs and supports math teachers at all grade levels, and her pay was set at the district minimum for her position based on her prior salary and the district's policy. However, when Aileen learned that several male colleagues with less experience than she had were being paid thousands of dollars more, she sued the district in 2014, claiming gender discrimination under the Equal Pay Act, a federal law designed to eliminate gender-based wage disparities that's been on the books since 1963. The federal judge who initially ruled on the case cited Bureau of Labor Statistics data that found women teachers are routinely paid less than male teachers and stated Fresno's pay structure was virtually guaranteed to perpetuate a discriminatory wage disparity, despite its good intentions.[2] In 2020, the federal Ninth Circuit Court of Appeals ruled in the case that it's illegal for an employer to use past salary history as justification for perpetuating gender-based wage disparities and that Fresno USD's policy was, in fact, discriminatory.[3]

A 2019 survey found that 60 percent of US employers are working to make pay more equitable, reducing disparities based on gender, race, ethnicity, and other demographic factors, with 93 percent of that group reviewing their pay scales to identify inequity and 77 percent instituting remediation plans and pay adjustments to correct pay wrongs.[4] Yet despite that, massive pay disparities still exist. Survey data show that only 22 percent of Americans—and only 15 percent of women—believe employers are doing enough to promote pay equity, while 71 percent of business owners believe they're doing enough.[5] The Fresno case shows us that thinking you're doing enough and actually doing enough are not the same thing. Plenty of well-meaning employers are perpetuating and even worsening wage gaps despite attempting to address the problem.

In 2015, Cindy Robbins, who was at the time the head of human resources for the tech company Salesforce, went to CEO Marc Benioff and told him that she believed the company was systematically paying women less than men. He insisted it wasn't but gave her the green light to look at the data. Her analysis proved that she was right: women were earning substantially less at all levels. When he saw the data clearly, Benioff agreed to adjust the pay for all women to make things equitable. It took three rounds of pay adjustments and cost the company $9 million to right its wrongs, but it was resolved not to perpetuate inequality in pay.[6] But what Salesforce did is not the norm across Silicon Valley. At the same time as Salesforce worked to make its pay more transparent and equitable, other giant tech companies like Google and Facebook were going to great lengths to conceal gender equity pay data.[7] In 2018, a group of women employees sued Google, arguing that they were systematically underpaid.[8] In response, Google went so far as to claim that it actually had a reverse pay gap, and that it underpaid some men, not women, because its analysis showed that women tended to be the most highly paid at their levels. The women countered that the data were deceiving, and that women only appeared to be more highly paid because they tended to be hired at lower levels than men doing the exact same work, and if you compared pay by task rather than by level, women were receiving less pay for the same work.

The data show clearly that we're not paying people equally for equal work, regardless of the many laws on the books requiring it and despite the large majority of employers who believe they're addressing the problem. Though the gender wage gap has shrunk slightly, in 2021, women were paid on average only $.82 to every $1 a man earned, resulting in an average of $850,000 in lost earnings over the course of a lifetime.[9] For many women of color, the wage gap is even more dramatic: Indigenous American and Alaska Native women earn $.60

for every $1 paid to white men; Black women, $.63; and Latina women just $.55. We see these wage gaps across nearly all demographic categories: men of color earn less than white men, those with disabilities earn less, mothers are penalized with lower pay while fathers tend to be paid more after having children, and wage gaps even exist based on weight and perceived attractiveness.[10]

In this "land of opportunity," perhaps the most upsetting thing of all is how little opportunity actually exists. Work is the place where we're supposed to be able to get ahead, to provide a good life for ourselves and our families, perhaps to live better than our parents did. And yet social mobility measures tell a different story, especially near the top of the income ladder. The biggest predictor of whether you'll one day be in the upper middle class is being born into the upper middle class, not how hard you work in school or at work.[11] A big part of the reason for that is opportunity hoarding by the upper classes, which applies every bit as much to behavior in the workplace as it does to behavior where you live. That's a big part of why wallet activism at work is important, too.

WHAT WALLET ACTIVISM LOOKS LIKE AT WORK

Your place of work may not feel like a space where wallet activism is even possible, let alone necessary, but consider: What if, instead of receiving a paycheck every few weeks, your boss handed you cash every hour you're at work? That might feel tacky, but in essence it's exactly what's happening: your employer or clients are buying services from you one hour or project unit at a time; they're just paying you in a way that makes it easy to forget about that transactional nature. Work is every bit as much a financial transaction as any purchase you make.

In a perfect world, we'd all be able to do work that feels ethical and noble, that lifts people up, and that contributes good to the world. But in reality, while we can do our best not to earn a living through work that is fundamentally unethical, there are few perfect employers out there, and most of us will have to compromise in some way to earn a living. That means, however, that we have another way to create change. As a customer of a big corporation that you want to pressure to change its ways, you have power to push that corporation, but only through certain avenues. As an employee on the inside, you have the power to push for change, whether directly or covertly, that customers don't have.

If you're part of management, you have more direct power, but you don't need to be a manager to make a difference. In 2020, Hachette Book Group,[12] one of the largest publishers in the world, was set to publish the memoir of Woody Allen, the filmmaker who has long been accused of molesting his adopted daughter Dylan Farrow. Books by controversial figures get published all the time and are often best sellers, so the notion of such a book deal was nothing new. Though management across the organization seemed to be in favor of publishing Allen's memoir, many lower-level employees were angry about the decision and decided they weren't going to stand for it. A month before the book was set to publish, dozens of employees staged a walkout, joining a protest outside Hachette's offices in midtown Manhattan and forcing management's hand. As a result, Hachette announced that it was dropping Allen and would not be releasing his book as planned. Protestors and Hachette customers had already been expressing outrage, and nothing changed. It was employees on the inside who made the difference.

Undertaking wallet activism at work could mean using your power over others in ways that are more positive. It could look like banding together with fellow employees to take collective action. Whatever it looks like for you, both now and in the future, never forget that you are more powerful than you think.

THE HISTORY OF EMPLOYMENT AND INEQUALITY

As long as humans have existed, there have been those who've exploited others for their own gain, something we see in feudal landowner exploitation of peasant farmers, in the general lack of investment throughout human history in services for the poor, and, most deplorably, in the practice of chattel slavery, in which Black people were brought from Africa to the Americas and treated as subhuman property for the benefit of white landowners. But the Industrial Revolution ushered in a massive rise in inequality, as people moved off the farms and into cities where factories were springing up, bosses and owners squeezed their workers, and workers rebelled, often violently. In other words, the rise in widespread inequality is directly tied to the rise of the employer-employee relationship.

Basic economic theory tells us that employers and employees should have equal power: the employee has something to sell (their labor), and the employer has money to offer for that. Either one can walk away if they don't like the other's terms. But in reality, workers who are desperate to earn money will accept low wages and inhumane treatment for lack of better options, and when employers realize that, many see the opportunity to take even more advantage of their disempowered workforce. The employer-employee relationship is inherently exploitative unless you deliberately work to change that dynamic.

Though inequality tends to be cyclical in nature, we're currently experiencing the biggest divide between rich and poor and the least social mobility between socioeconomic classes in more than a century.[13] The current trend began with the wage-productivity split in the 1970s. Throughout the mid-1900s, productivity increased steadily, thanks to technological advances and more women entering the workforce, and workers' wages increased steadily right alongside. During the period of the most rapid American economic growth and social mobility, the post-war 1950s and 1960s, employers focused on raising wages. This was the era that saw the rise of the middle class. However, beginning in the 1970s, and exploding in the 1980s under President Ronald Reagan, companies began putting most of the productivity gains into executive pay increases and shareholder dividends, a move that has been great for stock market investors, but terrible for workers. When adjusting for inflation, wages for most workers have been essentially flat for decades now, despite companies earning greater profits, CEO pay skyrocketing exponentially, and companies increasing their market value year over year.[14]

Economists recognize that everyone is better off economically when there is lower inequality, greater social mobility, and a thriving middle class. Companies are more profitable, because they have more customers and those customers have more money to spend, reinforcing Henry Ford's belief that he did better when he paid his employees enough to afford the cars they were making, even though it meant more money going out to them than he probably could have gotten away with paying.[15] Employers, however, often see their choice in the same false terms in which parents often see their choice of schools for their kids: you can either be a good citizen or a good businessperson. The truth, however, is that you can be both, and our society will only become more equal if employers change their mindset accordingly.

CHOOSING THE WORK YOU DO

You may have the power to influence pay policies in your work, or you may not. You may have the ability to push for greater diversity and inclusion, or you may not. But one thing you have control over, no matter where you are in your career, is choosing the work you do. Given our current lack of social mobility, not every opportunity is available to everyone. Understanding that many of us don't have an unlimited range of options, you can choose among the options you do have by considering several key factors.

We tend to choose jobs based on functional questions: Can I perform the actual job itself, am I qualified to do the job, and will I enjoy the work? We're less likely to consider what that work is contributing to. Just as we ask, in assessing whether to give business to companies, *What am I funding?* it's worth asking ourselves a parallel question when deciding on what work to do: *What am I contributing to?* A geologist may love the science of exploring for oil deposits, and therefore pay less attention to the fact that they're doing an objectively harmful thing by helping bring more oil out of the ground. (I've known several geologists to whom this applied, who later decided they couldn't stomach staying in the petroleum industry.) Avoiding work in harmful industries, or even those that don't contribute to our collective good, is another way to put pressure on industries to change. If companies can't attract top talent because too many find the work unsavory or unethical, that affects their bottom lines.

Next, consider the employer as carefully as you can. Even within industries that don't actively harm the collective good, or even within ones that contribute demonstrable good, not all employers behave the same. Some may very well still be bad guy companies. Consider the behaviors of good guy companies and bad guy companies we discussed in chapter five when deciding whether to go to work for someone. Companies that exploit one thing tend to exploit many things, so a poor environmental record is often a sign of poor employee treatment. Poor pay for people in their factories but good pay for those in the corporate office is a good indicator that they're not committed to equity or social justice, which will certainly manifest in many other ways. However, don't assume that big and corporate equals bad and smaller business equals good. Employees of small businesses on average earn significantly less than employees of large companies and corporations.[16] Large employers are also much more likely to provide benefits like retirement contribution matching, paid time off, and health insurance.[17] And small businesses are not immune from exploitation, with reports not uncommon of employers withholding compensation, refusing to pay overtime, mistreating immigrant workers, and subjecting workers to an abusive atmosphere (and often with no HR department an employee can go to for support).[18] Some may find the more nimble and less hierarchical work environment at a smaller company more desirable, but it's good not to assume that small is automatically better. If the work you do is client-based, you might ask these same questions and apply the same standards: Do you want to earn your living profiting off their behaviors? Work only for clients whose money doesn't make you feel like you're sacrificing your values.

If you have the choice, it's often a good idea to work for an organization that considers itself mission-driven. A similar concept is that of social entrepreneurship or social ventures, companies focused on solving social or environmental problems through a for-profit, capitalist framework. But given what we have already discussed about eagerness among profit-hungry companies to exploit consumers' (and potential employees') willingness to spend more on mission-aligned goods and services, it's also possible for those with a stated social mission to use that mission more as window dressing than as a true guiding principle. An organization being mission-driven does not automatically mean it never exploits anyone, and in fact it could end up being more exploitative, as employees are expected to work long hours and have no work-life balance, all to serve "the mission." So it's still important to ask a lot of questions to understand an organization's practices.

YOUR POWER IN THE WORKPLACE

Whether you currently have management responsibilities, you aspire to be a part of management in the future, or you have no interest whatsoever in taking on that responsibility, you have a role to play in creating a safe, equitable, and just workplace. Your power (now or in the future) will dictate the mechanisms available to you to create that change, but it's entirely up to you to decide what's most important to fight for.

Those with management responsibility have the most direct power to create change. Managers can work to change company policies, make decisions about hiring and pay, and influence public statements the company makes. However, depending on the company culture and team dynamics, many employees who aren't managers themselves still have the power to influence those who rank above them. It's always worth considering the "soft power" you may possess—even if it's informal—to influence the way things are done, whether it's setting a tone for newer employees or choosing how to treat customers.

Employees who feel they have no power whatsoever still have two major avenues available to them: collective action and whistleblowing. Hachette didn't cancel Woody Allen's memoir because managers spoke up but because junior-level employees walked out. If something unjust is happening in the workplace, you can be a part of collective action that seeks to push change, whether that's with a physical walkout, a virtual walkout like the one Facebook employees staged to push for increased moderation of extremist messages on the platform, or something more drastic like a unionization drive. The benefit of collective action is the relative safety it offers. If no one is seen as the instigator or figurehead, there's unlikely to be retaliation. If something unsafe, clearly unethical, or even illegal is happening, whistleblowing—alerting government regulators or the news media—is another option. While there are laws in place in most juris-dictions to protect whistleblowers, because most employment is at will (meaning either side can terminate the employment agreement for any reason), you may be putting your job at risk if you can easily be identified as the instigator of collective action or whistleblowing. It's not uncommon for people who are seen as leading unionization efforts to be fired. So you may decide to take steps to be anonymous if you move forward with actions like these. If you know that you are highly valued and your manager will protect you, you might use the privilege of your relative safety to stick your neck out for others, pro-viding them with cover to take collective action.

No matter what your role is in a company, almost everyone can ask management or human resources to provide a presentation on some-thing that troubles you, giving you and your coworkers the opportu-nity to ask questions, provide feedback, and ask for an anonymous employee survey to be conducted. Then, encourage your coworkers to take the survey seriously instead of blowing it off and share your views with management. Sharing criticism in a survey is far from a guaran-tee that anything will change, but it very well might be the thing that sets change in motion.

STANDING UP FOR EQUITY

When US Representative Alexandria Ocasio-Cortez first ran for office, she campaigned on paying workers higher wages, but after she won her race, she arrived on Capitol Hill with the task of hiring a staff where the culture is to pay people as little as possible. Most congres-sional interns are unpaid, and the starting salary for staff assistants is $35,000, despite Washington, DC, being an expensive place to live.[19] As a result, it's not uncommon for Hill staffers to work side jobs to get by. And that pay also tends to limit the diversity of staffers, making the job doable mainly for those who can get some parental help paying the bills, which in turn hurts the diversity of senior staffers because those positions tend to be filled by people with congressional experience.[20] But instead of continuing that tradition simply because that's how everyone else does things, or trying to stretch her budget as far as possible, Ocasio-Cortez announced before being sworn in that she would hire fewer staffers but pay each of them more: all interns in her office would get $15 an hour, and all of her staff at least $52,000 a year plus benefits—an unheard-of starting salary on the Hill.[21] Regardless of your views on her politics, she has indisputably seen that approach pay off, as she regularly goes into committee hearings the most prepared of anyone,[22] including her colleagues with many more staff members at their disposal. Her example shows that using your financial power to stand up for what's right can absolutely pay off.

No matter how you decide to push for change, based on your position at work, it's important for all of us to make pay equity a central principle of the change we're pushing for. Whether you push for them now, later as you rise in your career, or through some form of collective action, we should all be pushing for things like the following:

- Paying all staff at all levels a living wage, so they can afford to cover essentials without relying on public assistance or going into debt.

- Not asking job applicants for their salary history, a practice that only perpetuates existing wage gaps and one that's already banned in many states, cities, and other jurisdictions.

- Making pay more transparent, so everyone knows what everyone else earns, a practice that tends to lead to smaller pay gaps. At a minimum, this means including salary ranges in job listings, but ideally it means posting salary ranges for all staff publicly.

- Ensuring that women, mothers, people of color, disabled people, those reentering the workforce, and others who've historically been devalued at work are hired as often and paid as much as their white male counterparts.
- Making paid vacation, sick leave, and parental leave standard at all levels and in all roles.
- Changing the culture around internships to stop them from being a powerful barrier to entry to the upper middle class.

Richard Reeves asserts that the "informal allocation of internships" is a major form of opportunity hoarding that directly impacts who has access to the higher-paying jobs that provide access to the upper middle class. How a college student spends one summer may not seem that important in the grand scheme of things, until you consider some facts: HR professionals cite internship experience as the most important factor in deciding whether to hire a recent college graduate.[23] Significantly more of those who intern during college have a full-time job offer upon graduation (58 percent who interned versus 44 percent who didn't),[24] and half of employers say they regularly hire former interns.[25] Wealthier and whiter students are more likely to have internship experience, especially paid internships, than are students of color, who are less likely to have interned and more likely to have worked for free.[26] The historical trend of not paying interns has made it nearly impossible for people from low-income backgrounds to break into fields that require internships and widened the privilege gap more generally. Only students who can afford to work for free—with someone else paying their bills or the time to work a second, paid job—can dream of taking an unpaid internship, while those supporting themselves or their families are forced to find far less prestigious paid work while in school. Even with trends moving toward most internships being paid, the selection process still means that these opportunities are afforded only to certain students. If internships are how graduates get well-paid jobs, but only students from wealthy backgrounds and elite schools are offered the bulk of them, then an internship is a tool of maintaining the unjust status quo. In addition to paying interns a living wage, companies can change this by creating a new selection process that's not based on prior experience, where someone goes to school, or friend or family connections and instead focuses on students' initiative or creativity in completing a project or even on specifically selecting students who would not otherwise have a natural entry point into that industry or career path.

When we put an equity measure we support in theory into practice, it's important to keep track of its actual impact to ensure it works as intended. For example, parents and economists alike have been saying for years that organizations should adopt not just paid maternal leave policies that let women stay home from work after having a baby but also paid parental leave policies, so that dads or same-sex partners can stay home to support women who are healing and caring for their newborn child, and comparable policies should be instituted for adoption. (This is in the absence of federally mandated paid leave policies, which would be far better, and for which we must advocate.) On its face, this approach makes enormous sense and seems fairer. However, researchers have found that these policies can have knock-on effects that result in greater inequity. Economists found in one analysis that more equal-seeming parental leave policies in a higher education setting, in which the tenure clock stops while both men and women take parental leave, actually has the effect of disadvantaging women. Women are much more likely to use their maternity leave to care for their child and perform "mom duties," while dads use their paternal leave to provide some care but also to continue their academic work from home. The result is that men get ahead during their leave, while women tread water at best.[27] For another example, if the

Fresno school district had done a review of its supposedly bias-free process after a year or two, it would have seen that its policy was not, in fact, correcting gender inequality, and it could have tried a different policy. The problem isn't when an employer tries something and it doesn't work—it's when that employer assumes that one solution is the cure-all and then never bothers to check. That could explain why most employers think they're doing enough, while most employees harshly disagree. The only way to know if your company's policies are working is to audit the actual data and to do so regularly. If you're making demands, include impact-tracking in that list of demands, not just the policy change itself.

In addition to pay equity, another important principle is simply paying everyone fairly. Across the board, we see that the growing gap between rich and poor, the increasing levels of student debt that people can't pay off in a reasonable period, the decreasing rates of homeownership—all of it stems from our habit of paying people too little. And while many employers look strictly at the wages line on the balance sheet, striving to make that number as small as possible, underpaying employees also hurts businesses. Companies that pay a sub–living wage have higher employee attrition and have to commit more resources to ongoing recruitment and training, and their employees are less motivated and less loyal. Gravity Payments CEO Dan Price made the choice to take a big pay cut for himself but to begin paying all of his employees much more, making $70,000 the minimum salary for any position in the company, partly to recognize the high cost of living in Seattle, where the company is based, and partly to attract and retain the best people and show them that they're valued.[28] He frequently tweets that completely revamping the company pay structure has resulted in higher profits, employee satisfaction, productivity, and employee retention.[29] Paying people more is both the right thing to do and good for business.

Another important piece of reducing inequity is committing to true diversity and inclusion in the workplace, not just token efforts that let you check a box rather than actually changing outcomes, what we can sarcastically call Diversity™. That can happen at all levels, from the CEO's office down to the mailroom. Any employee can reach out to new hires who don't share the demographics with most of the other employees and offer to mentor, support, or advocate for them. Anyone can also work to push back against tokenism in work interactions, like when a lone female employee is expected to speak for all women, an Asian American employee is expected to speak for all Asian people, or a Black employee is only asked to weigh in on things that affect Black customers, while white male employees are asked for their input on a range of topics and never asked to speak on behalf of an entire demographic. This may seem like basic allyship, but it's more than that. You're looking out for someone else's paycheck and livelihood, as well as trying to make more workplaces inclusive to those who've traditionally been excluded, giving them a better chance at upward mobility. A 2016 study found that executives who were women or people of color and who pushed for diversity and inclusion got worse reviews than those who kept their heads down and followed the status quo, so it's especially on white men who don't pay a price for their advocacy to step up and do this work.[30] There's a wealth of data out there to help anyone make the business case for greater diversity and inclusion within an organization, from stats that show more diverse teams make better decisions and are more profitable,[31] to the latest research on employee retention at diverse and inclusive organizations.[32]

Many companies that have worked to boost their diversity have failed to retain diverse teams because their commitment only extended to bringing new employees in the door, not to making them feel welcome and needed when they got there. That's why it's diversity *and* inclusion. The inclusion piece may require more work and sustained commitment. In terms of making the business case for investing in inclusion, inclusive companies are much better at attracting and retaining top talent from all demographic backgrounds. Though the topic of inclusion is a big one warranting additional research specific to your industry, some beginning strategies are to take a close look at several aspects of company culture for clues about what it suggests to employees and prospective employees who don't match the dominant demographic. For example, you can examine the language the organization uses and look for hidden clues that might suggest it's turning off women, people of color, or other historically excluded groups. Organizations who use especially casual language can easily fall into this trap, assuming that the greeting *Hey, guys* is gender-neutral when many see it as male-centric.[33] (I call companies "good guys" and "bad guys" knowing it's not gender-neutral. More than 90 percent of Fortune 500 CEOs are men.[34])

Another way to identify exclusion signals you may be sending unintentionally is to analyze the company's and key leaders' social media followings to see what that tells you. For example, Anil Dash, the CEO of tech company Glitch, has a large Twitter following that he assumed was more or less evenly split between men and women. However, when he looked at the data, he found that 77 percent of them were men, which surprised him. Unsure at first how to correct that, and to better serve the women who he felt should be included in his audience, he resolved only to retweet women for a year. Not only did the gender balance of his followers shift, but he also got into more conversations with women, which broadened his perspective and helped him identify more of his unconscious biases.[35] Analyzing your organization's social media following can tell you a lot about who you're attracting, whether or not that's your intended target audience.

Companies that invest financially in their employees reap multiple dividends. That investment can take many forms or, ideally, all of these:

- Paying staff fairly and providing them with fair benefits, including an employer retirement contribution and comprehensive health care in countries where it's tied to work, including coverage for transgender employees and family members, and same-sex partners.
- Committing to ongoing enrichment for all staff that makes the work more interesting, especially for those who had fewer opportunities before arriving.
- Offering additional leadership training and mentoring to those who haven't had it before.
- Providing specific retraining to help underrepresented workers transition from a lower-paid job into your industry.
- Providing significant tuition assistance to those pursuing a degree or certificate.

Even if you meet resistance when fighting for change in the workplace, as you very well might, never forget that your work relationships are fundamentally about financial power, and even changes that seem small can still help a lot of people.

SUSTAINABILITY IN THE WORKPLACE

Though we've talked primarily about social good thus far, work is also a place where you can do a great deal to reduce environmental harm. Office spaces consume 18 percent of our total energy in the US, and with more workers shifting to permanent work-from-home arrangements, there's a lot of wasted energy being spent lighting and climate-controlling offices unnecessarily.[36] Here are some easy things to push for:

- Eliminate as many single-use plastics and other disposables as possible in the kitchen and break rooms, switching instead to washable and reusable cutlery and plates, or to compostable or biodegradable options if necessary.
- Get rid of the ever-so-convenient but environmentally disastrous pod-based coffee and tea makers, switching to traditional large-scale coffee makers.
- When ordering food for meetings or large events, don't order so much that there's food waste, and make sure you have a plan beforehand for distributing uneaten food to those who need it, identifying a local organization who can pick up would-be food waste and redistribute it to hungry families, or simply letting staff know in advance to bring containers they can use to take home leftovers.
- Watch how much swag and other free stuff the company produces, resisting the urge to print a bunch of T-shirts and other free junk that no one asked for, most of which will end up in the landfill before long.
- If the organization tends to communicate online, normalize not printing things out unnecessarily, especially if people are likely to read it on an electronic device.

Given energy demands of powering workspaces and employee commutes, instituting a broad work-from-home policy that allows employees to be off-site part or all of the time is also a sustainable move that reduces the total climate impact of a company's work. It also improves equity for parents and people with disabilities, who might otherwise miss more work than their colleagues to care for their children and themselves, or who may simply work most effectively remotely. If encouraging more people to work from home also allows a company to downsize an office or commercial space, leaving less space to heat and cool, or freeing it up to become housing, all the better. The same thing applies to business travel. Given the massive carbon emissions from airline travel in particular and the wasteful nature of large hotels that heat and cool even unoccupied rooms, reducing a company's reliance on travel can have a massive impact. Business travelers represent the bulk of all airline miles, so the more companies work to find technological solutions to replace physically transporting someone somewhere, the less environmental harm those businesses will cause.

———

Just as how you spend your money expresses your values in the world, how you spend your time does, too. Work is the place where most of us spend the bulk of our waking hours, so don't overlook your power to push for change there. Even if you are self-employed or do freelance work, you likely have interactions that provide opportunities to use your financial power for good, whether it's deciding how much to pay subcontractors, deciding who to work for, or asking clients about their pay equity and diversity policies before agreeing to work for them. Because a paycheck is always more than a paycheck: it's a vote for the type of business you want to see more of in the world.

CHAPTER 10

Where Your Money Lives

When you buy something, especially if you pay with a card, the transaction is not nearly as straightforward as you think. It's not just that money goes from your account or bank to the vendor's account. Instead, the money winds its way through a surprisingly outdated and slow-moving system of payment processors and computer systems, incurring mostly invisible costs along the way. The most well-known costs are those the vendors pay, but we still tend not to think about them when we choose between a debit card or a credit card—despite the fact that which one you choose will determine how much of your payment the vendor will actually receive. (Vendors keep more of the total with debit cards.) And many of these fees, like ATM fees, take a bigger toll on low- and middle-income earners than they do on wealthier people, because they're often a flat fee or a flat fee plus a percentage. A $3 or $4 ATM charge is insignificant when you can afford to take out $300 or $400 at a time, but when you can only take out $20 or $40, that charge is devastating. Lower-income people are also much more likely to pay overdraft fees that can top $100 each time, and it's rare for someone to find a free checking account without restrictive balance minimums, credit score requirements, or obligations to deposit monthly. Instead, they're charged $100 to $200 a year for the privilege, further eroding their financial resources.

Our system makes it very expensive not to have a lot of money. For many reasons, not the least of which is the expense for someone of limited income and resources to use a bank, the Federal Reserve estimates that 22 percent of households in America are unbanked or underbanked.[1] This means they rely on even more predatory systems like payday loans, which regularly take $15 or more out of every $100 borrowed, working out to an annualized interest rate of 400 to 700 percent,[2] as well as check-cashing services that charge several dollars for every check cashed.

Meanwhile, those with higher incomes encounter a financial system so different that it's almost unrecognizable. People with thousands of dollars to put in the bank have no trouble being offered a free checking account, and it's likely to pay a higher interest rate (or any interest rate at all) compared to the account options offered to those paying money for the privilege.[3] They're unlikely ever to face an overdraft fee, and if they happen to get careless and incur one, a quick call to the bank will quickly get that resolved, paired with a reminder of how much the bank values their business. (Technically any bank can reverse these fees, so it's always worth trying, though wealthier customers will tend to encounter more lenience.) And the use of credit cards is where the difference is most pronounced.

Those with poor or average credit scores and low to middle incomes are rarely offered any benefits for using a certain credit card (beyond the "benefit" of a few weeks' grace between buying something and having to pay for it). Wealthier individuals are offered an enormous array of valuable benefits for using a card, many of those benefits available even on cards with no annual fee—generous cash back, travel miles, and hotel points are the most common. Of course, if you do pay an annual fee, you get much more. Perhaps free access to the traveler's lounge at the airport. Free travel or rental car insurance. Free evacuation if you get stranded in a foreign country. Free TSA PreCheck or Global Entry to speed through airport security and immigration. The list goes on. Those benefits are paid for by the high interest rates charged on those who can't afford to pay their balance in full each month, the late fees they frequently get hit with, and the vendor fees that do more harm to small and medium businesses than to the big retailers. As former Treasury Department deputy assistant secretary Aaron Klein wrote, "The less money you have, the more money you spend just to be able to use the money you have."[4] But, the richer you are, the more that very same system gives you for free. *Is it too cheap?* If a financial institution is throwing lots of "free" extras at you, or if you pride yourself on "hacking" the system to collect big benefits, it's too cheap for you and too expensive for someone else.

Whether you simply need a bank account so you can collect a paycheck and pay bills or you're ready to level up your money and invest it, entrusting a company with your money means interacting with the financial services industry—an industry with a dark history of discrimination and predatory practices, plenty of which are in place to this day. While financial institutions will tell you that the benefits are there to lure in the people with the most money, which in turn lets the bank make more money, the effect is the wholesale exploitation and frequent exclusion of groups of people from our financial system on the basis of their skin color, country of origin, or gender. Choosing a bank or a lender is about more than just who is offering you the best terms or who has the closest branch or ATM to where you live. It's a question of whose practices you want to support and even directly fund.

JPMorgan Chase, a retail bank and issuer of a broad range of benefit-packed credit cards, for example, showers its high-end credit customers with benefits while actively discriminating against Black families seeking loans. An analysis of Chase's lending showed that only 1.9 percent of its loans in Chicago have gone into Black neighborhoods, despite the city being more than 30 percent Black.[5] The vast majority of mortgage loans have gone instead to white households, which make up less than half of the city.[6] While redlining is now technically illegal, many big banks find ways to avoid lending to people of color or lending in poorer neighborhoods, granting their best terms instead to those who are already ahead of everyone else financially. But while Chase is leery about investing in families to correct past and present injustice, there's one thing it apparently has no qualms about investing in: fossil fuels.[7]

As a bank customer, it's your money the bank lends out to people and businesses it deems worthy. You receive a small interest rate on the money sitting in your savings account as a partial payback for the much larger interest the bank receives from turning around and lending it out. So if someone like Chase invests in fossil fuels, and you are a customer with Chase, then you're investing in fossil fuels. When Chase refuses mortgages to Black households, you're refusing those mortgages, too. Most of the energy around personal finance and responsibility is in responsible investing. But you can't invest responsibly if you don't bank responsibly. Where we keep our money matters.

CHOOSING A BANK

Perhaps we should not be surprised that most of the companies whose core business is holding our money are those who put making money above everything else. But even knowing that, the misdeeds many have committed—and the brazen attempts they've made to hide those actions—are breathtaking. Wells Fargo is notorious for its attempts to dupe investors by opening false accounts in customers' names, only one of many things for which it's been hit with big federal fines.[8] HSBC, a bank with enormous culpability for the 2008 financial crisis, has financed Mexican drug cartels, an especially violent group of criminal organizations.[9] Even USAA, a bank set up specifically to serve military personnel and their families, which regularly receives top marks from its 13 million members for good service and low fees, has repeatedly faced state and federal action for discriminating against would-be borrowers. In 2019, during a federal government shutdown, USAA denied loans to members of the Coast Guard to help them get through the period without paychecks, or offered only loans with interest, while other military banks, like the Navy Federal Credit Union, offered their members interest-free loans.[10] And in 2020, the Office of the Comptroller of the Currency lowered USAA's rating from "satisfactory" to "needs to improve" on the basis of more than six hundred violations of the Community Reinvestment Act, infractions the regulator describes as "discriminatory or other illegal credit practices."[11] A week later, USAA announced a $50 million dollar initiative to "advance racial equality."[12] Its press released stated, "Black-owned non-employer businesses are less than half as likely to get financing as white-owned firms," while neglecting to mention USAA's own history of discriminatory lending and that it does not offer and doesn't plan to start offering small-business loans.[13] USAA is almost undoubtedly less evil than most of the big banks. But by actively engaging in behavior that we might call "woke-washing," it's demonstrating that, in banking, even those who seem like good guys are often just bad guys in disguise. Virtually every big bank operating today has committed grievous sins against its customers and would-be customers,[14] so there's no good way to place your money with a big bank and be assured that it's not being used for discriminatory or climate-destroying purposes. Fortunately, there are other options.

Credit unions perform essentially all the same functions that banks perform—offering checking and savings accounts and mortgages and small-business loans—but with much less exploitation of customers. Because credit unions are nonprofit, the rates they offer for loans are reasonable, and when they make a profit, that money is returned to members as higher interest rates on savings accounts, lower interest rates on loans, and reduced banking fees. The catch is that each credit union has an eligibility requirement for new members to join it. Some employers sponsor credit unions or have an arrangement with one that allows their employees to join. Some credit unions serve entire geographic regions, and the only requirement to join is that you live or work there. And some serve members of particular groups, like labor unions, schools, places of worship, or homeowner's associations. Unlike the big banks, which finance their lending not only with customers' deposits but also with money from Wall Street investors, credit unions have a much more direct relationship between lending and deposits: the money deposited by members of the community is reinvested in loans within the same community. Being a part of a credit union assures you that not only is your money not funding exploitative practices, it's also staying local. MyCreditUnion .gov has a locator tool to help you find a credit union nearby. If you wish to go a step further, seek out a community development credit union, which follows a mandate to support low- to moderate-income communities in particular. You can find a community development credit union at Inclusiv.org.

Another option is to go with a community bank. Community banks focus their services and lending primarily in a particular geographic area, rather than sending the money you deposited in St. Louis or Toronto halfway around the world to a fossil fuel project in Turkmenistan. Though community banks are for-profit, they operate much more like credit unions than the big banks do.

If you're especially interested in racial justice, you might seek out a Black-owned bank. Black banks have for more than a century been the only consistent investor in Black communities, while other banks have denied both mortgage and small-business loans through discriminatory practices. By depositing your money with a Black bank, you ensure that it will be lent out to support and uplift Black communities and help forge pathways to creating wealth for Black households, shrinking the disparity between the $171,000 median wealth for white families and $17,600 for Black families.[15] OneUnited Bank is the largest Black-owned bank in the United States, as well as the first to offer comprehensive online service, allowing customers to bank with them from anywhere. A variety of sites like BLACKOUT Coalition and BankBlackUSA.org have maps to locate a Black bank near you.

A final alternative is to do business with a bank that uses a different business model. Beneficial State Bank, for example, is not a credit union but a nonprofit organization owned by a foundation that offers free online checking accounts for individuals and businesses, as well as all the normal bank services at reasonable rates, and uses deposits to fund social justice and environmental sustainability projects. Amalgamated Bank is the only union-owned bank in America and one of the only banks with a unionized workforce. It also has an environmental and social justice mission, offering a 100 percent fossil fuel–free portfolio, as well as being a Certified B Corp and deriving 100 percent of its power from renewable energy. You can find other banks who do not put profits above everything else and who pledge to use deposits to fund projects that benefit the collective good at the Global Alliance for Banking on Values site.

If you can't find a credit union or community bank that meets your needs, and you need to go with a big bank, the good news is that a lot of people are keeping tabs on big banks' activities. It's easy to find information about who invests in what. JPMorgan Chase, Wells Fargo, Citi, and Bank of America are the four largest financiers of fossil fuel projects around the world.[16] Wells Fargo, for example, has been actively involved in funding the Dakota Access Pipeline[17] that crosses the land of Indigenous peoples without their consent, moving more than 500,000 barrels of crude oil a day through the region and risking large-scale environmental destruction when accidents occur. This involvement spurred the Seattle City Council to vote to sever ties with the bank.[18] Wells Fargo brags about its long-standing relationship with the Standing Rock Sioux Tribe and many other tribal entities, but when there's big money on the table, it sides with the fossil fuel project.[19] BankTrack.org is a good resource for identifying banks around the world to avoid, as is StopTheMoneyPipeline.com, or you can search for the biggest investors in the issue area of your choice and then do your best to avoid the worst of the worst.

CHOOSING A LENDER

When choosing a lender for a car purchase, a small-business loan, or a home mortgage, you may approach the institution you already bank with, or you may select another. In addition to using the same resources you use to select a regular bank, you may opt to dig into their lending-specific practices to ensure that you won't be mistreated, and, more importantly, to ensure that you won't be participating in a process that will help you get ahead at someone else's expense.

Check on service ratings for your would-be lender and find out if it services loans itself or sells them to a third-party service who you can't choose or research in advance—most of whom have poor service ratings. You also want to look into whether a particular lender has faced regulatory action for violations of the Equal Credit Opportunity Act (ECOA) or the Fair Housing Act (FHA). You can search the lender's name along with *ECOA violation*, *FHA violation*, *lending discrimination*, or *prosecution* to get a sense of whether it's a repeat offender, and that's a clear red flag. Some states' attorneys general also maintain a list of the institutions against whom they've taken action for discriminatory or predatory lending practices. Then, look more specifically at practices in your state or metro area. Search for the best geographical descriptor and the phrase *lending discrimination*, as well as the same search but with prospective lender names included. Some lenders may not be large-scale discriminators, but they may have a history of discriminating in your area, and if that's the case, run away as fast as you can. Choosing a lender with a bad history rewards that business for its bad behavior. Worse, if you choose a lender specifically in an area where it has discriminated against others, potentially driving down home values for families of color, for example, or disadvantaging those families as buyers, making it hard for them to compete in a competitive housing market, you're benefiting directly from that discrimination.

HOW TO INVEST, AND WHY YOU SHOULD

Investing has long been thought of as the domain of those who are already well-off, but in a world with fewer safety nets than prior generations had, we are each on our own far more than in the past. The programs you pay into your whole career are less likely than ever to provide you with a retirement in which you can afford to live, let alone live comfortably. Medicare does not cover the full cost of medical expenses that tend to cluster later in life, and it's projected that, within the next decade, the average retiree's out-of-pocket costs for medical care not covered by Medicare will consume at least half of their Social Security benefits.[20] We have to look out for ourselves, and that means investing, whether just for retirement or for other life goals. Saving money in a bank ensures that your money will decrease in spending power over time, while investing for the long term gives you the best chance of your money growing faster than the rate of inflation.

The common narrative that we hear in news stories is that millennials aren't investing, and this is misleading. Millennials are saving at higher rates and investing for retirement at earlier ages than Gen X. Many experts believe that more millennials and members of Gen Z would also invest if it were more transparent how to invest in good causes and avoid investing with bad guys.[21] The question we need to answer is how to invest your money responsibly, because the industry does not make it especially easy.

Like brands who try to greenwash themselves and their products, the investment industry is in a frenzy to "ethical wash" its offerings. Options labeled as socially responsible often come with significantly higher fees and lower returns than other comparable investments, in hopes that values-driven investors either won't notice, or they'll be willing to pay the premium to feel like they're not supporting or profiting off of bad guy companies. What's more, *socially responsible* and *environmentally sustainable* are not regulated terms with set definitions, so someone can call their investment offering socially responsible whether it actually is or not. Some socially responsible investment products have been found to include fossil fuel companies, gunmakers, producers of junk food, and any number of other bad guy companies.[22]

If you're not familiar with the principles of investing and how to select a portfolio that matches your needs, I cover the topic in-depth in my book *Work Optional*. It's a lot less complicated than most financial advisers would have you believe, because they want you to pay them to manage it all for you. (If you do decide to pay someone, search for a fee-only certified financial planner, or CFP, who adheres to the fiduciary standard. Search for those exact words.) The concept behind investing for retirement is that you're trying to grow your money faster than the rate of inflation, so that it grows not just in absolute number over time, but in spending power; you can save a manageable amount now and have it support you one day when you stop working. On average, inflation goes up 2 to 3 percent a year, so something that costs $100 this year will cost $102 or $103 next year. If you deposit $100 in a savings account that pays (if you're lucky) 1 percent interest, a year from now, it will be worth $101. That $100 today could buy the $100 object, but in a year, it no longer can. Inflation erodes the value of your money, and only investing allows you to sock money away with the likelihood that it will grow in spending power over time. Economist Thomas Piketty says that, since 1700, world economic growth has averaged 1.6 percent a year, but during that same period, the growth of capital—something you own that appreciates in value without you doing anything, in this case an investment—has averaged 4 to 5 percent a year, about triple the rate of the broader economy.[23] In the US stock markets in particular, over every ten-year period in history, the value of stocks in the markets has increased by more than the rate of inflation, meaning that if you invest for the long term, not for short-term gains, you stand a very good chance of growing your money over time. All of that sounds very capitalistic, and it is. Given how flawed our economy is, we have no choice but to engage with this imperfect system, but we can do it in a more principled way.

In traditional investing, you have only three real options: stocks, bonds, and mutual funds/exchange-traded funds (ETFs). Owning stock means owning a tiny slice of a company in hopes that it will grow in value over time or pay out dividends, a portion of corporate profits. Owning stock makes you a shareholder in a company. The money you pay for a stock goes to the company only if you buy it during an initial public offering (IPO), the very first time its stock is offered to the public on one of the exchanges. Otherwise, when you buy shares, the money you pay for them goes to the investor who is selling their shares to you. However, though you're likely not funding the company with your stock purchase price, you are profiting off whatever business it conducts when you receive dividends—the excess profits a company gives to shareholders—a few times a year. And then when you sell your shares, ideally many years later, the increase in share price will be driven by market perceptions of the work the company is doing.

While owning a share of stock is to own a small slice of a company, owning a bond is to be a lender. In essence, the bond is a promissory note for a loan issued by a company or government entity to fund some project, often things like building roads and bridges or updating school facilities. By buying the bond, you're lending the company or government entity money, and it promises to pay you back in full, plus the amount of interest specified at the time of purchase, on the bond's maturity date. In general, stock investing is considered more aggressive, meaning there's a much higher potential for growth but also to lose more money, while bond investing is seen as more conservative. This refers not to any political ideology, but simply to the fact that bonds have no potential to grow beyond the interest rate you bought it at, though you're unlikely to lose what you invested.

While it's important to understand what stocks and bonds are, and how they work, you never need to buy a single share of stock or a single bond certificate to invest successfully. That's where the mutual fund—and one specific type, the index fund—comes in.

A mutual fund—and the closely related ETF—is a bucket of stocks and/or bonds selected by a mutual fund manager. When you buy a share of that fund, you are a buying a tiny slice of all the stocks and/or bonds in that bucket. There are mutual funds of all shapes and sizes, with plenty to serve the most aggressive (risk-tolerant) and the most conservative (risk-averse) investors, others that focus on large companies or smaller companies, some that invest only in the US or the EU, others that invest only in developing countries, and on and on. But don't let that overwhelm you, because there are fundamentally only two types of mutual funds: actively managed and passively managed. Actively managed mutual funds are often organized around a goal, such as generating dividend income for shareholders or investing in companies that don't generate dividends so that you pay taxes only when it's time to sell shares. I'm not an investment adviser, and it's always best to consult with a pro who can advise you on your situation, but I can tell you that I do not invest in actively managed mutual funds. Mutual fund managers are always seeking to beat the markets, but research shows that, year over year, none do so consistently.[24] But they do charge more for all the time they put into picking companies to swap in and out of the fund, and actively managed funds therefore come with much higher fees that dramatically erode your gains over time.

Passively managed mutual funds, on the other hand, are treated more as a "set it and forget it" fund in which the mutual fund manager chooses stocks and/or bonds that match some existing index. The S&P 500 is the most commonly known index, composed of the five hundred largest publicly traded companies in America. The manager of an S&P index fund would simply put stocks in the bucket in proportion to their weight on the S&P 500 index, and then investors can buy shares of the bucket. Because that doesn't require ongoing research and management, passively managed index funds have much lower fees, which is better for you as an investor and can be the difference of hundreds of thousands of dollars by the time you retire. With index investing, you're not trying to beat the markets but only match them, which is still good enough to grow wealth over time.

The investments you own can be within a workplace retirement account, like a 401(k) or 403(b), which is like a bigger bucket that holds the smaller buckets of the mutual funds you select; they can be within an individual retirement account (IRA) or Roth IRA at the investment bank of your choice; they can be within a general investment account at an investment bank; or some combination of all three.

If you don't already invest, I encourage you to start as soon as you can, but learn a bit more first by doing additional reading to ensure that your approach matches your individual circumstances and goals. Don't hesitate to hire a pro for a one-time consultation if you just want some advice to get started. Securing your own future ensures that you can look after your own health and well-being the same way you're looking after the health and well-being of others through your wallet activism.

INVESTING RESPONSIBLY

Investing responsibly is just like any other form of investing, but it's investing with a much higher degree of discernment about what you're investing in and with a high degree of wariness about what you're told by people trying to sell you their investment products. If your only investing is through a workplace retirement account, you won't have infinite options of where to invest—instead you have only the choices your company and plan manager selected for you. In that case, do your best among your choices, but also speak up to your company and plan manager and demand more responsible options.

The simplest way to invest responsibly, without seeing your gains eroded to fees, is to seek out ESG index funds. ESG stands for *environment*, *social*, and *governance*, and it has become the universal parlance for investments that aren't environmentally destructive, socially exploitative, or run through exploitative governance. A 2019 report from the International Monetary Fund found that sustainable invest-ments like ESG funds match the performance of returns of regular funds, a good sign that it's not a choice between investing responsibly and investing for your financial security.[25] A fund that says *ESG* but not *index* is likely actively managed and comes with higher fees, so seek out a fund that is both. In most cases, these funds will simply mirror an index like the S&P 500, or the US total stock market, but with the worst companies removed. The big caution on ESG investing is that *ESG* is not a regulated term—therefore, what feels responsible to the fund manager and to you may not be the same. It's also a term that's being exploited to lure in investors under the same logic of com-panies greenwashing their physical products.[26] So it's important to do your homework to dig into what is inside each ESG index fund being offered. A company can be given a high ESG rating for its transpar-ency, labor practices, and environmental commitments, not its actual impact. For example, the Spanish oil company Repsol, whose main business remains oil extraction, gets consistently high governance and transparency marks, and thus is included in several European ESG funds.[27] You can research what's in any mutual fund by searching its ticker symbol, often composed of five letters, or you can search the name of the fund along with the term *social responsibility* to find out if others have spoken up to point out that it's not as responsible as it claims to be.

The woke-washing that happens in regular banking happens a lot in investment banking, too, so it's important to do a little homework before making an investment. BlackRock is the world's largest asset manager, with nearly $8 trillion under management, meaning it con-trols the investment vehicles in which other people have invested nearly $8 trillion of their own money. A few years ago, after too many deadly school shootings, BlackRock announced that it was introducing gun-free ESG index funds, which sounded like a positive development, especially coming from such a heavy hitter in the investment industry. The problem was that BlackRock also happens to be the largest single investor in the world, through its assets under management, in fossil fuel companies. And though it announced new ESG offerings, it has still made no effort or commitment to divest from fossil fuels. If you or I buy a few shares of a bad guy company like ExxonMobil, it has little to no effect on the markets. But when a behemoth like Black-Rock continues to invest in fossil fuels (largely by including them in its mutual funds), that sends massive signals to the markets and spurs large-scale investment in those stocks by others. BlackRock funds are notorious for their high fees, so if you buy into a BlackRock ESG fund expecting that you're doing a good thing, you're paying all those fees to support the work of a company that is actively bolstering the share price of fossil fuel companies.[28] *What am I funding?* In this case, you'd be indirectly supporting the fossil fuel industry.

More recently, a group of forty-three global financial institutions with $70 trillion combined assets under management have announced the Glasgow Financial Alliance for Net Zero (GFANZ), a pledge they claim will "mobilise the trillions of dollars necessary to build a global zero emissions economy and deliver the goals of the Paris Agreement."[29] Though announced with much fanfare and support from the UN and global leaders, the announcement has no commitments within it to stop funding fossil fuels, only to achieve "net zero" emissions (which can be done deceptively through bogus offsets, as we discussed in chapter four) by 2050, which is much too far in the future to achieve what's needed, and the announcement was roundly criticized by environmental groups.[30] If you choose to invest with an institution that touts its inclusion in the GFANZ pledge as a selling point, dig deeper to see if it's actually doing real work or just talking a big game.

A newer option for responsible investing is what is called direct indexing. It's not designed strictly for investors focused on social responsibility and sustainability, but it can work well for the purpose. With direct indexing, you start with a standard index fund like the S&P 500, and then you can decide which companies in the index you wish to exclude, because you don't want to endorse or profit off of their harmful work. So you could create something very similar to the S&P, but with Amazon, Facebook, fossil fuels, guns, tobacco, junk food, and mining subtracted, for example. As with any investments, aim to keep the fees on all of your investments under .25 percent (a quarter of 1 percent), and read all the fine print.

Another relatively new form of investing that's grown enormously in popularity is investing in cryptocurrencies like Bitcoin. Bitcoin and other cryptocurrencies exist entirely online, they aren't guaranteed by a country's central bank like traditional currencies are, and they tend to fluctuate wildly in value month to month or even day to day. If you care about investing responsibly, it's best to steer clear entirely. Bitcoin specifically is so energy-hungry that its network is responsible for carbon emissions of more than 20 million metric tons a year, equal to the entire country of Jordan,[31] and it consumes as much electricity as the entire country of Czechia (also called Czech Republic)[32]; soon it may exceed Australia's total energy use.[33] Making just one Bitcoin transaction has the same climate impact as watching more than fifty thousand hours of YouTube.[34] *What am I funding?* Nothing good.

The best way of all to invest responsibly has less to do with where you put your money and everything to do with the mindset you bring to it. Setting a goal amount that will let you retire comfortably but modestly, what we can call *enough*, and then stopping when you hit that number, is a powerful act.[35] Capitalism trains us to accumulate more, more, more—but stepping aside after you've covered your own needs leaves more for others. If everyone would stop trying to accumulate more after they have enough, there would be sufficient available money for everyone to have enough.

SHAREHOLDER ACTIVISM

After the mass shooting at Marjory Stoneman Douglas High School in Parkland, Florida, major news outlets reported on how much the gun manufacturers profit from mass murder and then shared something I should have known but didn't: two of the largest gunmakers in America are included on the S&P 500, an index in which my husband, Mark, and I had invested most of our retirement savings. Not long after that, BlackRock announced it was offering gun-free funds, but Vanguard, where we had our investments, would not commit to doing the same. So I started an online petition, and with the support of Change.org, it got nearly 100,000 signatures.[36] I sent the petition to Vanguard, reminding the company of our combined total investments with it, and demanded action. Though it wouldn't commit to anything to me directly—and it's entirely possible if not likely that Vanguard was already working on new funds before the Parkland shooting and my petition—a few months later the company announced a new set of ESG funds that excluded guns and other bad guy companies. The offerings were a big leap forward for responsible investing, as Vanguard is known for having some of the lowest fees around, which means you get to keep more of your gains and let them compound over time. They were also evidence that shareholder activism can work.

Whether you use your business with the investment companies to push them to be more socially and environmentally responsible or engage in the more traditional activism of showing up at shareholder meetings of the companies in which you own stock and demanding action, stakeholder activism absolutely can work. In 2021, a small group of ExxonMobil shareholders succeeded in getting three new directors with renewable energy backgrounds installed on Exxon-Mobil's board in defiance of its CEO, with the goal of forcing the company to transition away from fossil fuels. On the same day, Chevron's shareholders overruled the company's leadership and voted to be more aggressive in reducing its emissions.[37] Like with boycotts, shareholder activism works best if you can also get media coverage, so you make the company fear for its reputation, and if you can band together other shareholders to fight with you. If you're able to invest, even just a little, you have additional financial capital to deploy toward the collective good.

———

Even if you don't have a lot of money in a savings account or much money to invest now, don't underestimate the importance of choosing a financial institution that fits your values. Divesting your money from banks that fund fossil fuel projects is many times more powerful than changing how you shop. And the more money you have to save and invest, the bigger your impact becomes. More than in any other topic in this book, where you put your money dictates exactly what you're funding, so make sure you're funding the world you want to live in.

CHAPTER 11

Giving for Impact

Every few weeks, there is a new "heartwarming" story about someone in a dire financial situation because of health-care costs who has received help from coworkers, friends, or family, and is now getting the care they need. Maybe it's colleagues donating their vacation time so the sick person can be out of work without forgoing pay. Maybe it's someone hosting a successful GoFundMe campaign that will pay for their transplant surgery. I'm sure you've read these stories, too, but they're not heartwarming, they're heartbreaking. As a society, the US has decided that it's acceptable to let people fall into financial ruin over medical bills or, worse, to skip care altogether because they can't afford it.

We're hit up for donations constantly, and many of the things we may be asked to contribute to are outside of the realm of things we can research and get a definitive answer about. Maybe it's a panhandler asking if you can spare a dollar, or someone you know asking you to contribute to their crowdfunding campaign for a kid's surgery that insurance won't cover (a uniquely American phenomenon, as other countries consider health care a right, not a privilege), or a politician practically begging for your contribution so they can flip a seat and swing the balance of power. These requests are the product of a failed system, or, some would argue, a system that's working just as intended, which is to fail our most vulnerable neighbors.

More than perhaps any other in this book, we shouldn't need this chapter. We should not be in this dire state, with inequality skyrocketing, more people falling into poverty every year (or getting pushed into it), and the planet continuing to warm while our leaders do next to nothing. We should be able to focus our efforts on civic action and building an economy in which everyone can thrive. Capitalism is not incompatible with fair taxation on those with high incomes to fund safety-net programs that ensure everyone can have their basic needs covered. But we find ourselves in the most heartless version of capitalism: basic human needs aren't met, and a public commitment to fund the infrastructure needed to head off climate disaster is all but an impossibility. Even needing to talk about philanthropy means that public policy has failed. But this is the system we have, and so we must do our best within it to correct the crises we're facing. Because we can't shop our way out of this, there are times when the best thing we can do is give money to the causes and people who need it.

If you're going to stop spending money on manufactured goods or dramatically reduce your spending, that has a human cost, too. More than a billion workers in the world today work in manufacturing or a related field that's all about making more stuff. Billions more avoid poverty by virtue of the global economy continuing to grow. If we seriously commit to consuming less, as we must—or go further to embrace the "degrowth" economic approach that some say is our only path to climate resilience—many of those people, already many of the poorest and most disempowered people in the world, will lose their livelihood. Some of that is happening anyway with automation, and at least 375 million people in the world are expected to need to find a new line of work this decade, thanks to robots taking their jobs. And during the COVID-19 pandemic, the global economic contraction pushed 131 million people into poverty (defined as living on $2 a day or less, far below the US poverty line), demonstrating starkly the human cost of reduced consumption.[1] So instead of just sitting on the money you're no longer spending, you can donate some of it to causes that help retrain these workers for jobs in other industries like tech, health care, or the service sector, for instance, or that simply provide for their basic needs. That's a good start, but to talk about giving for real impact, we need to discuss the current philanthropy landscape.

THE PROBLEM WITH PHILANTHROPY

Many of our major societal issues stem from not taxing the wealthy enough, particularly the ultrawealthy or multinational corporations. They spend so much money lobbying Congress every year to fight against any tax increases, especially wealth taxes, that we might even be better off if they at least paid their lobbying budgets in taxes instead. However, in our current philanthropic system, the largest share of investments in social causes comes from private foundations funded by those ultrawealthy people. This means we're letting the same billionaires who don't pay their fair share in taxes turn around and set our social priorities without any accountability or input from voters. It's asking quite a lot to have us believe that the billionaires who got us into this mess are going to get us out of it.

The current philanthropic system is dominated by the largest foundations, those with endowments north of a billion dollars whose names you hear at the end of the programs on NPR and PBS. Our tax code allows individuals to make charitable donations that count as tax write-offs, and in the case of endowing a foundation, an ultrawealthy person can not only grant some large amount of money to form the foundation, getting a tax write-off on every dollar donated, they can also retain control over that money and how it is spent for as long as they wish. The only rule is that the foundation must give away roughly 5 percent of its endowment each year.[2] Even with that rule, most of the largest foundations continue to grow their endowments, becoming more influential in the nonprofit sphere and able to chart the course for the thousands of nongovernmental nonprofits in nearly every country who could not exist without those foundation dollars.

The Gates Foundation, funded by Microsoft money, is the largest philanthropic foundation in the world. Over the past three decades, it has granted more than $55 billion to programs internationally, especially in the areas of global health and development and US education reform. Many more children have been vaccinated thanks to the Gates Foundation's grantmaking. More children have access to clean drinking water, better nutrition, and a quality education. All of this is real and demonstrable good. The question is: Why do we let Bill Gates, a computer engineer with no education in humanitarian causes, set the priorities for spending such a massive sum of money meant to contribute good?

Nobel Prize–winning economist Joseph Stiglitz wrote in his book *People, Power, and Profits: Progressive Capitalism for an Age of Discontent*, "Perhaps the greatest failing of the American political system is the increasing power of money, so much so that our political system can be better described as one dollar, one vote than one person, one vote."[3] The wealthiest among us have the most political influence, and that money allows them to set social policy for the government through the political process and for the nongovernmental sphere through their philanthropic foundations.

That's the problem with philanthropy: not that it doesn't have good intentions, or that the people working for those foundations aren't putting real effort into finding solutions for our largest problems, or that rich people giving back isn't a good thing. It's that it does nothing to redistribute power, and instead it just further concentrates power in the hands of the few who get to set our global priorities. But even worse, by putting all that power in the hands of private individuals rather than world governments, we limit our own collective ability to make real change. Large foundations can't force all the big emitters of greenhouse gases in the world to clean up their act. They can help fund new clean energy infrastructure and educate people about the importance of renewable energy, but only government can institute policies that force the bad guys to change their ways.

Our reliance on philanthropic dollars not only keeps power concentrated among the wealthiest few but it also forces us to rely heavily on the worst abusers of capitalism—those who achieved nearly unthinkable levels of wealth—as our saviors, when they likely would not have amassed that wealth if they'd simply treated workers and customers fairly in the first place, or if we'd properly taxed their income and wealth.

THE IMPORTANCE OF INDIVIDUAL GIVING

Individual giving represents the largest share of philanthropic dollars in the US, with the biggest slice going to religious organizations, most often through a place of worship. Though the remainder is still larger than the total granted by the large foundations, individual donations are fragmented and irregular, making them hard for nonprofits to plan around. Foundation dollars are most predictable: they come for a promised period of time, normally several years, and usually go to fund specific programs. Because foundations give their money in big chunks, unlike most individual donors, they can offer it with a lot of strings attached. They can nudge or even push an organization to change its approach to one the foundation prefers. They can fund an organization for a number of years and demand that they hire more staff, only to abandon the organization completely later on, leaving everyone out of a job. They can move whole fields of activists to stop paying attention to something important and instead focus on this trendy thing the foundation decides it wants to be known for, simply because that's where the funding is.

People working for NGOs and nonprofits are doing some of our most important work, filling the gaps where governments fail us or simply cannot do that type of work. These organizations are to thank for raising awareness about global warming, for working directly with garment and factory workers to raise the alarm about inhumane labor conditions, and innumerable other causes. Most have honed their understanding on the ground, coming to understand the differences between the textbook version of something and its real-life equivalent. And for that, we thank them by paying them poorly. Nonprofit and social sector jobs pay well below average compared to for-profit positions the same workers would be eligible for. Much like teachers, they accept lower pay to make a difference in the world. Nonprofits are far from perfect, and much of what we've discussed throughout this book of imposing solutions on people rather than asking what they need has been driven by nonprofits and nongovernmental organizations, especially those working in poorer countries. But the social sector as a whole is working to improve its practices, which is promising. Even with those flaws, nonprofits are full of workers who've dedicated their careers and lives to a cause and who work directly with those in need, and they know far more about the issues we care about than those of us outside the social sector could hope to. So they are the ones we ought to trust to do the work that's needed. But instead, the foundation dollars dictate what they get to work on and how they approach it. (And in fairness to nonprofits, much of the most problematic behavior on their part has been driven by the foundations and their big checks.[4])

If we as individuals instead made the decision to step up and give more to organizations doing important work, they would be less reliant on foundation dollars and better able to steer their own course. Like all philanthropic endeavors, they still would not be accountable to voters, and in a perfect world, our tax dollars would fund this work and we would not need to. But in the world we've got, empowering those who've dedicated their lives to doing this hard work without the chance of personal enrichment is a whole lot better than letting a few billionaires call all the shots.

THE RIGHT WAY TO GIVE

When we talk about giving money, the words that we use matter, and changing some of our vocabulary can also help put us in the right frame of mind. For a long time, donations have been called *charitable*, and organizations doing work in the social sector have been called *charities*. This naming promotes "savior" narratives and takes agency away from those whom the donations are meant to serve, privileging the interests of the giver over those of the receiver. Edgar Villanueva, author of *Decolonizing Wealth: Indigenous Wisdom to Heal Divides and Restore Balance*, proposes that we instead call it *solidarity*. Instead of charitable giving, it's solidarity giving. Instead of charitable organizations, we're supporting solidarity organizations. It puts giver and receiver on equal levels instead of perpetuating a power imbalance, while helping better contextualize the role we should play in giving: meeting the needs someone says they have instead of telling them what they need.

If you're just starting out with philanthropic donations, the right way to give is just *to give*. If you have money to spare, it will go further in the hands of anyone doing solidarity work toward the collective good than it will in your pocket. But once you build up a bit more muscle around giving, you may wish to be more focused.

A question that I hear often is how to assess the effectiveness of a nonprofit organization. But like so many questions, it's based on a flawed premise, namely the fundamental belief that most nonprofit organizations are wasteful. In fact, like schools that stretch tiny budgets incredibly far, nonprofit organizations are masters at stretching their money, because they have to be. There is simply never enough money coming in to fund all the work they want to do or pay people what they're truly worth. So the question should be not how to find the effective few among many, but how to find those that are most effective among the many doing excellent and much-needed work. That begins by understanding the different ways organizations can operate.

It's oversimplifying things, but most nonprofit organizations either do most work themselves, which often means hiring staff to do whatever it is that they aim to do in the world, or they grant most of their money out to people on the ground who in turn do the work. Those are fundamentally different business models, as different as buying all your food at the store or moving to a farm and growing it all yourself. News stories confuse the issue, though, when they talk about how much an organization paid their staff, rather than giving that money away or spending it on physical things like food that can be given out to those who are hungry, implying that any money spent on staff is inherently bad. For some organizations, it might be. If you're running a food bank, we'd expect to see you spending more money on food than anything else. But if the thing that you offer *is* your staff, then it's ridiculous to suggest that paying those staff members is an extravagant expense. Keeping that in mind, if you aren't familiar with a nonprofit organization or its work, it's fair to look them up on GuideStar and Charity Navigator, two sites that assess nonprofit organizations' financials and give them ratings. Just understand that it's often not an apples-to-apples comparison if two organizations operate on fundamentally different models.

Unless you have millions of dollars to donate and can give to every cause that strikes your fancy, it's wise to look at the areas of greatest need. Though the wealthy give a high percentage of total philanthropic dollars, they tend to give to prestige causes, not to those that meet people's essential needs. Filmmaker and activist Peter Joseph's book *The New Human Rights Movement: Reinventing the Economy to End Oppression* includes a scathing critique of both philanthropic foundations and large-scale individual giving, and he shares that, in 2012 as in most years, not one of the top fifty individual gifts went to social services to help those facing existential need. Instead, the richest people who could afford to give most directly, outside of foundations, used their wealth to fund museums, symphonies, and the arts—the types of donations that get your name etched into a wall or onto a building.[5] While funding the arts is important, it's critical that we keep perspective and balance that giving with donations that meet essential human needs, too.

Also, pay attention to whether a cause is particularly well funded already. If you or someone in your family was affected by breast cancer, you may wish to donate to support breast cancer research. But a quick online search will reveal that breast cancer research is now among the most well-funded medical fields, thanks to decades of awareness campaigns and fundraising appeals by groups like the Susan G. Komen organization. The areas of greatest need are those that are both urgent and underfunded. For instance, though climate change is absolutely urgent, not every environmental organization working on the issue is underfunded because some do work that's more costly while others do work that's less expensive, and not every aspect of activism needs equal attention to move the needle. Those who focus on lobbying (or, more accurately, policymaker education, because lobbying is not allowed for most nonprofits) aren't underfunded, because the lack of lobbying on our side isn't the problem. The problem is the lack of political will. Voters aren't demanding action on climate change broadly, for the most part because the oil and gas industries are pouring millions into efforts to misinform the public, and so policymakers don't act. The organizations working to sway public opinion and build that public will are underfunded, because anything that involves outreach to the public is incredibly expensive.

Choose the handful of issues you think are most urgent and give to organizations doing work on them who you think are serving a current need. You don't need to overthink it, but if you need data before you can click the Donate button, check them out on one of the rating sites, search for the kind of news coverage they've gotten to see if they're breaking through with their work, and then go forth. Of course, there are times when priorities might need to change temporarily, when new problems arise that are more urgent. During the COVID-19 pandemic, for example, when millions of people lost their jobs and both homelessness and hunger spiked, it was a good time to divert money from other causes to organizations working to keep people fed and in their homes.

If you're tempted to give to faith-based philanthropic organizations, it's worth doing a bit more research on the work they do and especially the reception their efforts receive in the areas where they work. There's unfortunately a long history of faith-based groups bringing an imperialist mindset to their work, imposing a particular vision on people as a condition of providing aid or even requiring people to convert to their faith to receive assistance. This top-down approach to philanthropy rarely results in good or lasting outcomes, and the far better way to approach this work is to ask the people you wish to help what it is that they need, rather than telling them what they need. All types of organizations have taken this paternalistic approach, but it has a particularly dark history especially in faith-based work abroad. That said, the faith-based community is making great strides in reckoning with this history, and many organizations have gone to great lengths to reform their ways. Just do your homework first before you decide to support an organization's work.

The big names in the nonprofit sector tend to be traditional non-profit organizations that fund a staff, perhaps have local chapters, and do work through some combination of funding local projects and by using staff time directly. However, there are other avenues for traditional giving that take different forms and are worth supporting. Especially in times of great need, like during and after a natural disaster or crisis, you can donate money to mutual aid funds, which are meant to get money and resources into the hands of people as quickly as possible to pay rent, buy groceries, or cover other necessities. The organizations function as pass-throughs only, taking money in and getting it into the hands of those who need it most, rather than allocating staff time to long-term systemic change. Other mutual aid funds are specifically bail funds, collecting money to post monetary bail for those detained for unjust reasons, such as for protesting racial injustice or police violence. If you hope to claim your donation to a mutual aid fund as an income tax write-off, be sure that it is a registered charitable organization, as many but not all mutual aid funds qualify.

BEYOND FORMAL PHILANTHROPIC GIVING

Outside of formal giving, there are several ways you may be asked to give that can have an impact if done thoughtfully.

For example, you've likely been asked for money by someone who seems to be experiencing homelessness. Should you give them money directly, or donate to homeless service organizations? Direct giving to those who seem to be experiencing homelessness is a contentious issue, even among homelessness advocates: some argue that giving money helps people stay on the streets longer when we should be helping them get into social services, and others contend that you should give to a fellow human in need, especially because shelters are full and there's little help available. (Cynical people will insist that giving a dollar will just fuel someone's drug habit, despite ample evidence that most people experiencing homelessness do not have a drug or alcohol problem.[6]) And the best outcomes happen when we can get people into homeless services, ideally into permanent, supportive housing. (The *According to Need* podcast series is an excellent primer to better understand homelessness.) However, we have to be pragmatic. With rates of homelessness skyrocketing in virtually every city in recent years as housing becomes less and less affordable and wages fail to keep up, there simply isn't support available for everyone who needs it. Knowing that, go ahead and give money if you're inclined to help. Or, you can do what I do when I have time, mostly because I never carry cash: ask the person if you can buy them something to eat at a nearby store or restaurant. People experiencing homelessness are also likely to be hungry, and offering to feed them is compassionate and humane. If they say yes, ask them what they'd like, because people experiencing homelessness can have dietary restrictions, too, and then go buy it for them. Treating them as a person who is entitled to choices— something the experience of homelessness can quickly strip away—is a better way to help than telling them to go to the shelter that doesn't have space for them anyway. Of course, if you can also give money to your local shelters, especially those that don't enforce strict and invasive sobriety rules, that's even better.

Another common way you may be asked to contribute directly is with a crowdfunding campaign to pay for someone's medical care. When I'm approached to contribute this way, my first thought is always whether giving will just worsen the problem, giving policymakers permission not to improve our access to health care and its affordability. But given the scale of the need that's out there, that's all but impossible. Achieving meaningful shifts toward better health care requires getting the right people into office, not leaving vulnerable people out to dry. While you don't need to feel pressure to chip in, you're also not causing any harm if you do.

Because I used to work in politics, I often get the question from friends of whether their political donations make a difference, and the answer is: it depends. By and large, small donors, those who give $200 or less to a candidate in an election cycle, make up a small portion of the candidate's funding, with a majority coming from large individual donations and political action committees. There are exceptions, however. In 2012, President Barack Obama raised more from small donors than his opponent Mitt Romney raised from all donors combined.[7] If you're truly fired up to donate and you can spare the money, go ahead and do it and don't overthink it. But if you're focused on making the biggest impact you can, focus your money on seats that can realistically be flipped or held, and especially look to down-ballot races like those at the state level that aren't already saturated with funds. In the 2020 election, with Democratic enthusiasm (or fear) running high, there was an enormous surge of giving to House, Senate, and statehouse candidates in the final months of the campaign season.[8] Many groups publicized polling showing which seats were most likely to be flipped, and money poured into those races, despite there being almost no advertising inventory left to spend money on.[9] Donations also poured into the campaign for Amy McGrath, the Democratic challenger to Senate majority leader and major obstructionist Mitch

McConnell, despite ample polling showing that she had no realistic path to victory.[10] Donations that truly can make a major difference fund grassroots organizing and door-knocking to register new voters and turn out the vote. Get-out-the-vote efforts can make all the difference in close elections, and that's virtually guaranteed to be money well spent.

———

Perhaps in the future, we'll see a wholesale reimagining of what's possible under capitalism, with a real commitment to restoring a strong safety net, so no one goes bankrupt because of health-care bills, people don't end up without a home after they lose a job, and no one goes hungry while we toss out ample food waste every day. It's worth fighting for that future and holding out hope. But in the meantime, given what great needs we see going unmet in this broken system of ours, do what you can to give for solidarity.

CONCLUSION

> *Hope begins in the dark, the stubborn hope that if you just show up and try to do the right thing, the dawn will come. You wait and watch and work: you don't give up.*
> —Anne Lamott

> *Deje el mundo cambiarle y usted puede cambiar el mundo. (Let the world change you and you can change the world.)*
> —Ernesto "Che" Guevara

While he was a graduate student, social psychologist Paul Piff decided to try a little experiment. He brought students in to play the board game Monopoly, but instead of following the usual rules, they played a rigged version. And they knew it was rigged. Based on a coin flip, one student was made "rich," given $2,000 at the start of the game, an additional $200 each time they passed Go, and two dice to roll each turn, so they could move around the board faster. The other student was made "poor," beginning with $1,000, getting only $100 when passing Go, and having a single die to roll. The students played as researchers watched video of them down the hall, analyzing their behavior. Quickly, a pattern emerged: the students arbitrarily made rich acknowledged the unfairness of the situation at first, but soon began talking louder, making their moves faster, occasionally saying something obnoxious, and even eating more of the cookies researchers left out for them on the table.

When asked about the game afterward, the arbitrarily "rich" students said they believed they were better at playing Monopoly than their opponents, and that, even though everyone knew that the game had been rigged in their favor, they probably deserved to win anyway. Piff concluded, "When we watch patterns of human interactions, people who feel entitled and deserving of their own success are more willing to privilege their own interests above the interests of other people and often engage in ways that undermine other people's welfare so that they can get ahead." And, based on their behavior while playing, the "rich" students also didn't mind acting like jerks. An earlier paper Piff published, "Higher Social Class Predicts Increased Unethical Behavior," would support that notion.

But, Piff adds, "It's not about people who are rich, but rather that the experience of being relatively better off than someone seems to affect everyone, or would affect everyone, in the same way."[1] In other words, we believe that being better *off* than others makes us *better* than them, and therefore we can justify a whole range of bad behaviors toward them.

Research has documented time and time again that as people earn more and accumulate more wealth, they become less and less able to relate to people lower down the socioeconomic ladder from them and more apathetic to other people's struggles, a phenomenon sometimes called the "empathy gap."[2] Higher incomes are associated with less empathy, less compassion, and more unethical behavior.[3] In a capitalist society in which we entrust the most power to those with the most money, this is incredibly troubling. Those with the least empathy call the shots, when what we need most is more empathy.

Our world is rife with examples of this, some of which we've discussed in this book, from consumers in wealthy countries who are unbothered that the cheap junk they ordered online and expect to arrive promptly within two days is made by child labor in inhumane conditions, to the business owners and corporate leaders who have no problem squeezing those with far less power than they have to produce more for less pay, to the vast majority of us who go through life every day unconcerned with how our choices affect other people and the planet. Piff's research shows us that any of us can fall into this trap, and in fact, we've probably already fallen into it at least a little bit.

To be effective wallet activists, we must not only take action within our own lives but also within our own hearts. We must remember to constantly examine our own biases. We must remember that the reason we can take action at all isn't because we're better than those subjected to forced labor an ocean away—it's purely an accident of birth. You won the coin flip and got assigned the role of rich Monopoly player in life, even if you're only rich in a global sense, and you can either get complacent and eat all the cookies, or you can fight your way out of that mental trap and use your privilege for good.

———

As of a few years ago, in 2012, nearly half of the animals taken in by shelters in Los Angeles were ultimately euthanized. By 2018, only six years later, that number was down to 9 percent. Over that same period, Phoenix went from 46 percent to 4 percent, Philadelphia dropped from 36 percent to 13 percent, and Fort Worth went from 41 percent to 9 percent. We see this trend repeated in cities all over the US, with dramatic drops in nearly every city surveyed.[4] Experts believe that higher awareness of the need to spay and neuter pets did a lot to reduce animal euthanasia compared to its peak in the 1960s, when shelters routinely put down scores of animals every day, but what explains the dramatic drop in euthanasia rates in that short recent period? Consumer preferences. It became cool to adopt a shelter pet.

If we can make it trendy to adopt dogs and cats from the animal shelter, the very same animals we used to describe as "damaged goods" and "too much work," and especially if we can achieve that in only a handful of years, we can surely do the same for other causes. In a world and with a future that can seem bleak, it's important to remind ourselves of these examples, so that we don't feel naïve for being hopeful. There's reason to hope. There truly is. If you made it to the end of the book, and feel motivated to act, you can bet that lots of other people did, too, and they're ready to act alongside you. To be a wallet activist is to be deeply skeptical, but always to pair that skepticism with hope.

Even if we don't rise to the collective challenge and rapidly reduce our reliance on fossil fuels before 2030, change is still worth fighting for. The UN report outlining the differences between a 1.5°C average temperature rise and 2°C shows that even small increments matter for hundreds of millions or perhaps billions of people around the world. If we move the target and aim for 2°C instead of 2.5°C, or 2.5°C instead of 3°C, those differences affect how many will be impacted or killed by water shortages, droughts, famine, poverty, sea-level rise, the decline of whole industries, and the social unrest that will likely follow. As climate change worsens, inequality and social injustice will worsen, too, unless we push back forcefully. Never doubt that this is a fight worth fighting and that your efforts matter.

As you begin to practice wallet activism in your life, revisit the financial values statement that you wrote for yourself in chapter three.

Perhaps after reading the remainder of the book, some of what you wrote there has changed. You should expect that to happen in the future, too, as you take in new information and see things from more people's perspectives. The financial values statement is your document to carry with you through life, and you can revise it whenever you feel moved to do so.

I wish I could give you a definitive, permanent list of good financial choices and choices to avoid, but that's simply not possible. Our world changes every day, and your values play an important role in your decision-making process, too. So instead, here are some final reminders:

- We must always question both our own biases and intentions and the conventional wisdom, never trusting that something is "socially responsible" or "sustainable" just because someone says it is, or because we'd like it to be.
- Our two most urgent tasks are to decarbonize as quickly as possible and to address inequality in all its forms.
- We can make the best choices by asking ourselves the right questions: *For whom? Can everyone do this? Is it too cheap? What am I funding?*
- Our work as consumers is to create more demand for the world we want to live in and eliminate demand for everything harmful.
- Though we don't have to be perfect, we do the most good when we focus first on our biggest impacts and strive for consistent improvement, not perfection.
- Despite everything we can do as individuals to make financial choices in the interest of the collective good, we must never let policymakers off the hook. Putting pressure on them to act is just as urgent as any individual action you can take.

Wallet activism is important on its own, but its highest purpose is as a gateway to more engagement in society and governance generally. So don't stop here. If you feel fired up, explore how you can get involved on the local or state level and build from there, bringing more energy to all the good fights we must fight if justice is the goal.

If this book has inspired you to take action, don't stay silent about it. The more people we can engage to change their financial choices and to demand action from policymakers, the more impact we'll have collectively. The more attention we can bring to these issues, the more political will we can generate to drive new laws and regulations. So tell your friends and followers why you're making different choices. Use social media to tell companies the changes you want to see. Speak up often to your elected officials.

The more of us who speak up to say that we care and that we're willing to prove it with our money, the faster things will change.

ACKNOWLEDGMENTS

If you can help it, I highly recommend not writing a book during a pandemic. The fact that I couldn't travel, or even really leave the house, made this a different book than I originally convinced BenBella to publish, and I'm so grateful to my brilliant editor Claire Schulz, the thoughtful and talented Alyn Wallace, Sarah Avinger, Lindsay Marshall, Katie Hollister, Nichole Kraft, and the full BenBella team for their support as the shape of this project morphed along the way. Thank you for trusting me with this topic, even though it's not what I'm known for, and letting me live my dream of putting a book into the world that I'm proud to leave as my legacy.

Thanks to my incredible agent, Lucinda Halpern, for the help in shaping my messy ideas for this, for being the most incisive reader, and for the pep talks and hand-holding along the way. I aspire not to need such things, but I'm so grateful to have you there when I don't live up to that aspiration. I know it would have been an easier path to just keep writing straightforward personal finance books, so thank you for believing in me and this book.

Thanks to all the friends and allies who've lent support along the way, especially during the more-than-yearlong quarantine, and helped convince me that I could actually tackle this thing: Vicki Robin, Kiersten and Julien Saunders, Chris Browning, Bethany Bayless, Sherry

Petersik, Gemma Hartley, Matt Lane, Brian at *Done by Forty*, Amanda Holden, Ali and Alison Walker, Jill Thomas, Jordan England, Jackie Thai, Mike and Marissa Stender, Dave Donnelly, Stacy Holybee, Diana Moutsopoulos, Sarah Cady, and those I've undoubtedly left off purely by accident. Thanks to folks who've helped me find answers to the trickier questions, including Laura Zilverberg and the brilliant librarians at the Northwest Reno Library, part of Washoe County Libraries, where I wrote most of *Work Optional*, and where I would no doubt have written all of *Wallet Activism* if the pandemic hadn't forced me to stay home.

Thank you to past readers, whether from *Work Optional* or from my blog, *Our Next Life*, for coming along on this journey with me. I know it's a big departure from talking about early retirement! Knowing that so many of you were hungry to talk not just about becoming financially secure but also about using that financial security to benefit others gives me so much hope for the future.

Finally, and most of all, thank you to my husband, Mark Bunge, and my dad, Lewis Hester. The two of you are why I couldn't just sit back and fiddle away while the world burns. You've both pushed me to be the best version of myself, to value and trust others, to trust myself, and to fight for what's right, no matter the cost. You've listened patiently more times than I can count while I've ranted about patriarchy, white men, and boomers, and you've never taken it personally, because you two are the good ones. I don't know how I got so lucky to get not just one of you, but both of you.

RESEARCH TOOLS

While it can feel daunting to know whether a potential financial choice sup-ports your values, the good news is that you have plenty of help. Use the tools and resources listed here to help you do your research.

RESEARCH COMPANIES

Buycott—Mobile app to research boycott campaigns against companies and identify brands that are part of larger corporations.

CorpWatch—Organization that keeps tabs on companies' practices, especially around social justice. Their company profiles track labor violations, health violations, human rights violations, and more.

Glassdoor and Indeed—Job sites that let you read employee reviews of a company to help determine if they are an ethical employer.

Good On You—Mobile app that rates clothing companies on sustainability and social factors, along with letting you sort by price range.

Goods Unite Us—Provides better alternatives to shopping with bad guy companies.

InfluenceMap—Rates companies on their commitment to Paris Agreement–aligned climate measures.

OpenSecrets.org—Repository of political donation and lobbying spending for corporations and large companies.

Progressive Shopper—Information on company practices and support for causes that run counter to progressive values.

SourceWatch.org—Tool of the Center for Media and Democracy that tracks who is behind legislation, PR campaigns, corporate front groups, and so on.

RESEARCH FINANCIAL INSTITUTIONS

BankBlackUSA.org—Helps you find Black banks.

BankTrack.org—Tracks the involvement of banks in financing activities with a negative impact on people and the planet.

BLACKOUT Coalition—Helps you find Black banks.

Global Alliance for Banking on Values—Helps you find a bank committed to using its customers' deposits to fund social justice and environmental sustainability projects.

Inclusiv.org—Helps you find a community development credit union.

MyCreditUnion.gov—Helps you find a credit union you can join.

StopTheMoneyPipeline.org—Tracks banks' involvement in projects detrimental to the planet and climate and provides tools to help you switch to a good guy bank.

RESEARCH THIRD-PARTY CERTIFICATIONS (ALSO SEE THE NEXT SECTION FOR A LIST OF TRUSTWORTHY CERTIFICATIONS)

Ecolabel Index—Global directory that tracks more than four hundred different labels in two hundred countries to help you determine if a third-party certification is meaningful.

RESEARCH SPECIFIC PRODUCTS

Environmental Working Group guides—The originators of the Dirty Dozen and Clean Fifteen produce guides offer a range of consumer resources to find healthier and more environmentally responsible products, including the Skin Deep database, which rates products based on the safety of their ingredients, and the Healthy Living app, which lets you check products for unhealthy ingredients while you're out shopping.

Sweat & Toil app—US Department of Labor tool that lets you search by product type and country of origin to see if something is likely tied to exploitation or abuse.

Think Dirty app—Tool to identify products that are safe for consumers to use.

RESEARCH OFFSETS

Climate Action Reserve—Information on offset rigor.

Green-e Climate—Information on offset rigor.

RECYCLING

Earth911 Recycling Search—Allows you to find recycling locations near you for items that can't go in curbside recycling bins.

TerraCycle—Paid service that recycles more types of waste than can go into the bin.

MINIMIZE JUNK MAIL

Catalog Choice—Site that helps you get off mailing lists for catalogs and other junk mail.

DMAChoice.org—Registry to opt out of junk mail you don't wish to receive.

OptOutPrescreen.com—Registry to opt out of receiving prescreened credit and insurance offers, most often by mail.

PaperKarma—Like Catalog Choice, but app-based.

GIVING GIFTS

SoKind—Site that allows you to register for secondhand gifts, homemade gifts, and gifts of experience.

RESEARCH PHILANTHROPY

Charity Navigator—Site to research effectiveness and stewardship of nonprofit and philanthropic organizations.

GuideStar—Site to research effectiveness and stewardship of nonprofit and philanthropic organizations.

THIRD-PARTY CERTIFICATIONS

As of this writing, the following certifications for products are considered to be meaningful and trustworthy:

B Corp—A designation offered to companies who use business as a force for good, balancing profits alongside other goals like environmental stewardship or addressing inequality. The standards to qualify as a B Corp are high, requiring companies to report their social and environmental performance, assess how their business model impacts everyone in the chain, report on their supply chain, and share their philanthropic giving and employee benefits. B Corp certification also comes with the expectation that businesses build social and environmental considerations into their legal documents and structures.

Carbon Trust Standard—An internationally recognized certification that creates transparency about a company's energy usage, greenhouse gas emissions, water usage, and waste management.

Cradle to Cradle Certified—Considered the most comprehensive product certification available, Cradle to Cradle offers different levels of certification on five measures: (1) material health, meaning that something is made of substances not harmful to humans or the planet, (2) material reutilization, a measure focused on reducing waste and moving toward a circular life cycle of perpetual reuse, (3) renewable energy, dictating that products be manufactured with minimal greenhouse gas impacts, (4) water stewardship, ensuring that both water use and water pollution in manufacturing are minimized, and (5) social fairness, seeking to fairly compensate all those involved in a product's manufacture while not mistreating those impacted by it. Though it's an extremely helpful seal for customers, because there's a big bottleneck to get certified, the list of Cradle to Cradle Certified products is currently relatively short.

EPEAT—An electronics-specific certification from the Green Electronics Council that identifies environmentally preferable products. Electronics in general are among the least sustainable and most exploitatively produced products in the world, but the EPEAT seal identifies those that are most efficient, longest lasting, best designed for repair and/or recycling, and produced with the fewest harmful manufacturing chemicals.

EWG Verified—A certification offered by the Environmental Working Group, a consumer watchdog organization, affirming that a personal care product is free of chemicals associated with health concerns.

Fair Trade—Included on this list with reservations, as discussed in chapter five (see page 119).

Forest Stewardship Council (FSC)—This is considered the global standard for sustainably managed wood production, though the burden falls to the consumer to ensure that the steps taken between harvest and final product are also sustainable and nonexploitative.

Green Business—A certification offered by the nonprofit organization Green America, with an emphasis on small businesses, that affirms that a company is environmentally responsible, socially equitable, and accountable through continuous improvement and transparency.

Green Seal—A certification offered to both products and services such as restaurants and hotels denoting that they've met sustainability standards for the entire product or service life cycle.

Leaping Bunny—A seal affirming that a product is cruelty-free, having met high standards above and beyond national laws governing animal testing and verified by ongoing independent audits. Note that there are a variety of bunny logos and symbols out there, sometimes used by brands to trick consumers, so it's important to look for the actual Leaping Bunny seal, not just any bunny.

LEED—The US Green Building Council's Leadership in Energy and Environmental Design certification, the most widespread green building designation in the world, denotes that a building has met a certain grade of standards for energy efficiency and health, with platinum as its highest level. Critics say that it's become easy to buy LEED credits cheaply, similar to buying offsets without actually changing your practices, meaning that some with the certification may have cheated to obtain it. And monitoring of energy use in LEED-certified buildings shows that they usually don't save energy, because people behave more wastefully if they believe the building is inherently more efficient.[1] Therefore it's worth digging into the particulars of what a building is claiming earned it the LEED seal of approval. But LEED is still considered to be a reputable certification issued by a governing body with integrity.

Organic certifications (USDA organic, Canada organic, European Union organic, and so on)—Many countries now offer government-regulated certification of organic foods as well as products made from plant fibers, letting consumers know that they are free of synthetic pesticides and herbicides, they are free of genetic modification (i.e., they are GMO-free), and efforts have been made to practice agriculture in environmentally sustainable ways.

RECOMMENDED RESOURCES

Dream Hoarders: How the American Upper Middle Class Is Leaving Everyone Else in the Dust, Why That Is a Problem, and What to Do About It by Richard V. Reeves, 2017, Brookings Institution

The New Human Rights Movement: Reinventing the Economy to End Oppression by Peter Joseph, 2017, BenBella Books

The Color of Law: A Forgotten History of How Our Government Segregated America by Richard Rothstein, 2017, Liveright

Cradle to Cradle: Remaking the Way We Make Things by William McDonough and Michael Braungart, 2002, North Point Press

The Story of Stuff: The Impact of Overconsumption on the Planet, Our Communities, and Our Health—and How We Can Make It Better by Annie Leonard, 2010, Free Press

The Conscious Closet: The Revolutionary Guide to Looking Good While Doing Good by Elizabeth L. Cline, 2019, Plume

Nice White Parents podcast by Chana Joffe-Walt, Serial Productions and New York Times Company, 2020

According to Need podcast by Katie Mingle, 99% Invisible, 2020

There Goes the Neighborhood podcast by WYNC, WYNC Studios in partnership with WLRN, *The Nation*, and KCRW, 2016–2019

Vox and UCLA Climate Lab YouTube series

INTRODUCTION

1. United Nations Intergovernmental Panel on Climate Change (IPCC), "Global Warming of 1.5°C," 2018, https://www.ipcc.ch/sr15.

2. NASA, "Is It Too Late to Prevent Climate Change?" accessed April 22, 2021, https://climate.nasa.gov/faq/16/is-it-too-late-to-prevent-climate-change.

3. IPCC, "Global Warming of 1.5°C."

4. IPCC, "Global Warming of 1.5°C."

5. United Nations Department of Economic and Social Affairs (UNDESA), "UNDESA World Social Report 2020," October 24, 2019, https://www.un.org/development/desa/dspd/world-social-report/2020-2.html; UNDESA, "World Social Report 2020: Inequality in a Rapidly Changing World [executive summary]," 2020, https://www.un.org/development/desa/dspd/wp-content/uploads/sites/22/2020/02/World-Social-Report2020-ExecutiveSummary.pdf.

6. UNDESA, "World Social Report 2020."

7. Emmanuel Saez and Gabriel Zucman, "Exploding Wealth Inequality in the United States," VoxEU, October 28, 2014, https://voxeu.org/article/exploding-wealth-inequality-united-states.

8. Population Reference Bureau, "Summary: Family Income and Poverty, 2007-2017," KidsData.org, accessed April 22, 2021, https://www.kidsdata.org/topic/38/family-income-and-poverty/summary.

9. "People of color" is by no means a perfect term, and its meaning and usage are heavily debated, along with related abbreviations like "POC" and

"BIPOC" (usually meaning specifically Black and Indigenous people of color, though definitions vary). Where possible and appropriate, I've designated specific racial and ethnic designations. Where I have used it as a blanket term, I intend "people of color" to refer to all nonwhite people, but phrased affirmatively rather than as a deficit (possessing color rather than lacking whiteness).

10. Though the "womxn" spelling is often used to be more inclusive of trans and nonbinary people, I've opted to use the more traditional spelling of "women" throughout the book both for clarity and because of the argument made by many trans women that inventing a new word or spelling is actually less inclusive because it signals that they are not included in the typical spelling of the word. Trans women are women, and thus "women" is the spelling you'll see throughout the book.

11. The current trend is to use "people-first" language when describing someone's conditions—for example, saying "a person experiencing homelessness" instead of "homeless person"—so as not to define someone's entire identity by one fact that may not be permanent. However, certain communities have communicated a preference against this type of language, and I've chosen my words here in deference to those requests. When talking about disability, a community of which I am a part, the predominant sentiment at the time of this writing is to call an individual a "disabled person" or simply "disabled," not "a person with a disability," and to call it the "disability community." (Also, don't say "differently abled," "special needs," or use other euphemisms that may come from good intentions but have the effect of erasing a disabled person's experience or making their needs seem extravagant.) A similar sentiment exists, for example, within the autism community, asking people not to be afraid to use the word "autistic." When in doubt, ask people in the category you're describing how they wish to be referred to, and understand that individuals may not all have the same preferences.

12. Oxfam International, "Annual Income of Richest 100 People Enough to End Global Poverty Four Times Over," January 19, 2013, https://www.oxfam.org /en/press-releases/annual-income-richest-100-people-enough-end-global -poverty-four-times-over.

13. "LGBTQ+" stands for lesbian, gay, bisexual, transgender, queer, plus anyone nonbinary, intersex, asexual, two-spirit, and any other category marginalized for their gender and/or sexuality. I've used the "+" to be as inclusive as possible into the future should the term evolve further.

14. Robert Moss, "How Bottled Water Became America's Most Popular Beverage," Serious Eats, July 10, 2017, https://www.seriouseats.com/2017/07/how -bottled-water-became-americas-most-popular-beverage.html.

15. Cox Business, "Small Business Survey Shows Social Consciousness Pays Off—Cox Business 2018 Consumer Pulse Survey," accessed April 21, 2021, https://www.coxblue.com/2018-cox-business-consumer-pulse-survey/.

16. Nielsen, "Global Consumers Seek Companies that Care About Environmental Issues," November 9, 2018, https://www.nielsen.com/us/en/insights/article /2018/global-consumers-seek-companies-that-care-about-environmental -issues/.

17. Nielsen, "Consumer Goods Brands that Demonstrate Commitment to Sustainability Outperform Those That Don't," October 12, 2015, accessed via Archive.org, web.archive.org/web/20191007075526/https:/www.nielsen.com /us/en/press-releases/2015/consumer-goods-brands-that-demonstrate -commitment-to-sustainability-outperform/.

18. Nicole Lyn Pesce, "This Depressing Chart Shows the Jaw-Dropping Wealth Gap Between Millennials and Boomers," MarketWatch, December 28, 2019, https://www.marketwatch.com/story/this-depressing-chart-shows-the-jaw -dropping-wealth-gap-between-millennials-and-boomers-2019-12-04; Andrew Van Dam, "The Unluckiest Generation in U.S. History," *Washington Post*, June 5, 2020, https://www.washingtonpost.com/business/2020/05 /27/millennial-recession-covid/.

19. Business Wire, "First Insight Finds Expectations for Sustainable Retail Practices Growing with the Rise of Gen Z Shoppers," January 14, 2020, https:// www.businesswire.com/news/home/20200114005180/en/First-Insight -Finds-Expectations-for-Sustainable-Retail-Practices-Growing-with-the -Rise-of-Gen-Z-Shoppers.

20. Naomi Klein, "On Fire," in *All We Can Save*, ed. Ayana Elizabeth Johnson and Katharine K. Wilkinson (New York: One World, 2020), 41.

CHAPTER I

1. Justin Fox, "Bush's Economic Mistakes: Telling Us to Go Shopping," *Time*, January 19, 2009, https://content.time.com/time/specials/packages/article/0 ,28804,1872229_1872230_1872236,00.html.

2. Sheldon Garon, *Beyond Our Means: Why America Spends While the World Saves* (Princeton: Princeton University Press, 2013), 332.

3. BBC, "Reasons for the Cold War," accessed April 21, 2021, https://www.bbc .co.uk/bitesize/guides/z8qnsbk/revision/3.

4. Mark J. Perry, "Ten Reasons That Market-determined Wages Are Better Than Government-mandated Minimum Wages," American Enterprise Institute, November 29, 2015, https://www.aei.org/carpe-diem/ten-reasons -that-market-determined-wages-are-better-than-government-mandate -minimum-wages/.

5. Samantha Cooney, "Should You Share Your Salary With Co-Workers? Here's What Experts Say," *Time*, August 14, 2018, https://time.com/5353848/salary -pay-transparency-work/.

6. Cameron Huddleston, "Survey: 69% of Americans Have Less Than $1,000 in Savings," GOBankingRates, December 16, 2019, https://www.go bankingrates.com/saving-money/savings-advice/americans-have-less-than -1000-in-savings/.

7. Luca Ventura, "Household Saving Rates 2021," *Global Finance*, January 25, 2021, https://www.gfmag.com/global-data/economic-data/916lqg-household -saving-rates.

8. NASA, "Is It Too Late to Prevent Climate Change?" accessed April 22, 2021, https://climate.nasa.gov/faq/16/is-it-too-late-to-prevent-climate-change; Marlowe Hood, "Scientists Say It Is Too Late to Stop Climate Change," *Times of Israel*, November 28, 2019, https://www.timesofisrael.com/scientists-say-it -is-too-late-to-stop-climate-change/.

9. United States Environmental Protection Agency, "International Treaties and Cooperation about the Protection of the Stratospheric Ozone Layer," accessed April 21, 2021, https://www.epa.gov/ozone-layer-protection/international -treaties-and-cooperation-about-protection-stratospheric-ozone.

10. Joungn, "How the Ozone Hole Can Help Us Communicate Climate Change," PBS, April 15, 2019, https://www.pbs.org/wnet/peril-and-promise/2019/04 /how-the-ozone-hole-can-help-us-communicate-climate-change/.

11. Chelsea Harvey, "Closing the Ozone Hole Helped Slow Arctic Warming," *Scientific American*, January 22, 2020, https://www.scientificamerican.com /article/closing-the-ozone-hole-helped-slow-arctic-warming/.

12. Lloyd Alter, "In Defense of Carbon Footprints," Treehugger, August 27, 2020, https://www.treehugger.com/in-defense-of-carbon-footprints-5075880.

CHAPTER 2

1. United Nations High Commissioner for Refugees (UNHCR), "World Directory of Minorities and Indigenous Peoples – Ecuador," May 2018, https:// www.refworld.org/docid/4954ce3223.html.

2. Richard A. Houghton, Brett Byers, and Alexander Nassikas, "A Role for Tropical Forests in Stabilizing Atmospheric CO_2," *Nature Climate Change* 5 (December 2015): 1022–1023, http://doi.org/10.1038/nclimate2869.

3. Jeff Overton, "Fact Sheet: The Growth in Greenhouse Gas Emissions from Commercial Aviation," Environmental and Energy Study Institute, October 17, 2019, https://www.eesi.org/papers/view/fact-sheet-the-growth-in -greenhouse-gas-emissions-from-commercial-aviation.

4. Julian Brave NoiseCat, "The Environmental Movement Needs to Reckon with Its Racist History," Vice, September 13, 2019, https://www.vice.com /en/article/bjwvn8/the-environmental-movement-needs-to-reckon-with -its-racist-history; Adam Wernick, "Green Groups Grapple with a History of Racism and Exclusion," WBFO, August 11, 2020, https://news.wbfo.org /post/green-groups-grapple-history-racism-and-exclusion; Jedediah Purdy, "Environmentalism's Racist History," *The New Yorker*, August 13, 2015, https://www.newyorker.com/news/news-desk/environmentalisms-racist -history.

5. Maddi Miller, "The Implications of Commercialized Quinoa in Bolivia," *The Borgen Project* (blog), September 4, 2020, https://borgenproject.org/quinoa -in-bolivia.

6. Food and Agriculture Organization of the United Nations, "The Impact of the Quinoa Boom on Bolivian Family Farmers," accessed April 21, 2021, https://www.fao.org/resources/infographics/infographics-details/en/c /225070/.

7. "Quinoa Selection," *The Economist*, May 12, 2012, https://www.economist .com/the-americas/2012/05/12/quinoa-selection.

8. Emma McDonell, "The Quinoa Boom Goes Bust in the Andes," NACLA, March 12, 2018, https://nacla.org/news/2018/03/12/quinoa-boom-goes-bust -andes.

9. Jeremy Cherfas, "Your Quinoa Habit Really Did Help Peru's Poor. But There's Trouble Ahead," NPR, March 31, 2016, https://www.npr.org/sections/thesalt /2016/03/31/472453674/your-quinoa-habit-really-did-help-perus-poor-but -theres-trouble-ahead.

10. John Muir, *My First Summer in the Sierra* (Boston and New York: Houghton Mifflin Company, 1911), 277.

11. Charles C. Mann, "The Book That Incited a Worldwide Fear of Overpopulation," *Smithsonian*, January/February 2018, https://www.smithsonian mag.com/innovation/book-incited-worldwide-fear-overpopulation -180967499/.

12. The foundational text of the overpopulation frenzy was Paul Ehrlich's 1968 book *The Population Bomb*, which made him famous. Numerous global conferences followed, culminating in the International Conference on Population and Development (Cairo, Egypt, September 5–13, 1994). The United Nations Population Fund also formed during this time, though it now states its focus as reproductive and maternal health.

13. Caitlin Fendley, "Eugenics Is Trending. That's a Problem," *Washington Post*, February 17, 2020, https://www.washingtonpost.com/outlook/2020 /02/17/eugenics-is-trending-thats-problem/; Austin Ruse, "The Myth of Overpopulation and the Folks Who Brought it to You," United States Conference of Catholic Bishops, accessed April 21, 2021, https://www.usccb .org/committees/pro-life-activities/myth-overpopulation-and-folks-who -brought-it-you.

14. Khushbu Shah, "The Pandemic Has Exposed America's Clean Water Crisis," *Vox*, April 17, 2020. https://www.vox.com/identities/2020/4/17/21223565 /coronavirus-clean-water-crisis-america; Maura Allaire, Haowei Wu, and Upmanu Lall, "National Trends in Drinking Water Quality Violations," *Proceedings of the National Academies of Sciences*, February 27, 2018, 115 (9) 2078-2083, https://www.pnas.org/content/115/9/2078

15. The term "Latinx" has grown in popularity as a gender-neutral form of "Latino" or "Latina," intended to be a more inclusive to trans and nonbinary people. However, I've opted not to use it here because research shows that it is used predominantly by non-Latinos, and by only 3 percent of Latinos

(Source: Luis Noe-Bustamante, Lauren Mora, and Mark Hugo Lopez, "About One-in-Four US Hispanics Have Heard of Latinx, but Just 3% Use It," Pew Research Center, August 11, 2020, https://www.pewresearch.org/hispanic/2020/08/11/about-one-in-four-u-s-hispanics-have-heard-of-latinx-but-just-3-use-it). Some Latino activists have argued for a gender-neutral form of the word that would be understandable in Spanish, such as "Latine," but the word has also not yet achieved widespread use or acceptance. While the preferred term could certainly change, I have chosen terms that are most preferred among the group to which they refer, not just the terms popular among progressives more broadly.

16. Ihab Mikati et al., "Disparities in Distribution of Particulate Matter Emission Sources by Race and Poverty Status," *American Journal of Public Health* 108, no. 4 (April 2018): 480–485, https://doi.org/10.2105/AJPH.2017.304297.

17. Rachel Jones, "The Environmental Movement Is Very White. These Leaders Want to Change That," *National Geographic*, July 29, 2020, https://www.nationalgeographic.com/history/article/environmental-movement-very-white-these-leaders-want-change-that.

18. Emily Holden, "'A Lot at Stake': Indigenous and Minorities Sidelined on Climate Change Fight," *The Guardian*, March 10, 2019, https://www.theguardian.com/world/2019/mar/10/environment-climate-change-movement-indigenous-minorities-sidelined.

19. "NGOs in Africa: A Tainted History," *New African*, March 15, 2018, https://newafricanmagazine.com/16536/; Nicola Banks, David Hulme, and Michael Edwards, "NGOs, States, and Donors Revisited: Still Too Close for Comfort?" *World Development* 66 (February 2015): 707–718, https://doi.org/10.1016/j.worlddev.2014.09.028.

20. Olivia B. Waxman, "'It's a Struggle They Will Wage Alone.' How Black Women Won the Right to Vote," *Time*, updated August 17, 2020, https://time.com/5876456/black-women-right-to-vote/.

21. Yamissette Westerband, "Lesbian Feminism, 1960s and 1970s," Out History, accessed April 21, 2021, https://outhistory.org/exhibits/show/lesbians-20th-century/lesbian-feminism.

22. See note 13 in the introduction endnotes (page 305).

23. Grace Robertson, "Where J.K. Rowling's Transphobia Comes From," *Vanity Fair*, June 12, 2020, https://www.vanityfair.com/style/2020/06/jk-rowling-transphobia-feminism.

24. I use the terms "equality" and "equity" differently throughout the book. *Equality* means that people are paid the same, people have the same opportunities, people are treated the same under the law, etc. *Equity* has a meaning closer to reparations, focused on specifically lifting up those who have historically been oppressed or marginalized to level the playing field. Equality is more of an end state, while efforts to promote equity are the rebalancing actions required to get us to that end state.

25. Though "Native American" was most commonly used in media for decades, "Indigenous American" and "American Indian" are the more preferred blanket terms according to numerous Indigenous sources. When possible, refer to a person or group by their tribal designation, which is most preferred of all.

26. "Aboriginal" is not a commonly used term in US English, but in Canada, it is considered more inclusive than "First Nations," which is the preferred terminology for tribal groups, but which excludes groups like the Inuit.

CHAPTER 3

1. World Bank, "The World Bank in China," accessed April 21, 2021, https://www.worldbank.org/en/country/china/overview; Gaurav Datt et al., "China: From Poor Areas to Poor People: China's Evolving Poverty Reduction Agenda—An Assessment of Poverty and Inquality," World Bank, March 5, 2009, https://documents.worldbank.org/en/publication/documents-reports/documentdetail/816851468219918783/china-from-poor-areas-to-poor-people-chinas-evolving-poverty-reduction-agenda-an-assessment-of-poverty-and-inequality.

2. Datt et al., "China: From Poor Areas to Poor People."

3. Ivana Bozic, "5 Facts About Workers' Rights in China," *The Borgen Project* (blog), September 30, 2018, https://borgenproject.org/facts-about-workers-rights-in-china/.

4. Stephanie Nebehay, "U.N. Says It Has Credible Reports That China Holds Million Uighurs in Secret Camps," Reuters, August 10, 2018, https://www.reuters.com/article/us-china-rights-un/u-n-says-it-has-credible-reports-that-china-holds-million-uighurs-in-secret-camps-idUSKBN1KV1SU.

5. Data through 2019 (Source: World Bank, "Employment in Industry," accessed February 2021, https://data.worldbank.org/indicator/SL.IND .EMPL.ZS).

6. Anna Pujol-Mazzini, "How Vegetarianism Is Going Back to Its Roots in Africa," *The Guardian*, January 15, 2020, https://www.theguardian.com /global-development/2020/jan/15/how-vegetarianism-is-going-back-to-its -roots-in-africa.

7. Elie Gordon, "Reminder: The Roots of Veganism Aren't White," Atmos, January 14, 2021, https://atmos.earth/veganism-history-instagram-culture/.

8. Zach Hrynowski, "What Percentage of Americans Are Vegetarian?" Gallup, September 27, 2019, https://news.gallup.com/poll/267074/percentage -americans-vegetarian.aspx.

9. Lisa Betty, "Veganism* Is in Crisis. *As an Anti-oppressive Social (Justice) Movement," Medium, February 20, 2021, https://lbetty1.medium.com /veganism-is-in-crisis-36f78fa9a4b9.

10. Anya Zoledziowski, "Dear White Vegans, Stop Appropriating Food," Vice, August 13, 2020, https://www.vice.com/en/article/bv833z/dear-white -vegans-stop-appropriating-food.

11. PETA (People for the Ethical Treatment of Animals), "Award-Winning 'Captivity Is Slavery,'" July 1, 2015, https://www.peta.org/media/psa/captivity-is -slavery/; Jill Hamilton, "Using the 'Holocaust' Metaphor," Society of Professional Journalists, accessed April 21, 2021, https://www.spj.org/ecs14.asp.

12. Juliana Yazbeck, "The Problem with White Veganism," Medium, November 1, 2018, https://julianayaz.medium.com/the-problem-with-white-veganism -f86c0341e2a2.

13. Erin White, "Vegans: You Should Be Worried About the Working Conditions of Farm Workers If You're Really Against Cruelty," Afropunk, October 27, 2017, https://afropunk.com/2017/10/vegans-worried-working-conditions -farm-workers-youre-really-cruelty/.

14. Kendall J. Eskine, "Wholesome Foods and Wholesome Morals?: Organic Foods Reduce Prosocial Behavior and Harshen Moral Judgments," *Social Psychology and Personality Science* 4, no. 2 (2013): 251–254, https://doi.org /10.1177/1948550612447114.

15. See note 11 on "disabled" in the introduction endnotes (page 304).

16. See note 11 on "disabled" in the introduction endnotes (page 304).

17. Arwa Mahdawi, "Starbucks Is Banning Straws—But Is It Really a Big Win for the Environment?" *The Guardian*, July 23, 2018, https://www.theguardian .com/business/2018/jul/23/starbucks-straws-ban-2020-environment.

18. Laura Parker, "The Great Pacific Garbage Patch Isn't What You Think It Is," *National Geographic*, March 22, 2018, https://www.nationalgeographic.com /science/article/great-pacific-garbage-patch-plastics-environment.

19. Jason Bittel, "Hundreds of Endangered Sea Turtles Found Dead Off Mexico," *National Geographic*, August 29, 2018, https://www.nationalgeographic.com /animals/article/endangered-olive-ridley-sea-turtles-dead-mexico-news.

20. The Abolition Project, "Consumer Action (Boycotts of Sugar and Rum)," accessed April 21, 2021, https://abolition.e2bn.org/campaign_17.html.

21. Bill Radke, "Black History Month 2019: Are We Moving Forward or Sliding Back?" KUOW, February 25, 2019, https://www.kuow.org/stories/how-to -feel-less-like-a-victim-of-government-and-more-like-an-owner.

22. Clare Carlile, "History of Successful Boycotts," Ethical Consumer, May 5, 2019, https://www.ethicalconsumer.org/ethicalcampaigns/boycotts/history -successful-boycotts.

23. Carlile, "History of Successful Boycotts."

24. Carlile, "History of Successful Boycotts."

25. Brayden King, "Do Boycotts Work?" Northwestern University Institute for Policy Research, March 29, 2017, https://www.ipr.northwestern.edu/news /2017/king-corporate-boycotts.html.

26. King, "Do Boycotts Work?"

27. Bruce Watson, "Do Boycotts Really Work?" *The Guardian*, January 6, 2015, https://www.theguardian.com/vital-signs/2015/jan/06/boycotts-shopping -protests-activists-consumers.

28. Ana Swanson, "Nike and Coca-Cola Lobby Against Xinjiang Forced Labor Bill," *New York Times*, November 29, 2021, https://www.nytimes.com/2020 /11/29/business/economy/nike-coca-cola-xinjiang-forced-labor-bill.html.

29. Apparel Insider, "Patagonia Announces Plans to Exit Xinjiang Region," July 27, 2020, https://apparelinsider.com/patagonia-announces-plans-to-exit -xinjiang-region/.

CHAPTER 4

1. Singapore Building and Construction Authority, "Engineered Quartz Stone," accessed April 21, 2021, https://www.bca.gov.sg/Publications /EnhancementSeries/others/design2Ch2.pdf.

2. Osnat Shtraichman et al., "Outbreak of Autoimmune Disease in Silicosis Linked to Artificial Stone," *Occupational Medicine* 65, no. 6 (August 2015): 444–450, https://doi.org/10.1093/occmed/kqv073.

3. Katelynn Dodd et al., "Outbreak of Silicosis among Engineered Stone Counterop Workers in Four States," US Centers for Disease Control NIOSH Science Blog, October 29, 2019, https://blogs.cdc.gov/niosh-science-blog/2019 /10/29/silicosis-countertop/.

4. David Michaels, "Silicosis Outbreak Highlights the 'Malignant Neglect' of OSHA That Is Killing American Workers," STAT, October 10, 2019, https:// www.statnews.com/2019/10/10/silicosis-outbreak-malignant-neglect-of -osha/; Nell Greenfieldboyce, "A New Safety Program Takes on Silica Dust Amid a Possible Crisis," NPR, December 21, 2019, https://www.npr.org /sections/health-shots/2019/12/21/790298648/a-new-safety-program-takes -on-silica-dust-amid-a-possible-crisis.

5. Ihab Mikati et al., "Disparities in Distribution of Particulate Matter Emission Sources by Race and Poverty Status," *American Journal of Public Health* 108, no. 4 (April 2018): 480–485, https://doi.org/10.2105/AJPH.2017.304297.

6. Matt Richtel, "Three Headaches for the Recycling Industry," *New York Times*, March 25, 2016, https://www.nytimes.com/2016/03/29/science/three -headaches-for-the-recycling-industry.html.

7. Using 2018 data (Source: US Environmental Protection Agency, "Facts and Figures about Materials, Waste and Recycling [Plastics: Material-Specific Data]," accessed February 2021, https://www.epa.gov/facts-and-figures -about-materials-waste-and-recycling/plastics-material-specific-data).

8. Mitch Jacoby, "Why Glass Recycling in the US Is Broken," *Chemical & Engineering News* 97, no. 6 (February 11, 2019), https://cen.acs.org/materials /inorganic-chemistry/glass-recycling-US-broken/97/i6.

9. Jacoby, "Why Glass Recycling in the US Is Broken."

10. Jacoby, "Why Glass Recycling in the US Is Broken."

11. Jacoby, "Why Glass Recycling in the US Is Broken."

12. There are a few exceptions, like California's law mandating 50 percent recycled content in newsprint paper, but that's less of a true incentive (carrot); it's a legal requirement (stick).

13. Aliyah Kovner, "The Future Looks Bright for Infinitely Recyclable Plastic," Berkeley Lab, April 22, 2021, https://newscenter.lbl.gov/2021/04/22/infinitely-recyclable-plastic/.

14. Doug Struck, "Cap-and-Trade Program Creates Green Jobs," *Scientific American*, April 23, 2009, https://www.scientificamerican.com/article/cap-and-trade-creates-jobs/.

15. Forest Trends, "Demand for Nature-based Solutions for Climate Drives Voluntary Carbon Markets to a Seven-Year High," December 5, 2019, https://www.forest-trends.org/pressroom/demand-for-nature-based-solutions-for-climate-drives-voluntary-carbon-markets-to-a-seven-year-high/.

16. Lisa Song and Paula Moura, "An Even More Inconvenient Truth: Why Carbon Credits for Forest Preservation May Be Worse than Nothing," ProPublica, May 22, 2019, https://features.propublica.org/brazil-carbon-offsets/inconvenient-truth-carbon-credits-dont-work-deforestation-redd-acre-cambodia/.

17. Will Mathis and Ivan Levingston, "Startup That Rates Carbon Offsets Finds Almost Half Fall Short," Bloomberg, May 13, 2021, https://www.bloombergquint.com/markets/carbon-offsets-have-a-new-ratings-agency-with-startup-sylvera.

18. Brian Palmer, "Should You Buy Carbon Offsets?" National Resource Defense Council, April 28, 2016, https://www.nrdc.org/stories/should-you-buy-carbon-offsets.

19. Alex Blumberg and Ayana Elizabeth Johnson, "Cold Hard Cash for Your Greenhouse Gas," October 22, 2020, in *How to Save a Planet*, produced by Lauren Silverman, podcast, MP3 audio, https://gimletmedia.com/shows/howtosaveaplanet/kwhnz8b/cold-hard-cash-for-your-greenhouse-gas.

20. Palmer, "Should You Buy Carbon Offsets?"

21. Data through 2020 (Source: Environmental Working Group, "Corn Subsidies in the United States Totaled $116.6 Billion from 1995-2020," accessed April 23, 2021, https://farm.ewg.org/progdetail.php?fips=00000&progcode=corn).

22. One study found that hamburger meat could cost as much as $35 a pound without agricultural and water subsidies (Source: Aviva Shen, "Why We Should Stop Obsessing Over How Expensive the World's First Test-Tube Hamburger Is," *ThinkProgress*, August 5, 2013, https://archive.thinkprogress .org/why-we-should-stop-obsessing-over-how-expensive-the-worlds-first -test-tube-hamburger-is-c4e7011f52f4/).

23. Homeowners are less white than they used to be, but that's simply reflecting changing demographics overall, and not representing a proportional shift in who owns versus who rents (Source: Jenny Schuetz, "Who Is the New Face of American Homeownership?" Brookings Institution, October 9, 2017, https://www.brookings.edu/blog/the-avenue/2017/10/09/who-is-the-new -face-of-american-homeownership/).

24. Schuetz, "Who Is the New Face of American Homeownership?"

25. David Leonhardt, "The Rich Really Do Pay Lower Taxes Than You," *New York Times*, October 6, 2019, https://www.nytimes.com/interactive/2019/10 /06/opinion/income-tax-rate-wealthy.html.

26. Margery Austin Turner, Eric Toder, Rolf Pendall, and Claudia Shary-gin, "How Would Reforming the Mortgage Interest Deduction Affect the Housing Market?" Urban Institute, March 2013, https://www.urban.org /sites/default/files/publication/23431/412776-How-Would-Reforming-the -Mortgage-Interest-Deduction-Affect-the-Housing-Market-.PDF.

27. Turner et al., "How Would Reforming the Mortgage Interest Deduction Affect the Housing Market?"

28. Jim Tankersley and Ben Casselman, "As Mortgage-Interest Deduction Van-ishes, Housing Market Offers a Shrug," *New York Times*, August 4, 2019, https://www.nytimes.com/2019/08/04/business/economy/mortgage-interest -deduction-tax.html.

29. Christine Smith, "Why Economists Don't Like the Mortgage Interest Deduction," Federal Reserve Bank of St. Louis, May 9, 2018, https://www .stlouisfed.org/open-vault/2018/may/why-economists-dont-like-mortgage -interest-deduction.

30. Clayton Coleman and Emma Dietz, "Fact Sheet | Fossil Fuel Subsidies: A Closer Look at Tax Breaks and Societal Costs," Environmental and Energy Study Institute, July 29, 2019, https://www.eesi.org/papers/view/fact-sheet -fossil-fuel-subsidies-a-closer-look-at-tax-breaks-and-societal-costs.

31. Ellen Ruppel Shell, *Cheap: The High Cost of Discount Culture* (New York: Penguin Press, 2009), 209.

32. Shell, *Cheap*, 140–141.

33. Eric Holthaus, "Lawns Are the No. 1 Irrigated 'Crop' in America. They Need to Die," Grist, May 2, 2019, https://grist.org/article/lawns-are-the-no -1-agricultural-crop-in-america-they-need-to-die/.

CHAPTER 5

1. BP has spent at least $5 million a year lobbying the US government, backed anti-climate lobbying groups despite pledging not to, successfully pushed for the reduction of impact assessments before environmentally destructive projects can proceed, and has spent more than $50 million a year lobbying world governments following the Paris Agreement. (Sources: Open Secrets, "Top Spenders," accessed February 2021, https://www .opensecrets.org/federal-lobbying/clients/summary; Lawrence Carter, Zach Boren, and Alexander Kaufman, "Revealed: BP and Shell Back Anti-climate Lobby Groups Despite Pledges," Greenpeace, September 28, 2020, https:// unearthed.greenpeace.org/2020/09/28/bp-shell-climate-lobby-groups/; Jillian Ambrose, "Trump Weakened Environmental Laws After BP Lobbying," *The Guardian*, January 23, 2020, https://www.theguardian.com/business /2020/jan/23/trump-weakened-environmental-laws-after-bp-lobbying; InfluenceMap, "Big Oil's Real Agenda on Climate Change," March 2019, https://influencemap.org/report/How-Big-Oil-Continues-to-Oppose-the -Paris-Agreement-38212275958aa21196dae3b76220bddc.)

2. Climate Accountability Institute, "Carbon Majors Report," updated October 8, 2019, climateaccountability.org/carbonmajors.html; Paul Griffin, "The Carbon Majors Database: CDP Carbon Majors Report 2017," Rackcdn.com, 2017, https://b8f65cb373b1b7b15feb-c70d8ead6ced550b4d987d7c03fcdd1d .ssl.cf3.rackcdn.com/cms/reports/documents/000/002/327/original/Carbon -Majors-Report-2017.pdf?1499691240.

3. Richard Heede, "Climate Accountability Institute Report," Climate Accountability Institute, October 9, 2019, https://climateaccountability.org /pdf/CAI%20PressRelease%20Top20%20Oct19.pdf; Matthew Taylor and Jonathan Watts, "Revealed: The 20 Firms Behind a Third of All Carbon Emissions," *The Guardian*, October 9, 2019, https://www.theguardian.com /environment/2019/oct/09/revealed-20-firms-third-carbon-emissions.

4. History.com, "Andrew Carnegie," November 9, 2009 (updated February 9, 2021), https://www.history.com/topics/19th-century/andrew-carnegie.

5. History.com, "Labor Movement," October 29, 2009 (updated March 31, 2020), https://www.history.com/topics/19th-century/labor.

6. Christopher Klein, "Andrew Carnegie Claimed to Support Unions, But Then Destroyed Them in His Steel Empire," History.com, July 29, 2019, https://www.history.com/news/andrew-carnegie-unions-homestead-strike.

7. Taylor Nicole Rogers, "The AOC Adviser Behind the 'Every Billionaire Is a Policy Failure' Slogan Says There's a Critical Issue with Depending on the Richest People to Fix the World's Biggest Problems," *Insider*, July 16, 2019, https://www.businessinsider.com/aoc-adviser-dan-riffle-every-billionaire-policy-failure-billionaires-philanthropy-2019-7.

8. Center for Media and Democracy, "Keep America Beautiful," SourceWatch, edited December 25, 2019, https://www.sourcewatch.org/index.php/Keep_America_Beautiful.

9. Laura Sullivan, "How Big Oil Misled the Public Into Believing Plastic Would Be Recycled," NPR, September 11, 2020, https://www.npr.org/2020/09/11/897692090/how-big-oil-misled-the-public-into-believing-plastic-would-be-recycled.

10. "Mission-driven" is an imperfect term, and a company using it does not guarantee that it is a good guy. We'll come back to this in chapter nine. But I'm using it here because it is the preferred and most commonly understood term for this approach as of this writing.

11. Many people have written about Walmart's multitude of sins, from its involvement in human trafficking, to its effect of driving down wages by outsourcing jobs, to its displacement of hundreds of thousands of US manufacturing jobs to China, to its effects on crushing small and local businesses. (Sources: John Sifton, "Walmart's Human Trafficking Problem," Human Rights Watch, September 17, 2012, https://www.hrw.org/news/2012/09/17/walmarts-human-trafficking-problem; Travis Waldron, "Report: Walmart Drives Down American Wages by Outsourcing Jobs," ThinkProgress, June 6, 2012, https://archive.thinkprogress.org/report-walmart-drives-down-american-wages-by-outsourcing-jobs-40bfb6680a7c/; Robert E. Scott, "The Wal-Mart Effect," Economic Policy Institute, June 25, 2007, https://www.epi.org/publication/ib235/; Charles Fishman, "The Wal-Mart You Don't Know," *Fast Company*, December 1, 2003, https://www.fastcompany.com/47593/wal-mart-you-dont-know.)

12. Andy Kroll, "Are Walmart's Chinese Factories as Bad as Apple's?" *Mother Jones*, March/April 2020, https://www.motherjones.com/environment/2012/03/walmart-china-sustainability-shadow-factories-greenwash/; Elizabeth Sturcken, "Breathless in China: Walmart, Sustainability and Why You Should Care," Environmental Defense Fund, April 12, 2018, https://business.edf.org/insights/breathless-in-china-walmart-sustainability-and-why-you-should-care/.

13. Stacy Mitchell and Walter Wuthmann, "Walmart Spews a Huge Amount of Climate Pollution with Its Shipping, but Doesn't Report Any of It," Grist, June 2, 2015, https://grist.org/business-technology/walmart-spews-a-huge-amount-of-climate-pollution-with-its-shipping-but-doesnt-report-any-of-it/.

14. Stephen Stapczynski and Akshat Rathi, "Walmart Aims to End Emissions from Global Operations by 2040," Bloomberg Green, September 20, 2020, https://www.bloomberg.com/news/articles/2020-09-21/walmart-aims-to-end-emissions-from-global-operations-by-2040.

15. PBS, "Store Wars: When Wal-Mart Comes to Town," accessed February 2021 via Archive.org, https://web.archive.org/web/20121110155037/https://www.pbs.org/itvs/storewars/stores3.html.

16. Stacy Jones and Grace Donnelly, "Walmart's New Jobs Approach Could Be Undermined by Gender Bias," *Fortune*, April 4, 2017, https://fortune.com/2017/04/04/walmart-jobs-gender-bias/.

17. US Government Accountability Office, "Federal Social Safety Net Programs: Millions of Full-Time Workers Rely on Federal Health Care and Food Assistance Programs," October 19, 2020, https://www.gao.gov/products/GAO-21-45.

18. Dennis Green, "A $13 Billion Part of Walmart's Business Could Be About to Take a Critical Hit from Trump," *Insider*, April 9, 2018, https://www.businessinsider.com/walmart-could-take-hit-from-snap-benefits-reduction-2018-4.

19. US Bureau of Labor Statistics, "Nonunion Workers Had Weekly Earnings 81 Percent of Union Members in 2019," February 28, 2020, https://www.bls.gov/opub/ted/2020/nonunion-workers-had-weekly-earnings-81-percent-of-union-members-in-2019.htm.

20. Jacob Goldstein, "When Reagan Broke the Unions," NPR, December 18, 2019, https://www.npr.org/transcripts/788002965.

21. It will likely require federal legislation to outlaw states' so-called right-to-work laws. This is something you can demand your congressional representative and senators support.

22. Elise Gould and Will Kimball, "'Right-to-Work' States Still Have Lower Wages," Economic Policy Institute, April 22, 2015, https://www.epi.org/publication/right-to-work-states-have-lower-wages/.

23. I taught yoga myself for nearly a decade, and while I tried to acknowledge its origins regularly, I did not at the time give back to India in any way. I've attempted to correct that by donating in more recent years to various humanitarian causes in India. If you are a student now, you may urge your teachers and/or the locations where you practice to donate a portion of their proceeds as well, and to avoid any naming or messaging that implies they "invented" any aspect of yoga.

24. Lisa Girion, "Johnson & Johnson Knew for Decades That Asbestos Lurked in Its Baby Powder," Reuters, December 14, 2018, https://www.reuters.com/investigates/special-report/johnsonandjohnson-cancer/.

25. Tiffany Hsu and Roni Caryn Rabin, "Johnson & Johnson to End Talc-Based Baby Powder Sales in North America," *New York Times*, May 19, 2020, https://www.nytimes.com/2020/05/19/business/johnson-baby-powder-sales-stopped.html.

26. Labor Union Report, "The Majority of America's Favorite Grocery Chains Are (Mostly) Non-Union," April 23, 2019, https://laborunionreport.com/2019/04/23/eight-of-the-top-10-favorite-grocery-chain-are-non-union/; FoodIndustry.com, "A List of the Top Ten Grocery Chains in the United States," November 2020, https://www.foodindustry.com/articles/a-list-of-the-top-ten-grocery-chains-in-the-united-states/.

27. Whole Foods also quashed a unionization attempt in 2002, well before Amazon was in the picture (Source: Aaron Nathans, "Love the Worker, Not the Union, A Store Says As Some Organize," *New York Times*, May 24, 2003, https://www.nytimes.com/2003/05/24/business/love-the-worker-not-the-union-a-store-says-as-some-organize.html).

28. Jay Peters, "Whole Foods Is Reportedly Using a Heat Map to Track Stores at Risk of Unionization," The Verge, April 20, 2020, https://www.theverge.com/2020/4/20/21228324/amazon-whole-foods-unionization-heat-map-union; Bryan Menegus, "Amazon's Aggressive Anti-Union Tactics Revealed

in Leaked 45-Minute Video," Gizmodo, September 26, 2018, https://gizmodo.com/amazons-aggressive-anti-union-tactics-revealed-in-leake-1829305201.

29. Michael Sainato, "Whole Foods Cuts Workers' Hours After Amazon Introduces Minimum Wage." *The Guardian*, March 6, 2017, https://www.theguardian.com/us-news/2019/mar/06/whole-foods-amazon-cuts-minimum-wage-workers-hours-changes; Aine Cain, "Whole Foods Denies That It Is Cutting Employees' Hours," *Insider*, March 7, 2019, https://www.businessinsider.com/whole-foods-cutting-worker-hours-2019-3.

30. Arjun Panchadar, "Amazon Raises Minimum Wage to $15, Urges Rivals to Follow," Reuters, October 2, 2018, https://www.reuters.com/article/us-amazon-com-wage/amazon-raises-minimum-wage-to-15-urges-rivals-to-follow-idUSKCN1MC15Z.

31. Seventh Generation, "Product Responsibility & Packaging," Seventh Generation.com, accessed March 17, 2021, https://www.seventhgeneration.com/insideSVG/packaging.

32. Colleen Haight, "The Problem with Fair Trade Coffee," *Stanford Social Innovation Review*, Summer 2011, https://ssir.org/articles/entry/the_problem_with_fair_trade_coffee; Bruce Wydick, "10 Reasons Fair-Trade Coffee Doesn't Work," *Huffington Post*, January 28, 2016, https://www.huffpost.com/entry/10-reasons-fair-trade-coffee-doesnt-work_b_5651663.

33. Alina Brad et al., "The False Promise of Certification," Changing Markets Foundation, May 2018, https://changingmarkets.org/wp-content/uploads/2018/05/False-promise_full-report-ENG.pdf.

34. Brad et al., "The False Promise of Certification."

35. Brad et al., "The False Promise of Certification."

36. Alex Mayyasi and Priceonomics, "How Subarus Came to Be Seen as Cars for Lesbians," *The Atlantic*, June 22, 2016, https://www.theatlantic.com/business/archive/2016/06/how-subarus-came-to-be-seen-as-cars-for-lesbians/488042/.

37. OpenSecrets, "Amazon.com," accessed December 1, 2020, https://www.opensecrets.org/orgs/amazon-com/totals?id=D000023883.

38. OpenSecrets, "Amazon.com."

39. Paul Abowd and John Dunbar, "North Carolina Governor's Race Awash in Out-of-State Funds," The Center for Public Integrity, September 5, 2012 (updated May 19, 2014), https://publicintegrity.org/politics/north-carolina-governors-race-awash-in-out-of-state-funds/.

40. Daniel Beekman and Matt Day, "Seattle City Council Votes 9-0 for Scaled-down Head Tax on Large Employers," *Seattle Times*, May 14, 2018, https://www.seattletimes.com/seattle-news/politics/seattle-city-council-votes-9-0-for-scaled-down-head-tax-on-large-employers/.

41. Hannah Knowles, "Amazon Spent $1.5 Million on Seattle City Council Races. The Socialist It Opposed Has Won," *Washington Post*, November 10, 2019, https://www.washingtonpost.com/nation/2019/11/10/amazon-spent-million-seattle-city-council-races-socialist-it-opposed-has-won/.

42. Kerry Flynn, "Refinery29 Is Reeling from Claims of Racism and Toxic Work Culture. Employees Say It's Even Worse Behind the Scenes," CNN, June 11, 2020, https://www.cnn.com/2020/06/11/media/refinery29-workplace-culture/index.html; Todd Spangler, "Refinery29 Top Editor Christene Barberich Steps Down After Backlash Over Lack of Diversity, 'Racist Aggressions,'" *Variety*, June 8, 2020, https://variety.com/2020/digital/news/refinery29-editor-christene-barberich-steps-down-diversity-racial-discrimination-1234627692/.

43. US Federal Trade Commission, "Cases and Proceedings," accessed April 21, 2021, https://www.ftc.gov/enforcement/cases-proceedings.

CHAPTER 6

1. Paul Ringel, "Why Children Get Gifts on Christmas: A History," *The Atlantic*, December 25, 2015, https://www.theatlantic.com/business/archive/2015/12/why-people-give-christmas-gifts/421908/.

2. James Hardy, "The History of Marketing: From Trade to Tech," History Cooperative, September 14, 2016, https://historycooperative.org/the-evolution-of-marketing-from-trade-to-tech.

3. Norman Myers and Jennifer Kent, "New Consumers: The Influence of Affluence on the Environment," *Proceedings of the National Academy of Sciences* 100, no. 8 (April 15, 2003): 4963–4968, https://doi.org/10.1073/pnas.0438061100.

4. According to the UN IPCC, every projection that has us meeting our climate goals includes nuclear power. There's no real path to heading off the worst climate impacts without nuclear power (Source: United Nations Intergovernmental Panel on Climate Change [IPCC], "Global Warming of 1.5°C," 2018, https://www.ipcc.ch/sr15).

5. References to emissions from here forward are pulled from credible sources, but they may sometimes seem to conflict as it's impossible to completely separate different drivers or sources of emissions. For example, food must not only be grown, it must be transported, and therefore, when we talk about the emissions of food production, that overlaps with the emissions associated with transportation. Households rely on energy generation, as well as transport of both themselves and the goods they buy, so household emissions will overlap with both energy generation and transportation (and with food production, manufacturing, and so on).

6. United National Environment Programme (UNEP), "Emissions Gap Report 2020," December 9, 2020, https://www.unep.org/interactive/emissions-gap -report/2020/.

7. UNEP, "Emissions Gap Report 2020."

8. Data as of 2019 (Source: US Energy Information Administration, "What Is US Electricity Generation by Energy Source?" accessed February 1, 2021, https://www.eia.gov/tools/faqs/faq.php?id=427&t=3).

9. Brady Seals and Andee Krasner, "Gas Stoves: Health and Air Quality Impacts and Solutions," Rocky Mountain Institute, 2020, https://rmi.org/insight/gas -stoves-pollution-health.

10. Philip J. Landrigan, Howard Frumkin, and Brita E. Lundberg, "The False Promise of Natural Gas," *New England Journal of Medicine* 382 (January 9, 2020): 104–107, https://doi.org/10.1056/NEJMp1913663.

11. Rita Steyn, "The 10 Hidden Plastics You Didn't Know About," The Marine Diaries, June 10, 2019, https://www.themarinediaries.com/tmd-blog/the-10 -hidden-plastics-you-didn-t-know-about.

12. Ji-Su Kim, Hee-Jee Lee, Seung-Kyu Kim, and Hyun-Jung Kim, "Global Pattern of Microplastics (MPs) in Commercial Food-Grade Salts: Sea Salt as an Indicator of Seawater MP Pollution," *Environmental Science & Technology* 52, no. 21 (October 4, 2018): 12819–12828, https://doi.org/10.1021/acs.est .8b04180.

13. Jim Morris, "Study Spotlights High Breast Cancer Risk for Plastics Workers," Center for Public Integrity, November 19, 2012 (updated May 19, 2014), https://publicintegrity.org/inequality-poverty-opportunity/workers-rights /study-spotlights-high-breast-cancer-risk-for-plastics-workers/.

14. Amy Westervelt, "Phthalates Are Everywhere, and the Health Risks Are Worrying. How Bad Are They Really?" *The Guardian*, February 10, 2015, https://www.theguardian.com/lifeandstyle/2015/feb/10/phthalates-plastics-chemicals-research-analysis.

15. Emily Charles-Donelson, "The Truth About Biodegradable and Compostable Bags Is Out—But No One Is Asking the Right Questions," Water Docs, May 4, 2019, https://www.waterdocs.ca/water-talk/2019/5/2/do-compostable-and-biodegradable-items-break-down-in-marine-environments.

16. Mark Miodownik, "How Did Disposable Products Ever Become a Thing?" BBC, accessed April 21, 2021, https://www.bbc.co.uk/programmes/articles/nB9mTWPPJ4mDNS6wtV76bP/how-did-disposable-products-ever-become-a-thing.

17. Modern landfills are pretty good at containing the things within them, and we can even get useful value out of landfill space after the trash within it has been buried and the soil atop it replanted. And not everything we throw away ends up in the landfill. In some countries, trash is burned for electricity generation, and in others, trash is dumped into the ocean. If you aren't sure where something you're throwing away will end up, it's always best to check first.

18. University of Southern Indiana, "Solid Waste & Landfill Facts," accessed April 21, 2021, https://www.usi.edu/recycle/solid-waste-landfill-facts.

19. Clean Clothes Campaign, "Fashion's Problems," accessed April 21, 2021, https://cleanclothes.org/fashions-problems.

20. Irene San Segundo, "Do You Know How Much Garment Workers Really Make?" Fashion Revolution, 2020, https://www.fashionrevolution.org/usa-blog/how-much-garment-workers-really-make/.

21. Will Evans, "How Amazon Hid Its Safety Crisis," Reveal, September 29, 2020, https://revealnews.org/article/how-amazon-hid-its-safety-crisis/.

22. Data as of 2019 (Source: Daniel Workman, "Flower Bouquet Exports by Country," World's Top Exports, accessed April 23, 2021, https://www.worldstopexports.com/flower-bouquet-exports-country/).

23. Gaby Del Valle, "The Hidden Environmental Cost of Valentine's Day Roses," Vox, February 12, 2019, https://www.vox.com/the-goods/2019/2/12/18220984/valentines-day-flowers-roses-environmental-effects.

24. Lucy Rodgers, "Where Do Your Old Clothes Go?" BBC, February 11, 2015, https://www.bbc.com/news/magazine-30227025.

25. Natalie Delgadillo, "Anonymous Note Decrying Little Free Libraries Sparks Gentrification Debate," DCist, November 4, 2019, https://dcist.com/story/19 /11/04/anonymous-note-decrying-little-free-libraries-sparks-gentrification -debate/.

CHAPTER 7

1. Reed Tucker, "The Terrifying Secrets Behind Your Favorite Foods," *New York Post*, January 16, 2018, https://nypost.com/2018/01/16/the-terrifying -secrets-behind-your-favorite-foods/.

2. Wonjung Yun, "2018 Will Be the Most Difficult Year for Garlic Export: Chinese Garlic at Risk," Tridge, July 10, 2018, https://www.tridge.com/stories /2018-will-be-the-most-difficult-year-garlic-export-chinese-garlic-at-risk.

3. National Resources Defense Council, "Industrial Agriculture 101," January 31, 2020, https://www.nrdc.org/stories/industrial-agriculture-101.

4. While industrialization of agriculture has undoubtedly led to the production of more food, the economics of the current system rely heavily on government subsidies that lower the price of inputs and raise the prices farmers receive for their commodities. In addition, the current system does not price in health externalities like the public health costs of widespread pesticide use and the pollution of fertilizer runoff, or the resource depletion inherent in the extractive nature of industrialized agriculture. Finally, widespread industrialized agriculture has not addressed the global hunger crisis as promised. (Sources: Paula Bustos, Bruno Caprettini, and Jacopo Ponticelli, "Does Agricultural Productivity Favor Industrialization?" Barcelona GSE Focus, July 10, 2014, https://focus.barcelonagse.eu/agricultural-productivity -favor-industrialization; Union of Concerned Scientists, "The Hidden Costs of Industrial Agriculture," July 11, 2008, https://www.ucsusa.org/resources /hidden-costsindustrial-agriculture; John Ikerd, "Can Industrial Agriculture Provide Global Food Security?" University of Missouri, April 26, 2013, https://web.missouri.edu/~ikerdj/papers/California%20-%20IPDC%20-%20 Small%20Farms.htm; Food and Agriculture Organization of the United Nations [FAO], International Fund for Agricultural Development [IFAD] and World Food Programme [FAP], "The State of Food Insecurity in the

World. Meeting the 2015 International Hunger Targets: Taking Stock of Uneven Progress," 2015, https://www.fao.org/3/i4646e/i4646e.pdf.)

5. Harvard School of Public Health, "Eating Healthy vs. Unhealthy Diet Costs About $1.50 More a Day," December 5, 2013, https://www.hsph.harvard.edu /news/press-releases/healthy-vs-unhealthy-diet-costs-1-50-more/.

6. Shilpi Gupta et al., "Characterizing Ultra-Processed Foods by Energy Density, Nutrient Density, and Cost," *Frontiers in Nutrition* (May 28, 2019), https://doi.org/10.3389/fnut.2019.00070.

7. US Department of Agriculture Food and Nutrition Service (FNS), "Child Nutrition Tables," April 16, 2021, www.fns.usda.gov/pd/child-nutrition -tables; FNS, "National School Lunch Program: Participation and Lunches Served," April 2, 2021, https://fns-prod.azureedge.net/sites/default/files /resource-files/slsummar-4.pdf.

8. Kathryn Doyle, "Foods from Subsidized Commodities Tied to Obesity," Reuters, July 5, 2016, https://www.reuters.com/article/us-health-diet-farm -subsidies/foods-from-subsidized-commodities-tied-to-obesity-idUSKCN 0ZL2ER.

9. Rob Smith, "These Are the Countries That Eat the Most Meat," World Economic Forum, August 29, 2018, https://www.weforum.org/agenda /2018/08/these-countries-eat-the-most-meat-03bdf469-f40a-41e3-ade7-fe4 ddb2a709a/.

10. Nathan Halverson, "This Is What Would Happen If the Rest of the World Ate the Way America Does," *Mother Jones*, May 3, 2016, https://www .motherjones.com/environment/2016/05/world-already-would-be-out-water -if-everyone-ate-americans/.

11. Doyle, "Foods from Subsidized Commodities Tied to Obesity."

12. Dan Nosowitz, "Chinese Regulations Are Pushing American Pork Producers to Remove Feed Additives," *Modern Farmer*, October 24, 2019, https:// modernfarmer.com/2019/10/chinese-regulations-are-pushing-american -pork-producers-to-remove-feed-additives/.

13. Ashley Broocks et al., "Carbon Footprint Comparison Between Grass- and Grain-finished Beef," Oklahoma State University Extension, March 2017, https://extension.okstate.edu/fact-sheets/carbon-footprint-comparison -between-grass-and-grain-finished-beef.html.

14. Shawn Fremstad, Hye Jim Rho, and Hayley Brown, "Meatpacking Workers Are a Diverse Group Who Need Better Protection," Center for Economic

and Policy Research, April 29, 2020, https://cepr.net/meatpacking-workers
-are-a-diverse-group-who-need-better-protections.

15. Jeffrey Passel and D'Vera Cohn, "Industries of Unauthorized Immigrant
    Workers," in *Share of Unauthorized Immigrant Workers in Production,
    Construction Jobs Falls Since 2007*, Pew Research Center, March 26, 2015,
    https://www.pewresearch.org/hispanic/2015/03/26/chapter-2-industries-of
    -unauthorized-immigrant-workers/.

16. Food Empowerment Project, "Slaughterhouse Workers," accessed April 21,
    2021, https://foodispower.org/human-labor-slavery/slaughterhouse-workers/.

17. Abigail Abrams, "House Democrats Launch Investigation of OSHA, Meat
    Plants over COVID-19 Outbreaks," *Time*, February 1, 2021, https://time
    .com/5935089/democrats-investigation-meatpacking-coronavirus/.

18. Fremstad, Rho, and Brown, "Meatpacking Workers Are a Diverse Group
    Who Need Better Protection."

19. Economic Policy Institute, "Economists in Support of a Federal Mini-
    mum Wage of $15 by 2024," accessed April 21, 2021, https://www.epi.org
    /economists-in-support-of-15-by-2024/.

20. Chris Heasman, "Here's How Much Fast Food Workers Really Make,"
    Mashed, July 23, 2019, https://www.mashed.com/159615/heres-how-much
    -money-fast-food-workers-really-make/.

21. Jessica Marati, "Behind the Label: Where In-N-Out's Beef Really Comes
    From," Ecosalon, August 1, 2012, https://ecosalon.com/behind-the-label-in
    -n-out-burger-2.

22. National Farm Worker Ministry, "Issues Affecting Farm Workers," accessed
    April 21, 2021, https://nfwm.org/farm-workers/farm-worker-issues/.

23. Zoe Willingham and Silva Mathema, "Protecting Farmworkers From Coro-
    navirus and Securing the Food Supply," Center for American Progress, April
    23, 2020, https://www.americanprogress.org/issues/economy/reports/2020
    /04/23/483488/protecting-farmworkers-coronavirus-securing-food
    -supply/.

24. Farmworker Justice, "US Labor Law for Farmworkers," accessed April 21,
    2021, https://www.farmworkerjustice.org/advocacy_program/us-labor-law
    -for-farmworkers/.

25. Madeline Buiano, "A Push to Equalize Labor Laws for Child Farmwork-
    ers, Who Are Often Immigrants," Center for Public Integrity, July 3, 2019,
    https://publicintegrity.org/inequality-poverty-opportunity/immigration
    /immigration-employment/child-farmworkers-labor-laws/.

26. State of California Department of Industrial Relations, Division of Labor Standards Enforcement, "California Child Labor Laws," 2013, https://www.dir.ca.gov/dlse/childlaborlawpamphlet.pdf.

27. Susan Cosier, "The World Needs Topsoil to Grow 95% of Its Food—but It's Rapidly Disappearing," *The Guardian*, May 30, 2019, https://www.theguardian.com/us-news/2019/may/30/topsoil-farming-agriculture-food-toxic-america.

28. FoodPrint, "How Industrial Agriculture Affects Our Soil," accessed April 24, 2021, https://foodprint.org/issues/how-industrial-agriculture-affects-our-soil/.

29. United States Environmental Protection Agency, "Human Health Issues Related to Pesticides," updated March 7, 2017, https://www.epa.gov/pesticide-science-and-assessing-pesticide-risks/human-health-issues-related-pesticides.

30. Liza Gross, "What Pesticide Monitoring Misses," Food and Environment Reporting Network, March 20, 2019, https://thefern.org/2019/03/what-pesticide-monitoring-misses/.

31. Marcus Zeiger and Nicola Fohrer, "Impact of Organic Farming Systems on Runoff Formation Processes—A Long-term Sequential Rainfall Experiment," *Soil and Tillage Research* 102, no. 1 (January 2009): 45–54, https://doi.org/10.1016/j.still.2008.07.024.

32. Ketty Mobed, Ellen B. Gold, and Marc B. Schenker, "Occupational Health Problems Among Migrant and Seasonal Farm Workers," *Western Journal of Medicine* 157, no. 3 (September 1992): 367–373, https://www.ncbi.nlm.nih.gov/pmc/articles/PMC1011296/; Aaron Blair and Laura Beane Freeman, "Epidemiologic Studies of Cancer in Agricultural Populations: Observations and Future Directions," *Journal of Agromedicine* 14, no. 2 (May 2009): 125–131, https://doi.org/10.1080/10599240902779436; Hans-Peter Hutter et al., "Indicators of Genotoxicity in Farmers and Laborers of Ecological and Conventional Banana Plantations in Ecuador," *International Journal of Environmental Research and Public Health* 17, no. 4 (February 2020), https://doi.org/10.3390/ijerph17041435.

33. Dan Charles, "A Giant Organic Farm Faces Criticism That It's Harming the Environment," NPR, May 3, 2021, https://www.npr.org/2021/05/03/989984124/a-giant-organic-farm-faces-criticism-that-its-harming-the-environment.

34. Anuradha Varanasi, "Is Organic Food Really Better for the Environment?" *State of the Planet* (Columbia Climate School blog), October 22, 2019, https://blogs.ei.columbia.edu/2019/10/22/organic-food-better-environment/.

35. University Corporation for Atmospheric Research (UCAR) Center for Science Education, "The Changing Nitrogen Cycle," 2011, https://scied.ucar.edu/learning-zone/climate-change-impacts/changing-nitrogen-cycle.

36. Melinda Wenner Moyer, "How Drug-Resistant Bacteria Travel from the Farm to Your Table," *Scientific American*, December 1, 2016, https://www.scientificamerican.com/article/how-drug-resistant-bacteria-travel-from-the-farm-to-your-table/.

37. Tod Marks, "The Cost of Organic Food," *Consumer Reports*, March 19, 2015, https://www.consumerreports.org/cro/news/2015/03/cost-of-organic-food/index.htm.

38. Associated Press. "Good News if You Buy Organic Food—It's Getting Cheaper," MarketWatch, January 24, 2019, https://www.marketwatch.com/story/heres-why-prices-of-organic-food-are-dropping-2019-01-24.

39. Emily Cassidy, "Claims of GMO Yield Increases Don't Hold Up," Environmental Working Group, March 25, 2015, https://www.ewg.org/news-insights/news/claims-gmo-yield-increases-dont-hold.

40. Patricia Cohen, "Roundup Maker to Pay $10 Billion to Settle Cancer Suits," *New York Times*, June 24, 2020, https://www.nytimes.com/2020/06/24/business/roundup-settlement-lawsuits.html.

41. Daiane Cattani et al., "Mechanisms Underlying the Neurotoxicity Induced by Glyphosate-based Herbicide in Immature Rat Hippocampus: Involvement of Glutamate Excitotoxicity," *Toxicology* 320 (June 2014): 34–45, https://doi.org/10.1016/j.tox.2014.03.001; Lupping Zhang et al., "Exposure to Glyphosate-based Herbicides and Risk for Non-Hodgkin Lymphoma: A Meta-analysis and Supporting Evidence," *Mutation Research/Reviews in Mutation Research* 781 (July–September 2019): 186–206, https://doi.org/10.1016/j.mrrev.2019.02.001; Juan P. Muñoz, Tammy C. Bleak, and Gloria M. Calaf, "Glyphosate and the Key Characteristics of an Endocrine Disruptor: A Review," *Chemosphere* 270 (May 2021): 128619, https://doi.org/10.1016/j.chemosphere.2020.128619.

42. Ramdas Kanissery et al., "Glyphosate: Its Environmental Persistence and Impact on Crop Health and Nutrition," *Plants* 8, no. 11 (November 13, 2019): 499, https://doi.org/10.3390/plants8110499.

43. Sharon Rushton, Ann Spake, and Laura Chariton, "The Unintended Consequences of Using Glyphosate," January 2016, https://content.sierraclub.org /grassrootsnetwork/sites/content.sierraclub.org.activistnetwork/files/teams /documents/The_Unintended_Consequences_of_Using_Glyphosate_Jan -2016.pdf.

44. Cecelia Smith-Schoenwalder, "What to Know About Glyphosate, the Pesticide in Roundup Weed Killer," *U.S. News & World Report*, August 19, 2019, https://www.usnews.com/news/national-news/articles/what-to-know-about -glyphosate-the-pesticide-in-roundup-weed-killer.

45. Laura Medalie et al., "Influence of Land Use and Region on Glyphosate and Aminomethylphosphonic Acid in Streams in the USA," *Science of The Total Environment* 707 (March 10, 2020): 136008, https://doi.org/10.1016 /j.scitotenv.2019.136008.

46. Paul J. Mills, Izabela Kania-Korwel, and John Fagan, "Excretion of the Herbicide Glyphosate in Older Adults Between 1993 and 2016," *Journal of the American Medical Association* 318, no. 16 (October 24/31, 2017): 1610–1611, https://doi.org/10.1001/jama.2017.11726.

47. Olga Naidenko and Alexis Temkin, "In New Round of Tests, Monsanto's Weedkiller Still Contaminates Foods Marketed to Children," Environmental Working Group report, June 19, 2019, https://www.ewg.org/childrens health/monsanto-weedkiller-still-contaminates-foods-marketed-to -children.

48. Rajendra K. Pachauri et al., "Climate Change 2014: Synthesis Report," IPCC, 2014, https://www.ipcc.ch/site/assets/uploads/2018/02/SYR_AR5_FINAL _full.pdf.

49. Emine Saner, "Almond Milk: Quite Good for You—Very Bad for the Planet," *The Guardian*, October 21, 2015, https://www.theguardian.com/lifeandstyle /shortcuts/2015/oct/21/almond-milk-quite-good-for-you-very-bad-for-the -planet.

50. More than 90 percent of the world's almonds are grown in California. You could have a vigorous debate about whether California's limited water supply should be used to irrigate crops that just get shipped overseas, but that's a whole other topic.

51. Leah Blunt, "Recycling Mystery: Milk and Juice Cartons," Earth 911, November 14, 2018, https://earth911.com/home-garden/recycling-mystery -milk-and-juice-cartons/.

52. According to the UN Food and Agriculture Organization, livestock agriculture is responsible for 14.5 percent of all human-caused greenhouse gas emissions. Cattle represent 65 percent of that, or 9.4 percent of emissions, and sheep add a small amount to that (Source: Food and Agriculture Organization of the United Nations [FAO], "Key Facts and Findings," accessed April 24, 2021, https://www.fao.org/news/story/en/item/197623 /icode/).

53. Broocks et al., "Carbon Footprint Comparison Between Grass- and Grain-finished Beef."

54. Diana Rodgers and Robb Wolf, *Sacred Cow: The Case for (Better) Meat* (Dallas: BenBella Books, 2020): 142–146.

55. Tatiana Schlossberg, "An Unusual Snack for Cows, a Powerful Fix for Climate," *Washington Post*, November 27, 2020, https://www.washington post.com/climate-solutions/2020/11/27/climate-solutions-seaweed -methane/.

56. Julia Moskin et al., "Your Questions About Food and Climate Change, Answered," *New York Times*, April 30, 2019, https://www.nytimes.com /interactive/2019/04/30/dining/climate-change-food-eating-habits.html.

57. The Nature Conservancy, "The Aquaculture Opportunity," September 24, 2017, https://www.nature.org/en-us/what-we-do/our-insights/perspectives /the-aquaculture-opportunity/.

58. Rebecca Clarren, "Is Your Eco-Label Lying?" *Mother Jones*, November/ December 2019, https://www.motherjones.com/environment/2009/11/your -eco-label-lying/.

59. Office of Assistant Director-General (Natural Resources Management and Environment Department), "Food Wastage Footprint: Impacts on Natural Resources," Food and Agriculture Organization of the United Nations, 2013, https://www.fao.org/3/i3347e/i3347e.pdf.

60. Lana Bandoim, "The Shocking Amount of Food US Households Waste Every Year," *Forbes*, January 26, 2020, https://www.forbes.com/sites/lanabandoim /2020/01/26/the-shocking-amount-of-food-us-households-waste-every-year /?sh=53501fd7dc8e.

CHAPTER 8

1. Erika C. Poethig et al., "Inclusive Recovery in US Cities," Urban Institute, April 25, 2018, https://www.urban.org/research/publication/inclusive-recovery-us-cities/view/full_report.

2. Richard V. Reeves, *Dream Hoarders: How the American Upper Middle Class Is Leaving Everyone Else in the Dust, Why That Is a Problem, and What to Do About It* (Washington, DC: Brookings Institution Press, 2017), 107. Note that Reeves uses "affluent" and "best schools" as synonyms. While there are strong correlations between school funding and school quality, I've clarified that we're really talking about the best funded schools.

3. Charles Tilly, *Durable Inequality* (Berkeley: University of California Press, 1999), 10.

4. Joe Pinsker, "Why Are American Homes So Big?" *The Atlantic*, September 12, 2019, https://www.theatlantic.com/family/archive/2019/09/american-houses-big/597811/.

5. Carl Elefante, "Existing Buildings: The Elephant in the Room," *Architect*, October 1, 2018, https://www.architectmagazine.com/aia-architect/aiaperspective/existing-buildings-the-elephant-in-the-room_o.

6. Jennifer L. Rice et al., "Contradictions of the Climate-Friendly City: New Perspectives on Eco-Gentrification and Housing Justice," *International Journal of Urban and Regional Research* 44, no. 1 (March 1, 2019): 145–165, https://doi.org/10.1111/1468-2427.12740.

7. US Environmental Protection Agency (EPA), "Sources of Greenhouse Gas Emissions," updated April 14, 2021, https://www.epa.gov/ghgemissions/sources-greenhouse-gas-emissions. Note: There is plenty of overlap in sectors, like transportation overlapping with agriculture and manufacturing because it moves their products, making this data feel muddy. It's helpful to look at credible sources for better understanding.

8. James R. Elliott, Phylicia Lee Brown, and Kevin Loughran, "Racial Inequalities in the Federal Buyout of Flood-Prone Homes: A Nationwide Assessment of Environmental Adaptation," *Socius* (January 2020), https://doi.org/10.1177/2378023120905439.

9. Rachel Krantz, "Can You Be a Good Neighbor If You're a Gentrifier?" Bustle, July 7, 2016, https://www.bustle.com/articles/171201-can-you-be-a-good-neighbor-if-youre-a-gentrifier-9-tips-from-advocates.

10. Mike Owen Benediktsson, Brian Lamberta, and Erika Larsen, "Taming a 'Chaotic Concept': Gentrification and Segmented Consumption in Brooklyn, 2002-2012," *Urban Geography* 37, no. 4 (December 1, 2015), 590–610, https://doi.org/10.1080/02723638.2015.1096113.

11. Chana Joffe Walt, "Episode One: The Book of Statuses," July 30, 2020, in *Nice White Parents*, produced by Julie Snyder, podcast, MP3 audio, https://www.nytimes.com/2020/07/30/podcasts/nice-white-parents-serial.html.

12. Harry Brighouse and Adam Swift, *Family Values: The Ethics of Parent-Child Relationships* (Princeton: Princeton University Press, 2016), 128.

13. Todd Kominiak, "When It Comes to Parent Involvement, Income Matters," *K12 Insight*, September 11, 2017, https://www.k12insight.com/trusted/comes-parent-involvement-income-matters/.

14. Michael J. Petrilli, "One Reason Why Affluent, Liberal Parents Often Choose Segregated Schools, Even When That May Not Be Their Intention," Fordham Institute, May 3, 2017, https://fordhaminstitute.org/national/commentary/one-reason-why-affluent-liberal-parents-often-choose-segregated-schools-even.

15. Reeves, *Dream Hoarders*, 14.

16. Margaret A. Hagerman, "Op-Ed: White Progressive Parents and the Conundrum of Privilege," *Los Angeles Times*, September 30, 2018, https://www.latimes.com/opinion/op-ed/la-oe-hagerman-white-parents-20180930-story.html.

17. Reeves, *Dream Hoarders*, 15.

18. Kevin Drum, "Corruption and Bubbles in New York: How the Taxi Medallion Scam Ruined Thousands," *Mother Jones*, May 19, 2019, https://www.motherjones.com/kevin-drum/2019/05/corruption-and-bubbles-in-new-york-how-the-taxi-medallion-scam-ruined-thousands/.

19. Jill Filipovic, "The Ride from Hell," *Marie Claire*, August 10, 2020, https://www.marieclaire.com/politics/a32757898/lyft-sexual-assault/.

20. Lawrence Mishel, "Uber and the Labor Market," Economic Policy Institute, May 15, 2018, https://www.epi.org/publication/uber-and-the-labor-market-uber-drivers-compensation-wages-and-the-scale-of-uber-and-the-gig-economy/.

21. Mishel, "Uber and the Labor Market."

22. Kate Conger, "A Worker-Owned Cooperative Tries to Compete with Lyft and Uber," *New York Times*, May 28, 2021, https://www.nytimes.com/2021/05/28/technology/nyc-uber-lyft-the-drivers-cooperative.html

23. Union of Concerned Scientists, "Getting There Greener: The Guide to Your Lower-Carbon Vacation," December 2008, https://www.ucsusa.org/sites /default/files/2019-10/greentravel_report.pdf.

24. No White Saviors, "How to Be an Advocate Without Perpetuating the White Savior Complex," December 19, 2019, https://nowhitesaviors.org/how-to-be -an-advocate-without-perpetuating-the-white-savior-complex/.

25. Lubega Wendy, "The Ethics of Volunteering and Voluntourism," No White Saviors, September 24, 2019, https://nowhitesaviors.org/the-ethics-of -volunteering-and-voluntourism/.

CHAPTER 9

1. Helen Christophi, "En Banc 9th Circuit Takes Up California Teacher's Pay-Inequity Case," Courthouse News Service, December 12, 2017, https://www.courthousenews.com/en-banc-9th-circuit-takes-up-california -teachers-pay-inequity-case/.

2. Christophi, "En Banc 9th Circuit Takes Up California Teacher's Pay-Inequity Case."

3. Kate Gold and Cole D. Lewis, "9th Circuit Holds that Prior Salary Is Not a Defense to an Equal Pay Act Claim," *National Law Review* 11 no. 59 (February 28, 2020), https://www.natlawreview.com/article/9th-circuit-holds -prior-salary-not-defense-to-equal-pay-act-claim.

4. Stephen Miller, "US Companies Are Working to Fix Pay-Equity Issues," Society for Human Resource Management, May 13, 2019, https://www .shrm.org/resourcesandtools/hr-topics/compensation/pages/companies-are -working-to-fix-pay-equity-issues.aspx.

5. QuickBooks, "Are We Closing the Wage Gap? Employers and Employees Sound Off," accessed April 24, 2021, https://quickbooks.intuit.com/time -tracking/resources/equal-pay-survey/#modal-id.

6. Sissi Cao, "Q&A with Cindy Robbins, Marc Benioff's Ex-HR Chief Who Closed Salesforce's Gender Pay Gap," Observer, November 16, 2019, https:// observer.com/2019/11/salesforce-cindy-robbins-interview-pay-gap-men -women/.

7. Bryce Covert, "Even Google Can No Longer Hide Its Gender Pay Gap," *New York Times*, March 7, 2019, https://www.nytimes.com/2019/03/07/opinion /google-pay-gap.html.

8. Kari Paul, "Women at Google Miss Out on Thousands of Dollars as a Result of Pay Discrimination, Lawsuit Alleges," *The Guardian*, July 22, 2020, https://www.theguardian.com/technology/2020/jul/22/google-gender-pay-discrimination-lawsuit.

9. PayScale, "The State of the Gender Pay Gap in 2021," March 24, 2021, https://www.payscale.com/data/gender-pay-gap.

10. PayScale, "The State of the Gender Pay Gap"; Jessica Dickler, "First-Time Moms See a 30% Drop in Pay. For Dads, There's a Bump Up," CNBC, April 30, 2019, https://www.cnbc.com/2019/04/30/first-time-moms-see-a-30percent-drop-in-pay-for-dads-theres-a-bump-up.html; Tanya Tarr, "Weight Widens the Pay Gap," *InStyle*, May 14, 2019, https://www.instyle.com/lifestyle/weight-widens-pay-gap.

11. World Economic Forum, "The Global Social Mobility Index 2020: Why Economies Benefit from Fixing Inequality," January 19, 2020, https://www.weforum.org/reports/global-social-mobility-index-2020-why-economies-benefit-from-fixing-inequality.

12. Hachette Books, an imprint of Hachette Book Group, published my first book, *Work Optional*.

13. Xi Song et al., "Long-term Decline in Intergenerational Mobility in the United States Since the 1850s," *PNAS* 117, no. 1 (January 7, 2020): 251–258, https://doi.org/10.1073/pnas.1905094116; Marcus Lu, "Is the American Dream Over? Here's What the Data Says," World Economic Forum, September 2, 2020, https://www.weforum.org/agenda/2020/09/social-mobility-upwards-decline-usa-us-america-economics/.

14. CEO compensation has grown 940 percent since 1978, and stock markets have grown 707 percent, while workers' wages have grown only 12 percent (Source: Lawrence Mishel and Julia Wolfe, "CEO Compensation Has Grown 940 Percent Since 1978," Economic Policy Institute, August 14, 2019, https://www.epi.org/publication/ceo-compensation-2018/).

15. Sarah Cwiek, "The Middle Class Took Off 100 Years Ago . . . Thanks To Henry Ford?" National Public Radio, January 27, 2014, https://www.npr.org/2014/01/27/267145552/the-middle-class-took-off-100-years-ago-thanks-to-henry-ford.

16. Matt Bruenig, "Small Businesses Are Overrated," *Jacobin*, January 16, 2018, https://jacobinmag.com/2018/01/small-businesses-workers-wages.

17. US Department of Labor Bureau of Labor Statistics, "Employee Benefits in the United States—March 2020," September 24, 2020, https://www.bls.gov /news.release/pdf/ebs2.pdf.

18. Samantha Yenger Cremean, "America Worships Mom-and-Pops—But They Can Mistreat Employees, Too," Medium, January 25, 2018, https://medium .com/the-establishment/america-worships-mom-and-pops-but-they-can -mistreat-employees-too-c9af48c50ce8.

19. Marilyn Icsman, "Here Are the Congressional Offices That Pay Staffs the Highest and Lowest Salaries," *USA Today*, March 23, 2018, https:// www.usatoday.com/story/news/politics/onpolitics/2018/03/23/here -congressional-offices-pay-staffs-highest-and-lowest-salaries/450064002/.

20. Alex Gangitano, "Report: Nearly Three Quarters of the House Have No Senior Staffers of Color," *Roll Call*, September 11, 2018, https://www.rollcall .com/2018/09/11/report-nearly-three-quarters-of-the-house-have-no-senior -staffers-of-color/.

21. Stephanie Akin, "Alexandria Ocasio-Cortez's Call for a 'Living Wage' Starts in Her Office," *Roll Call*, February 22, 2019, https://www.rollcall.com /2019/02/22/alexandria-ocasio-cortezs-call-for-a-living-wage-starts-in-her -office/.

22. Elie Mystal, "Ocasio-Cortez and the New House Members Showed How to Do a Hearing Right," *Washington Post*, March 1, 2019, https://www .washingtonpost.com/outlook/2019/03/01/ocasio-cortez-new-house-members -showed-how-do-hearing-right/; Cory Stieg, "AOC Uses These Smart Tactics to Organize and Focus for Congressional Hearings—and You Can Steal Them," CNBC, August 25, 2020, https://www.cnbc.com/2020/08/25/how-alexandria -ocasio-cortez-prepares-for-congressional-hearings-tips.html; Daniel Merans and Paul Blumenthal, "Behind Alexandria Ocasio-Cortez's Masterful Inter-rogation of Michael Cohen," *Huffington Post*, updated March 14, 2019, https:// www.huffpost.com/entry/alexandria-ocasio-cortez-mastered-michael-cohen -testimony-preparation-staff_n_5c78605ee4b0de0c3fbf4eb9.

23. Kathryn Anne Edwards and Alexander Hertel-Fernandez, *Paving the Way Through Paid Internships: A Proposal to Expand Educational and Economic Opportunities for Low-Income College Students* (New York: Dēmos, 2010), https://www.demos.org/sites/default/files/publications/PavingWay_Paid Internships_Demos.pdf.

24. National Association of Colleges and Employers (NACE), "Job Offers for Class of 2019 Grads Impacted by Internship Experience," May 13, 2019, https://www.naceweb.org/job-market/trends-and-predictions/job-offers-for-class-of-2019-grads-impacted-by-internship-experience/.

25. Society for Human Resource Management (SHRM), "SHRM Survey Findings: Internships," Project Leader: Christina Lee, November 6, 2013, https://www.shrm.org/hr-today/trends-and-forecasting/research-and-surveys/pages/shrm-2013-internships.aspx.

26. NACE, "Racial Disproportionalities Exist in Terms of Intern Representation," July 24, 2020, https://www.naceweb.org/diversity-equity-and-inclusion/trends-and-predictions/racial-disproportionalities-exist-in-terms-of-intern-representation/; NACE, "Minority College Students Underrepresented in Paid Internships," September 9, 2020, https://www.naceweb.org/about-us/press/minority-college-students-underrepresented-in-paid-internships.

27. Heather Antecol, Kelly Bedard, and Jenna Stearns, "Equal but Inequitable: Who Benefits from Gender-Neutral Tenure Clock Stopping Policies?" *American Economic Review* 108, no. 9 (September 2018): 2420–2021, https://doi.org/10.1257/aer.20160613.

28. Dan Price, "3 Things I Learned by Paying a $70,000 Minimum Wage," Gravity Payments, https://gravitypayments.com/blog/3-things-i-learned-by-paying-a-70000-minimum-wage/.

29. Dan Price (@DanPriceSeattle), "6 years ago today I raised my company's min wage to $70k. Fox News called me a socialist whose employees would be on bread lines. Since then our revenue tripled, we're a Harvard Business School case study & our employees had a 10x boom in homes bought," Twitter, April 13, 2021, https://twitter.com/DanPriceSeattle/status/1382018355985588228?s=20.

30. David R. Hekman et al., "Does Diversity-Valuing Behavior Result in Diminished Performance Ratings for Non-White and Female Leaders?" *Academy of Management Journal* 60, no. 2 (March 3, 2016), https://doi.org/10.5465/amj.2014.0538.

31. Vivian Hunt, Lareina Yee, Sara Prince, and Sundiatu Dixon-Fyle, "Delivering Through Diversity," McKinsey & Company, January 18, 2018, https://www.mckinsey.com/business-functions/organization/our-insights/delivering-through-diversity.

32. Karen Brown, "To Retain Employees, Focus on Inclusion—Not Just Diversity," *Harvard Business Review*, December 4, 2018, https://hbr.org/2018/12/to-retain-employees-focus-on-inclusion-not-just-diversity.

33. Tom Wells, "10 Strategies to Build Diversity and Inclusion in the Workplace," Talaera, September 14, 2020, https://blog.talaera.com/strategies-diversity-inclusion-workplace.

34. Laura Mather, "Dear White Men: Five Pieces of Advice for 91 Percent of Fortune 500 CEOs," *Huffington Post*, updated August 4, 2016, https://www.huffpost.com/entry/dear-white-men-seven-piec_b_7899084.

35. Anil Dash, "The Year I Didn't Retweet Men," Medium, February 12, 2014, https://medium.com/the-only-woman-in-the-room/the-year-i-didnt-retweet-men-79403a7eade1.

36. US Energy Information Administration, "How Much Energy Is Consumed in US Buildings?" updated February 11, 2012, https://www.eia.gov/tools/faqs/faq.php?id=86&t=1.

CHAPTER 10

1. US Federal Reserve, "Report on the Economic Well-Being of US Households in 2018," updated June 5, 2019, https://www.federalreserve.gov/publications/2019-economic-well-being-of-us-households-in-2018-banking-and-credit.htm.

2. Megan Leonhardt, "This Map Shows the States Where Payday Loans Charge Nearly 700 Percent Interest," CNBC, August 3, 2018, https://www.cnbc.com/2018/08/03/states-with-the-highest-payday-loan-rates.html.

3. Aaron Klein, "America's Poor Subsidize Wealthier Consumers in a Vicious Income Inequality Cycle," Brookings Institute, February 6, 2018, https://www.brookings.edu/opinions/americas-poor-subsidize-wealthier-consumers-in-a-vicious-income-inequality-cycle/.

4. Klein, "America's Poor Subsidize Wealthier Consumers in a Vicious Income Inequality Cycle."

5. Linda Lutton, "Activists Want Reparations from Chase Bank for Chicago's Black Neighborhoods," National Public Radio, June 16, 2020, https://www.npr.org/local/309/2020/06/16/878136763/activists-want-reparations-from-chase-bank-for-chicago-s-black-neighborhoods.

6. Lutton, "Activists Want Reparations from Chase Bank for Chicago's Black Neighborhoods."

7. Jamie Henn, "Chase Lends to Fossil Fuel Companies—But Not Black Communities," Stop the Money Pipeline, June 18, 2020, https://stopthe moneypipeline.com/chase-lends-to-fossil-fuels-companies-but-not-black -communities/.

8. Danielle Chemtob, "Wells Fargo Fined Again. This Time the Bank Owes $35 Million over Investment Advice," Charlotte Observer, February 28, 2020, https:// www.charlotteobserver.com/news/business/banking/article240728241.html.

9. Lawrence White, "HSBC Draws Line Under Mexican Cartel Case After Five Years on Probation," Reuters, December 11, 2017, https://www.reuters.com /article/us-hsbc-usa/hsbc-draws-line-under-mexican-cartel-case-after-five -years-on-probation-idUSKBN1E50YA.

10. Soo Youn, "USAA, a traditional safeguard for military families, is under fire for denying loans to Coast Guard clients during the government shutdown," ABC News, January 3, 2019, https://abcnews.go.com/US/usaa-traditional -safeguard-military-families-fire-denying-loans/story?id=60090846.

11. Patrick Danner, "San Antonio's USAA Bank Receives Failing Grade from Bank Regulator," San Antonio Express-News, October 5, 2020, https:// www.expressnews.com/business/local/article/San-Antonio-s-USAA-Bank -receives-failing-grade-15622526.php.

12. USAA, "USAA Announces 3-Year, $50 Million Commitment to Advance Racial Equality," October 12, 2020, https://www.prnewswire.com/news -releases/usaa-announces-3-year-50-million-commitment-to-advance-racial -equality-301150343.html.

13. I'm a longtime USAA member and have been told numerous times over many years that they do not plan to offer accounts for small business, both by senior marketing team members and frontline customer service representatives.

14. Joris Luyendijk, "Big Banks Still Have a Problem with Ethics and Morality," The Guardian, January 18, 2016, https://www.theguardian.com/sustainable -business/2016/jan/18/big-banks-problem-ethics-morality-davos.

15. Kriston McIntosh, Emily Moss, Ryan Nunn, and Jay Shambaugh, "Examining the Black-White Wealth Gap," Brookings Institution, February 27, 2020, https://www.brookings.edu/blog/up-front/2020/02/27/examining-the-black -white-wealth-gap/.

16. David Vetter, "JPMorgan Chase Tops Dirty List of 35 Fossil Fuel-Funding Banks," *Forbes*, March 18, 2020, https://www.forbes.com/sites/davidrvetter /2020/03/18/jpmorgan-chase-tops-dirty-list-of-35-fossil-fuel-funding-banks/.

17. Wells Fargo, "Wells Fargo's Involvement in Funding the Dakota Access Pipeline," February 8, 2017, https://stories.wf.com/wells-fargos-involvement -funding-dakota-access-pipeline/.

18. Bill Chappell, "2 Cities to Pull More Than $3 Billion from Wells Fargo over Dakota Access Pipeline," National Public Radio, February 8, 2017, https:// www.npr.org/sections/thetwo-way/2017/02/08/514133514/two-cities-vote-to -pull-more-than-3-billion-from-wells-fargo-over-dakota-pipelin.

19. Wells Fargo, "Wells Fargo's Involvement in Funding the Dakota Access Pipeline."

20. Juliette Cubanski, Tricia Neuman, Anthony Damico, and Karen Smith, "Medicare Beneficiaries' Out-of-Pocket Health Care Spending as a Share of Income Now and Projections for the Future," Kaiser Family Foundation, January 26, 2018, https://www.kff.org/report-section/medicare -beneficiaries-out-of-pocket-health-care-spending-as-a-share-of-income -now-and-projections-for-the-future-report/.

21. Fidelity Charitable, "Study: 77% of Millennials Have Made an Impact Investment, but Only 53% of Advisors Understand the Concept Well," September 18, 2019, https://www.fidelitycharitable.org/about-us/news/77-percent -millennials-made-impact-investment-only-53-percent-advisors-say-they -understand-concept-well.html.

22. Victor Ferreira, "The Inconvenient Truth About Responsible Investing: An FP Investigation," *Financial Post*, November 25, 2019, https://financialpost .com/investing/the-inconvenient-truth-about-responsible-investing-an-fp -investigation.

23. Thomas Piketty, *Capital in the Twenty-First Century* (Cambridge: Harvard University Press, 2017), 94, 68.

24. Mark J. Perry, "More Evidence That It's Really Hard to 'Beat the Market' Over Time, 95% of Finance Professionals Can't Do It," American Enterprise Institute, October 18, 2018, https://www.aei.org/carpe-diem/more -evidence-that-its-really-hard-to-beat-the-market-over-time-95-of-finance -professionals-cant-do-it/; Jeff Sommer, "Mutual Fund Winners Don't Stay Ahead for Long," *New York Times*, July 31, 2020, https://www.nytimes.com /2020/07/31/business/mutual-fund-winners-stocks-bonds.html.

25. Elizabeth Schulze, "'Sustainable' Investors Match the Performance of Regular Investors, New IMF Research Finds," CNBC, October 10, 2019, https://www.cnbc.com/2019/10/10/imf-research-finds-esg-sustainable-investment-funds-dont-underperform.html.

26. Pippa Stevens, "ESG Investing Is a 'Complete Fraud,' Chamath Palihapitiya Says," CNBC, February 26, 2020, https://www.cnbc.com/2020/02/26/chamath-palihapitiya-esg-investing-is-a-complete-fraud.html.

27. Grist Creative, "Removing the Blindfold from Sustainable Investing," June 29, 2020, https://grist.org/sponsored/removing-the-blindfold-from-sustainable-investing/.

28. Trevor Hunnicutt, "BlackRock Faces Lawsuits over 'Disproportionately Large' Fees," *InvestmentNews*, January 9, 2015, https://www.investmentnews.com/blackrock-faces-lawsuits-over-disproportionately-large-fees-57735; Jasper Jolly, "BlackRock Holds $85bn in Coal Despite Pledge to Sell Fossil Fuel Shares," *The Guardian*, January 13, 2021, https://www.theguardian.com/business/2021/jan/13/blackrock-holds-85bn-in-coal-despite-pledge-to-sell-fossil-fuel-shares.

29. United Nations Environment Programme Finance Initiative, "Mark Carney, UN Race to Zero Campaign and COP26 Presidency Launch Net Zero Financial Alliance With World's Biggest Banks, Asset Owners, Asset Managers and Insurers," April 21, 2021, https://www.unepfi.org/wordpress/wp-content/uploads/2021/04/GFANZ-Launch-press-release.pdf.

30. Sierra Club, "Sierra Club and Rainforest Action Network Statement on Net-Zero Banking Alliance (NZBA) and Glasgow Financial Alliance for Net Zero (GFANZ)," April 21, 2021, https://www.sierraclub.org/press-releases/2021/04/sierra-club-and-rainforest-action-network-statement-net-zero-banking-alliance.

31. Christian Stoll, Lena Klaaßen, and Ulrich Gallersdörfer, "The Carbon Footprint of Bitcoin," *Joule,* June 12, 2019, https://www.cell.com/joule/fulltext/S2542-4351(19)30255-7.

32. Digiconomist, "Bitcoin Energy Consumption Index," accessed April 21, 2021, Digiconomist, https://digiconomist.net/bitcoin-energy-consumption.

33. Ben Deacon, "Bitcoin May Soon Consume More Power Than Australia—Almost 10 Times More Than Google, Microsoft and Facebook Combined," Australian Broadcasting Corporation, March 17, 2021, https://www.abc.net.au/news/2021-03-18/bitcoin-has-a-climate-problem/13210376.

34. Lauren Aratani, "Electricity Needed to Mine Bitcoin Is More Than Used by 'Entire Countries,'" *The Guardian*, February 27, 2021, https://www.the guardian.com/technology/2021/feb/27/bitcoin-mining-electricity-use -environmental-impact.

35. My book *Work Optional* has detailed guidance on determining this number and making a plan to achieve it.

36. Tanja Hester, "Vanguard Group, Dump Your Gun Stocks. We Don't Want to Profit Off Mass Murder" (Change.org petition), 2018, https://www.change .org/p/vanguard-group-dump-your-gun-stocks-we-don-t-want-to-profit -off-mass-murder.

37. Steven Mufson, "A Bad Day for Big Oil," *Washington Post*, May 26, 2021, https://www.washingtonpost.com/climate-environment/2021/05/26 /exxonmobil-rebel-shareholders-win-board-seats/.

CHAPTER II

1. Rakesh Kochhar, "The Pandemic Stalls Growth in the Global Middle Class, Pushes Poverty Up Sharply," Pew Research Center, March 18, 2021, https:// www.pewresearch.org/global/2021/03/18/the-pandemic-stalls-growth-in -the-global-middle-class-pushes-poverty-up-sharply/.

2. National Center for Family Philanthropy, "What Is the 5% Payout Rule?" October 15, 2008, https://www.ncfp.org/2008/10/15/what-is-the-5-payout-rule/.

3. Joseph Stiglitz, *People, Power, and Profits: Progressive Capitalism for an Age of Discontent* (New York: W.W. Norton & Company, 2019), 167.

4. Cheryl Dorsey et al., "Overcoming the Racial Bias in Philanthropic Funding," *Stanford Social Innovation Review*, May 4, 2020, https://ssir.org/articles /entry/overcoming_the_racial_bias_in_philanthropic_funding.

5. Peter Joseph, *The New Human Rights Movement: Reinventing the Economy to End Oppression* (Dallas: BenBella Books, 2017), 105.

6. Krystina Murray, "Homeless and Addiction," Addiction Center, March 24, 2021, https://www.addictioncenter.com/addiction/homelessness.

7. Dan Eggen, "Obama Fundraising Powered by Small Donors, New Study Shows," *Washington Post*, February 8, 2012, https://www.washingtonpost .com/politics/obama-fundraising-powered-by-small-donors-new-study -shows/2012/02/08/gIQANfKIzQ_story.html.

8. Rebecca R. Ruiz and Rachel Shorey, "Democrats See a Cash Surge, With a $1.5 Billion ActBlue Haul," *New York Times*, October 16, 2020, https://www.nytimes.com/2020/10/16/us/politics/senate-democrats-actblue-fundraising.html.

9. Sean J. Miller, "Ad Options Tightening for Campaigns as Election Day Nears," *Campaigns & Elections*, October 2, 2020, https://www.campaignsandelections.com/campaign-insider/ad-options-tightening-for-campaigns-as-election-day-nears.

10. McGrath raised $94 million to McConnell's $71 million, despite FiveThirtyEight giving her only a 4 percent chance of winning. (Sources: OpenSecrets, "Kentucky Senate 2020 Race," accessed February 2021, https://www.opensecrets.org/races/summary?cycle=2020&id=KYS1; FiveThirtyEight, "McConnell Is *Clearly Favored* to Win Kentucky's Senate Election," accessed April 21, 2021, https://projects.fivethirtyeight.com/2020-election-forecast/senate/kentucky/).

CONCLUSION

1. *Capital in the Twenty-First Century*, directed by Justin Pemberton, based on the book by Thomas Piketty (Netflix, 2020), streaming video.

2. Daisy Grewal, "How Wealth Reduces Compassion," *Scientific American*, April 10, 2012, https://www.scientificamerican.com/article/how-wealth-reduces-compassion/.

3. Peter Joseph, *The New Human Rights Movement: Reinventing the Economy to End Oppression* (Dallas: BenBella Books, 2017), 100–111.

4. Alicia Parlapiano, "Why Euthanasia Rates at Animal Shelters Have Plummeted," *New York Times*, September 3, 2019, https://www.nytimes.com/2019/09/03/upshot/why-euthanasia-rates-at-animal-shelters-have-plummeted.html.

THIRD-PARTY CERTIFICATIONS

1. Michael Mehaffy and Nikos Salingaros, "Toward Resilient Architectures: Why Green Often Isn't," April 4, 2013, *Metropolis*, https://www.metropolismag.com/sustainability/toward-resilient-architectures-2-why-green-often-isnt/.

INDEX

ABOUT THE AUTHOR

Tanja Hester is the author of *Wallet Activism: How to Use Every Dollar You Spend, Earn, and Save as a Force for Change* and *Work Optional: Retire Early the Non-Penny-Pinching Way.* After spending most of her career as a consultant to Democratic politics and progressive issue campaigns, and before that as a public radio journalist, Tanja retired early at the age of thirty-eight. She documented the process on her award-winning financial independence/retire early (FIRE) blog, *Our Next Life.* She's been an outspoken voice in the personal finance media community to consider systemic barriers and opportunity gaps, rather than simply pushing people with lots of advantages already to accumulate more wealth, part of why the *New York Times* called her "the matriarch of the women's FIRE movement." She hosts a podcast also called *Wallet Activism*, writes an occasional opinion column for *MarketWatch*, and lives in a burgeoning permaculture food forest she's growing in North Lake Tahoe, California, with her husband, Mark Bunge, and a flock of tiny rescue dogs. You can follow her on Twitter and Instagram at @our_nextlife and visit her blog at OurNextLife.com.